GREGG SPEED STUDIES

By

JOHN ROBERT GREGG

Anniversary Edition

THE GREGG PUBLISHING COMPANY

NEW YORK CHICAGO BOSTON SAN FRANCISCO TORONTO LONDON

17a-K-100

SHORTHAND PLATES WRITTEN BY
WINIFRED KENNA RICHMOND

PRINTED IN THE UNITED STATES OF AMERICA

PREFACE

"Gregg Speed Studies" first appeared in 1917 as a companion text to the Gregg Shorthand Manual. The best pedagogic thinking at that time called for the welding of shorthand theory with speed practice from the first lesson. "Gregg Speed Studies" was prepared to enable shorthand teachers to follow this new method of teaching the principles of shorthand.

The publication of the Anniversary Edition of the Shorthand Manual has made it necessary to revise "Speed Studies," for the supplementary drills and dictation material given in Part I correlate chapter by chapter with those of the Manual.

In the Preface to the first edition we said:

In planning the "studies" preceding each section of the book, the method adopted by the great industries in developing efficiency has been followed. Just as the best method of performing any mechanical operation is first established in a factory by scientific test, and each new workman is required to conform to that method, so in this plan of teaching skill in writing shorthand we endeavor from the first to teach the student the most effective method of performance. He is taught the correct posture for writing, the correct manner of holding the pen, the correct manner of turning the pages, the quickest and easiest way to make the various combinations, the importance of compactness in writing, to make rapid transitions between the forms, and to eliminate what Herbert Spencer called "unregistered movements of the pen."

An examination of the book will, we believe, disclose many notable contributions to the pedagogy of shorthand; but the two outstanding features are.

First, the presentation of practice material *in its shorthand form*, instead of in print as is done in most dictation books.

Second, the development of a large and varied writing vocabulary through the unique plan of incorporating *vocabulary drills* with the work in dictation.

The first of these features can hardly be overemphasized. Much observation in teaching shorthand has convinced me that the best results are obtained through the *reading* of shorthand. The reasons may be summarized briefly:

1. The student is more interested in reading shorthand than in reading print, and interest in a subject is of the first importance in securing results.

2. As he may be called upon to read the shorthand notes at any point in the assignment, he will naturally give more time to preparing himself to read fluently.

In doing this he familiarizes himself with the correct forms for words and phrases, and every new form makes a vivid impression on his mind.

3. The visual impression of the outline secured through reading enables him to write it readily when the matter is dictated to him. This inspires confidence, which is an important factor in the development of skill.

4. Through reading shorthand that has been written instead of *drawn*, he becomes familiar with the modifications in length, slant, curvature, etc., that outlines undergo in various joinings. He thus becomes impressed with the importance of accuracy, because his success in reading depends largely upon the accuracy of his notes.

5. In reading from his own notes he is helped, to a certain extent, by memory of the subject matter and even of the actual dictation; but in reading shorthand that has not been dictated to him he must depend entirely upon his knowledge of the system and of the forms. This stimulates his mind to greater alertness and leads to much greater fluency in reading his own notes.

6. The student trained in this way finds shorthand a real medium of communication, and learns the application of the word-building principles through almost effortless absorption. In any art, imitation plays an important part. It is fully utilized by this plan.

The original plan of organization of the teaching material that has made "Speed Studies" so successful in the classroom has been retained in the Anniversary Edition. Teachers will welcome these additional features:

1. The increased amount of analytical and comparative word drills.

2. The introduction of drills on the derivatives of brief forms as soon as the derivatives can be written according to principle.

3. The inclusion of frequent-phrase drills, enabling the teacher to build up the phrasing habit along with the skill in writing the brief forms that make up the phrases in the drills.

4. The large increase in the supplementary graded dictation material for each chapter of the Manual, consisting mostly of business letters written in shorthand.

5. An entirely new feature—a page or two of sentences and letters in type at the end of each Speed Study, to be used as a writing exercise supplementing the writing exercise at the end of each chapter of the Manual.

In this Anniversary Edition, the vocabulary, for the most part, is based on the Horn List* of the five thousand most frequently recurring words of the language. The theory underlying this procedure is that the student should *obtain skill* in writing the words he will be called upon to write instead of practicing words that, in all likelihood, will be but remotely connected with his experience. These words are introduced, as far as possible, in the order of their frequency. The power to write meaningful matter, with the added advantage of a constantly growing interest in the study, is vastly increased by this procedure, as will be realized when it is understood that 42 per cent of the running words in ordinary non-technical matter can be written with the prin-

* University of Iowa Monographs in Education, First Series No. 4.

ciples and brief forms presented in the first chapter of the Gregg Shorthand Manual.

The acquirement of skill in writing shorthand, however, does not end with that accomplishment. Consequently, attention has been given to developing, through adequate drills, such a complete understanding of all the principles that the student will acquire facility in constructing the forms for any word that he may be called upon to write in shorthand. We believe that these features of "Gregg Speed Studies" will do more toward enriching the student's writing vocabulary and increasing technical skill than any other method that has been devised.

The content of the business letters and articles deserves special mention. The letters are new and direct from the files of today's business firms. Every expression that does not comply with modern usage has been eliminated. The articles are rich in literary, informational, and vocabulary-building value.

In the preparation of this book the author has been assisted by suggestions from teachers in all parts of the country, and he desires to make grateful acknowledgment to them for their cooperation. In particular, he desires to acknowledge the assistance he has received in the preparation of the book for the press from the executive, managerial, and editorial staffs of The Gregg Publishing Company, to Mr. Charles L. Swem, Mr. Albert Schneider, and Mr. Martin J. Dupraw for posing for the photocuts illustrating the various methods of performing the work, which add so much to the value of the book, and to Mrs. Winifred Kenna Richmond for the artistic shorthand plates.

JOHN ROBERT GREGG

GREGG SPEED STUDIES

FOUNDATIONS OF SPEED AND ACCURACY

An introductory study of some of the basic principles and practices in the acquisition of speed in shorthand

The student must understand many of the principles of speed and accuracy in shorthand in a general way before any real work can be done toward acquiring the technique of writing. In other words, the principles are of general application. Some of these features will be discussed in this introduction to the Studies.

The Right Start. Today, the student of shorthand enjoys extraordinary opportunities. The learning of shorthand has been tremendously simplified by the almost universal adoption of a modern system, by improved methods of pedagogy and improved textbooks, and by the increased efficiency of schools and teachers. Formerly, the study of shorthand was accompanied by a constant struggle with the inconsistencies and complexities of unscientific systems. Only the most hardy were able to survive the ordeal. Today, students may study a system that has been brought to a degree of perfection that leaves little more to be hoped for. Every facility for becoming an expert writer, save one, lies ready at hand. That missing factor can be supplied only by the student himself—namely, his own study and application. The words of Emerson, "Thou shalt be paid exactly for what thou hast done, no more, no less," apply with striking force to the study of shorthand. The student will get out of shorthand just what he puts into it—no more, no less—and what he gets out of it will depend very largely upon his attitude of mind.

If he approaches the subject with enthusiasm for it, with the aim in view of perfecting himself in it for the sheer joy of achievement, without thought of the ultimate results, his success is assured. Some of the most prominent men and women in commercial and professional life today got their start in the world through the opportunities that shorthand offered; but they were invariably good stenographers *first.* They threw their whole energy into becoming experts in the profession they had selected, and the habit formed of doing things well extended to all their other activities. The result was that when the big opportunities came they were ready for them. Their skill in shorthand and typewriting had attracted the attention of those higher up, and they were given opportunities that were denied those of lesser skill.

Correct Habits Vital. The late Professor James, the great psychologist of Harvard University, describes the power of habit most graphically in his book on psychology. He lays down some maxims that every student of stenography should heed. He says:

> Could the young but realize how soon they will become mere walking bundles of habits, they would give more heed to their conduct while in the plastic state. We are spinning our fates, good or evil, never to be undone.
>
> The great thing in all education, is to make our nervous system our ally instead of our enemy. We must make automatic and habitual as many useful actions as we can, and guard against growing into ways that are likely to be a disadvantage to us. The

more the details of our daily life we can hand over to the effortless custody of automatism, the more our higher powers of mind will be set free for their own proper work.

He lays down three principles that are vitally important:

First: In the acquisition of a new habit, or the leaving-off of an old one, we must take care to launch ourselves with as strong and decided an *initiative* as possible.

Second: Never suffer an *exception* to occur till the new habit is rooted in your life.

Third: Seize the very first possible opportunity to act on every resolution you make and on every emotional prompting you may experience in the direction of habits you aspire to gain.

Writing shorthand expertly is merely a matter of acquiring correct habits, both mental and physical. Each step in your work, therefore, should be considered very carefully, so that such habits may be acquired at the start, for it is next to impossible to overcome habits that have once become fixed—transferred to the automatic process. The object to be sought in studying the art of shorthand writing is to build up a set of automatic actions as quickly and as thoroughly as possible. Every detail leading to this end must be studied and practiced. There is hardly another practical art in which the study of economical habits of movement and of efficient methods yields such large returns as in the technique of shorthand writing. Such mechanical details as the kind of materials you use—pen, pencil, notebook, etc.—become of great importance; but of greater importance still are the personal habits of thought, of posture, of execution, etc.

Materials. The good workman invariably demands good tools. He knows that the best work is only possible when the material necessities are of high quality. Careful attention should, therefore, be given to your working materials.

Notebooks. The notebook is especially important. The surface of the paper should be firm and smooth so that a light touch—the lighter the better—may be used. The paper should be free from imperfections in texture. The size most generally recommended by the best writers is 6 by 9 inches. The lines, preferably, should be one-third of an inch apart, as this spacing will tend to develop a more compact style of writing. The page should have a vertical ruling down the middle, so as to provide two columns for writing on each page. A column 3 inches wide enables you to write correctly across the line of writing without shifting the arm to any appreciable degree. If a pencil is used, a slightly rougher surface is necessary.

Pen or Pencil. Whether the pen or pencil is the better instrument for shorthand writing is a much discussed question, but it is the opinion of the most experienced and fastest writers that the pen is preferable. The pen gives a firm, distinct, easily recognized outline. The small circles and hooks, especially, can be much more readily and accurately executed with the pen than with the pencil. Pen writing is also very much easier to read, because it is generally more accurate. Also the more distinct lines of pen writing impose less strain on the eyes in reading.

The pen selected should have a fairly fine, but smooth, point. The style of point best adapted to the individual can only be ascertained by a little experimentation. The fountain pen has so many advantages that it is to be recommended in all cases.

If a pencil is used—and many writers prefer it in spite of its known disadvantages—the student should be supplied with a sufficient number of well-sharpened pencils to obviate the necessity of writing with a dull point. Pencil notes are apt to be large and inaccurately formed, and as the pencil dulls, this tendency grows, making the notes very difficult to read.

Posture. Perhaps no other feature of shorthand writing contributes so much to the ease, speed, and accuracy of writing as does the position the writer assumes at the table. In the teaching of penmanship great emphasis is laid upon the correct posture. Posture becomes of even greater importance in shorthand writing, for shorthand not only must be written correctly, but to become highly useful it must be *written at a very rapid rate of speed.* The shorthand writer is often required to write at a high rate of speed for long periods of time. Sustained effort is necessary.

Illustrations of the position of some of the best writers of the system are given on pages 6, 9, and 11. The illustrations, and a study of the technique of these writers, show that they sit squarely in front of the desk with both forearms resting on it. The notebook or paper is placed in a line with the right forearm, so that the hand can be moved across the line of writing without shifting the arm. The body is bent from the hips. In no case does the writer "slump" over his work, with the shoulders pressed forward, thus interfering with free breathing. The writer should sit far enough away from the table so that the edge of the table does not press against his body. The feet should be planted firmly on the floor. Many beginners twist their feet around the legs of the chair and assume awkward and erratic positions that make ease in writing impossible.

When the body is bent slightly forward a little weight will be resting on the elbows and forearms. The back should

UNDERWOOD & UNDERWOOD STUDIOS

MR. CHARLES L. SWEM

The writing position of Mr. Charles L. Swem, formerly personal stenographer and official reporter to President Woodrow Wilson. Winner of the World's Shorthand Championship in 1923 and 1924; official reporter, New York State Supreme Court.

be perfectly straight from the hips to the shoulders. The weight of the arm will then be carried by the heavy muscles of the forearm, and the movements of the hand, wrist, and fingers can be executed with the minimum of effort. It does not follow that a comfortable position is a correct one. Through habit you may have accustomed yourself to an awkward position. To find out whether you are assuming an incorrect position, ask your teacher to watch you closely while you are taking notes and to offer suggestions for improving your posture.

Position of Hand and Arm. The position of the right hand and arm is of as great importance as is that of the body. Study particularly the slant of the pen, the position of fingers, and the method of grasping the pen shown in the illustrations on pages 6, 9, and 11. The hand and arm must have the maximum of flexibility and freedom. Since the fastest writers of shorthand use the muscular movement for the heaviest work in writing, this method should be cultivated from the very beginning of the study of the art.

The large muscles of the arm are much more capable of sustained effort than are the muscles of the fingers, but unfortunately they cannot be trained to as high a degree of nicety of movement as can those of the fingers. A study of the writing movements of the most rapid writers shows that both finger and wrist movements are used. The best results can be obtained when a judicious blending of these movements is employed. For example, such characters as *p*, *b*, *f*, *v* can be executed much more readily and quickly if the downward sweep is a combination of arm and finger movement. The circles and hooks can also be executed with greater speed if the finger movement is combined with arm and wrist movement.

Keep the wrist and ball of the hand from touching the paper or the desk, but the whole forearm from the elbow to the wrist should rest on the table. With the second, third, and fourth fingers turned in, as shown in the illustrations, the hand will be in a position to glide easily on the nails of these fingers.

Hold the pen with just enough pressure to give you command of it, but do not grip it so firmly that all flexibility of movement is destroyed. Gripping the pen with a deathlike hold, one of the commonest habits of the young and inexperienced writer, is fatal to high speed and to ease of execution.

In all arts "form" or "technique" is of vast importance. Study the work of the violinist, the pianist, the golfer, the tennis player, and it will be seen that the experts have acquired a certain grace of form, an art in execution, that at once appeals to us because of its obvious effectiveness.

The late David Wolfe Brown, the famous congressional reporter, says:

> Pen gripping, involving as it does needless muscular effort, tends to promote an inartistic style of writing, interferes with the acquisition of speed, and induces undue and premature fatigue, to say nothing of the ultimate danger of pen paralysis from the unnecessary, excessive, and long-continued muscular strain.

Light Touch. A light touch of pen or pencil upon the paper is necessary to high speed. No more pressure should be exerted than is necessary to make a clear, definite outline. Using a heavy touch means gripping the pen; it destroys all flexibility of movement, retards the development of speed, and leads to inaccuracy—all results to be avoided.

UNDERWOOD & UNDERWOOD STUDIOS

MR. MARTIN J. DUPRAW

At the age of nineteen, Mr. Dupraw won the World's Shorthand Championship in 1925. By repeating his victories in 1926 and 1927, Mr Dupraw won permanent possession of the World's Championship Trophy.

Efficiency Methods. Much of the speed of the fast writers of shorthand has been acquired by the study and practice of efficiency methods in performing their work. The elimination of waste mechanical motion has almost as much to do with speed in writing as does the shortening of outlines or the application of the abbreviating principles of the system, phrasing, etc. The position of the notebook, the turning of the leaves, the passing from one outline to another, the spacing between the outlines, the passing from the bottom of a column to the top of the next, the distance the hand travels above or below the line of writing—all are factors that should be considered very carefully and analyzed by the student who wishes to acquire high speed as well as accuracy. The proper time to make a study of these features of the writing *is at the start, before incorrect habits are formed.*

Turning the Leaves of the Notebook. To the inexperienced writer the turning of a leaf of his notebook is always attended with a sense of hurry and fear that something will be lost, especially if the dictation is pushing him to the limit of his speed. A little study and practice will enable the writer to turn the leaves without appreciable loss of time.

The following description of the proper method of turning the leaves is the result of much study and practice on the part of the talented reporter, Thomas Allen Reed. He says:

> While writing on the upper half of the leaf introduce the second finger of the left hand between it and the next leaf, keeping the leaf just being written on steady by the first finger and thumb. While writing on the last part of the page shift the leaf by degrees until it is about halfway up the book; when it is convenient, lift the first finger and thumb and the leaf will turn by itself. This is the best plan while writing on a desk or table. When writing on the knee, the first finger should be introduced instead of the second.

HARRIS & EWING

MR. ALBERT SCHNEIDER

The writing position of Mr. Albert Schneider, winner of the World's Shorthand Championship, 1921, now member of the shorthand reporting staff of the Congress of the United States.

and the leaf be shifted up only about two inches. The finger should be introduced at the first pause the speaker makes or at any convenient opportunity that presents itself.

Isaac S. Dement, one of the most expert shorthand writers the world has ever known, preferred handling the notebook much as Mr. Reed has described, but he kept shifting the page upon which he was writing constantly upward, so that when he had finished one page he would be in a position to begin the following page without having to move the hand from the bottom of the notebook to the top of the next page.

Passing from One Outline to Another. It is axiomatic that the shortest distance between two points is a straight line. The shorthand writer should cultivate from the start the art of passing directly from one outline to another without any preliminary or useless movements. The best time to practice this method is while taking dictation that has been practiced, as the attention can then be concentrated entirely on the movement used in passing from one word to another, and the mind not diverted by trying to recall unfamiliar outlines or in constructing new ones.

The work of poorly trained writers shows that the pen makes several unnecessary movements at the completion of each word form—the writer seemingly trying to get a running start by making several movements in the air. These movements result in a loss of valuable nervous energy. They are generally the result of the hesitation caused by trying to recall principles or brief forms of which the writer has but a hazy recollection.

By memorizing a short passage and writing it repeatedly from memory, passing *directly from one outline to the next*, much may be done to overcome this very wasteful habit. Determined effort must be made to acquire continuity of movement. In acquiring this habit, a certain deliberation must at first be cultivated; the desire to keep the hand moving, except in performing the actual act of writing outlines, should be repressed.

In passing from one outline to another do not raise the pen higher than is necessary to clear the paper, for the farther the pen travels the longer it takes, and unnecessary travel records itself in decreased efficiency.

From the first, aim to acquire an easy, rapid—but accurate—formation of the characters and to make each character with a *continuous* movement. "Continuous" does not necessarily imply *rapid* movement, however. It is well to make a mental picture of the entire shorthand form of a word or phrase before writing it. If you are about to write the word "make," for example, think of the consonants *m* and *k* and where the vowel should go—outside the angle—and then write the entire word with an easy, flowing movement. If you cannot write the word form without a jerky movement the first time you attempt it, keep on writing it until you can. That is one of the most important of the "speed secrets." Acquire the habit early and it will help you immensely all through the Studies and enable you to reach a higher degree of skill than would be possible without it. The same principle applies to phrasing.

Spacing Between Outlines. The spacing between outlines should be no more than is necessary to give a proper clearance, and it should be uniform.

Size of Notes. Adopt a size of notes that seems natural to you. The characters given in this text and in *The Gregg Writer* are a good standard to follow. As a general thing, students make characters too large, and, as this tendency is magnified in rapid writing, much is to be gained by starting with notes that are rather small. The size of notes, however, is a point that must be determined largely by the writer himself, but he should consult with his teacher and aim to adopt a size best suited to his hand. The size should be such as to give a natural freedom of movement, but this should be determined only after earnest analysis.

Correcting Outlines. While practicing for speed and accuracy, or taking dictation, the writer should never under any circumstances *correct or change word forms while writing*. Making incorrect outlines is mostly a matter of habit. It is just as easy to acquire the habit of writing correctly as it is to write incorrectly. The loss of time in crossing out words incorrectly written is equivalent to that of writing several words correctly, to say nothing of the mental disturbance it causes. The time to make corrections in outlines is *while reading or transcribing the notes*. Then every poorly executed outline should receive careful attention and sufficient practice be obtained in writing the *correct form* to establish ease of execution.

Concentrating the Attention. Facility in writing reaches the highest point only when the writer can give his undivided attention to the work in hand. The writer should never let his attention be diverted if he can possibly avoid it. He should even accustom himself to continue his writing when the most startling causes for interruption appear. Holding command of the attention is an art that cannot be too strongly emphasized.

Systematic Methods of Arranging the Notebook. By following a systematic method, the notebook of the stenographer can be arranged so that any letter or any piece of dictation can be referred to quickly. The notebook should be dated at the beginning of each day's work. The beginning of each dictation or letter should be indicated by some landmark. If the dictation consists of letters, the name of each firm should begin on a new line and be indented. Form the habit of writing names in shorthand. Only the name of unusual spelling needs to be written in longhand.

As each piece of dictation is transcribed, draw a vertical line down through it to indicate that the matter has been transcribed or read. In reading, circle each outline that has been imperfectly executed and afterwards practice the correct form for each of these circled word forms. A rubber band should be slipped over the leaves of the notebook preceding the beginning of a day's work, so that the place of writing can be quickly found when it is desired to refer to any of the early dictation of the day.

General Principles to be Applied. To become expert in writing and in reading shorthand, the following principles should be kept in mind:

1. The principles of the system must be applied accurately and intelligently in order to give the required brevity of form and to produce uniformity in writing.

2. The proportion of the characters must be constantly observed; that is, a careful distinction must be made in the length of strokes and in the size of circles.

3. Much practice must be obtained in applying principles and in the execution of the characters in order to secure facility.

4. Everything written must be read—even the forms made in practicing the simple characters of the alphabet. The shorthand characters should be analyzed, criticized, and studied until an accurate style of writing has become a habit.

5. Frequent and thorough reviews are essential to rapid and

sure progress. The review should not be confined solely to "mental" review, but should be accompanied by much practice in writing. A deep impression of the principles can be acquired only by such reviews intelligently conducted. Each time the writer goes over a principle thoughtfully with the mind concentrated on it, the deeper will become the impression of that principle.

6. Shorthand writing skill is based upon correct habits; habits are acquired not by doing a thing once, but by repetition with attention.

7. As much as possible of actual writing should be done from dictation, or from copying well-written shorthand. Copying from printed matter is useful, but since shorthand writing is nearly always done from dictation it is evident that dictation is preferable. The student, however, should form the habit of writing all of his original compositions and notes in shorthand. We learn shorthand by *using* it.

SPEED STUDY I

Speed and accuracy in shorthand writing begin with the very first lesson. They depend almost wholly upon two things: first, the clearness of the mental picture of each form the student has in mind; and, second, his ability to execute correctly and rapidly the movements necessary to reproduce the picture. A good shorthand style depends eventually not upon what the writer has in mind, but upon what he can put on paper. It demands clear vision plus *mastery of movement.*

An analysis of Gregg Shorthand shows certain elementary combinations that are repeated, with slight variations, over and over again—even in the most advanced writing. A mastery of these combinations will therefore give the writer a firm foundation upon which to build his structure of speed and accuracy.

In studying the drills, aim first at securing a *clear mental picture* of the form to be executed; analyze carefully the movement necessary to make it rapidly; and then repeat the movement until facility is acquired and all hesitation is removed.

At the beginning a careful comparison of the notes written with the correct forms in the text is essential. The comparison should be carried on until the habit of correct movement has been established. The characters are to be *written*, not drawn. Two important features to be constantly watched are: first, comparative length of consonant strokes; and, second, relative size of vowels.

1. Consonants. In practicing the following drill, make a positive distinction in the length of strokes. By writing the curves with the natural longhand movement, *k* and *g* will be curved more at the end, while *r* and *l* will have the deeper curve at the beginning. These natural curves promote speed and ease of joining. Repeat to yourself the word for which the sign stands, as *can*, *go*, *are*, *will*, *in*, *am*, etc.

Drill

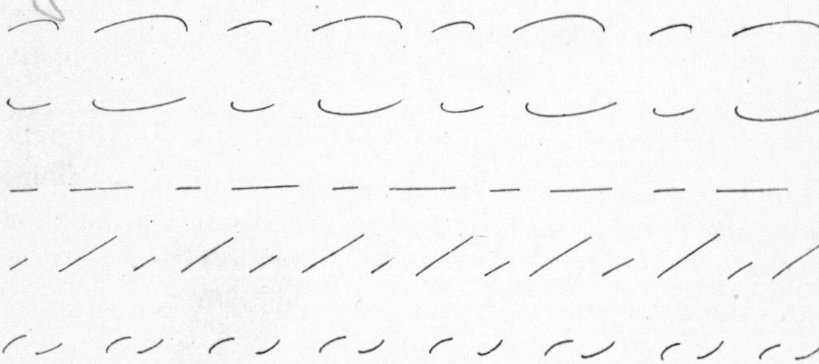

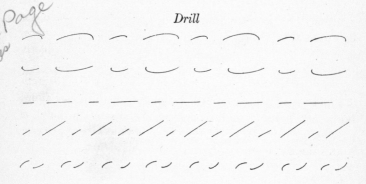

2. Circle Vowels. In writing the circle vowels distinguish carefully between sizes. Circles are written with either right motion or left motion, depending on the nature of the joining in which they occur. When they appear alone, they are written with left motion.

Drill

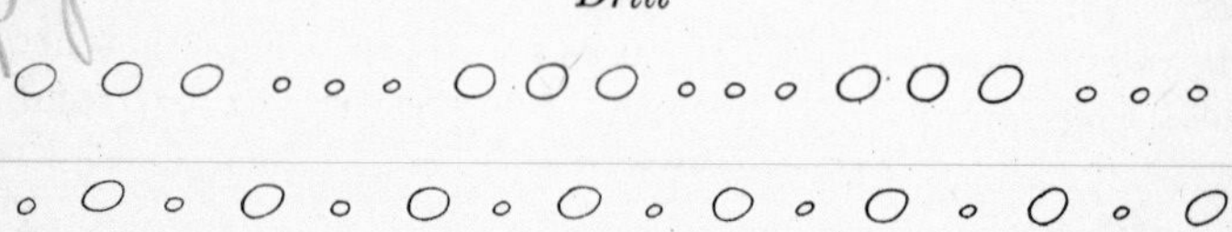

3. Circles Joined to Curves. In joining circles to curves, no part of the circle should be retraced. Observe carefully the movement used in starting and finishing the circles in the following outlines, as indicated by the dotted arrow:

Right:

Much time is wasted by retracing the circle, as in the following illustration:

Wrong:

Practice the joining of both large and small circles at the beginning and end of each consonant. Form the habit of *completely closing the circle*; there should be no space between it and the consonant.

Drill

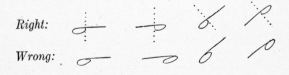

4. Circles Joined to Straight Strokes. In joining the circle to straight strokes, start or finish the circle in the way shown by the dotted lines in the following illustration:

Right:

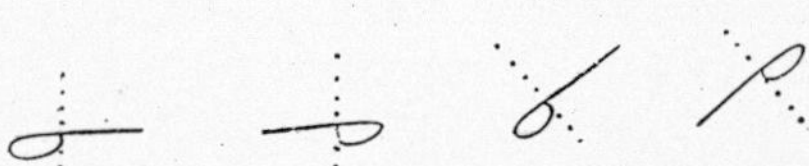

Wrong:

In the following drill the circle is joined with the right motion:

Drill

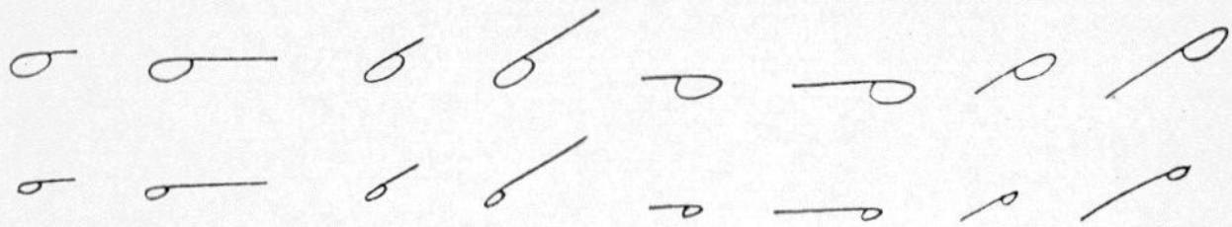

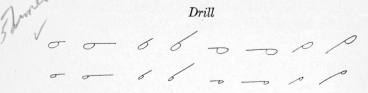

5. Outside Angles. In joinings of the following type, the circle cuts the line of writing:

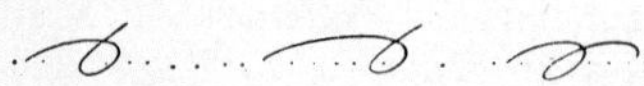

Drill

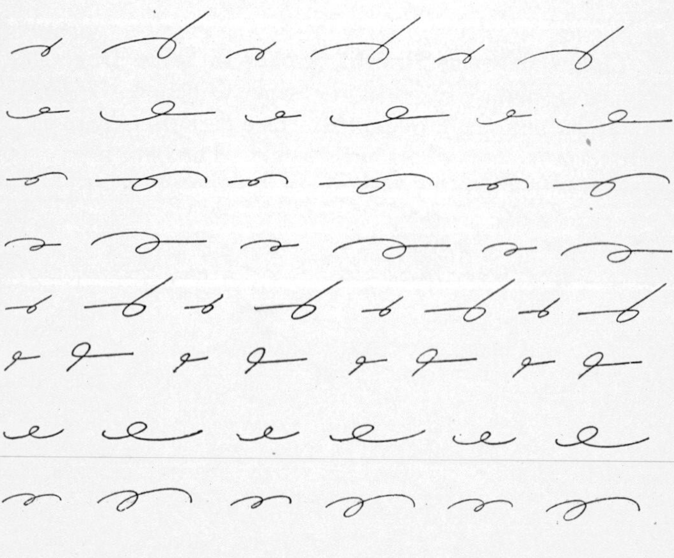

6. Straight Strokes Joined to Curves without Angle. In joinings of the following type, the blending of curve with straight line should be so smooth that the circle appears to have been inserted afterwards:

Right:

Wrong:

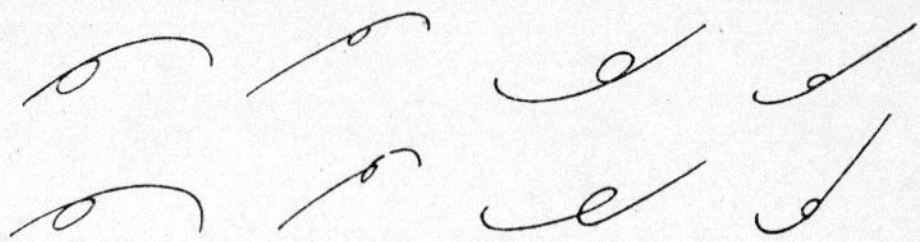

Drill

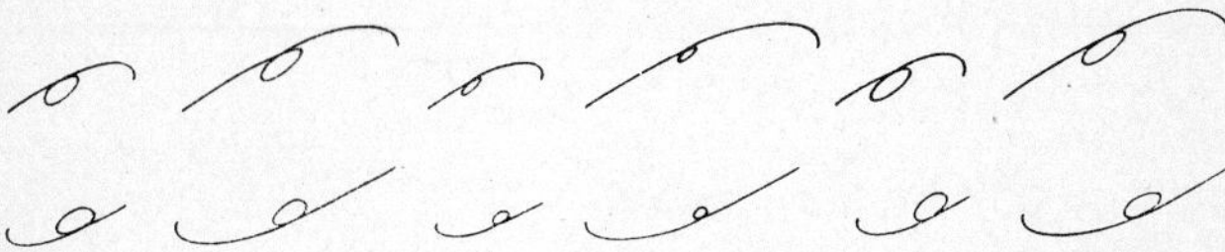

7. Circles Between Straight Strokes in Same Direction. Between straight strokes in the same direction the circle tends to flatten out into an oval. This permits the straight line to form the upper part of the circle. The right motion is used in this joining:

Right:

Wrong:

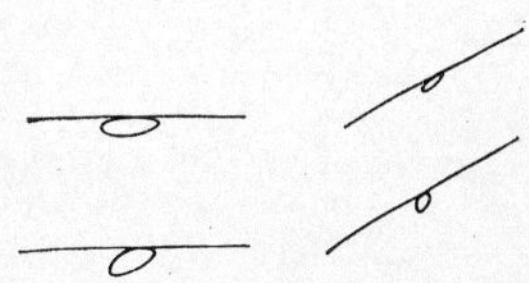

Drill

8. Circles Between Opposite Curves. When a circle occurs between opposite curves, the circle should join snugly, thus:

Right: 

If the circle were erased, the curves would still retain their correct formation.

If the joining has not been skillfully executed, the outlines would have had this appearance.

Wrong: 

Drill

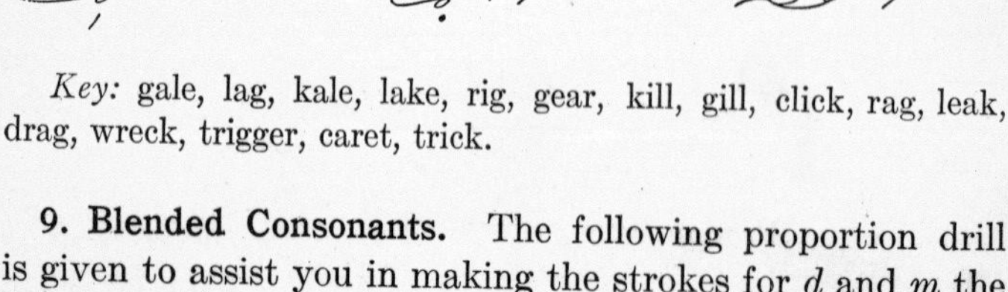

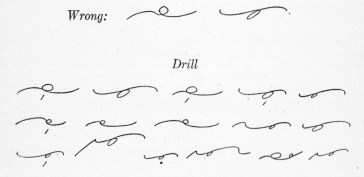

Key: gale, lag, kale, lake, rig, gear, kill, gill, click, rag, leak, drag, wreck, trigger, caret, trick.

9. Blended Consonants. The following proportion drill is given to assist you in making the strokes for *d* and *m* the proper length. Up to this point you have had in mind that *d* is longer than *t* and that *m* is longer than *n*, but you have not had to distinguish between these characters and a third one, which is as long as the combined length of the other two.

It is now necessary that you definitely restrict the length of the *d* and the *m* as shown in this drill. This drill will also furnish you an opportunity to practice the "get-away" ending of the strokes, one of the speed secrets of the rapid writer.

Drill

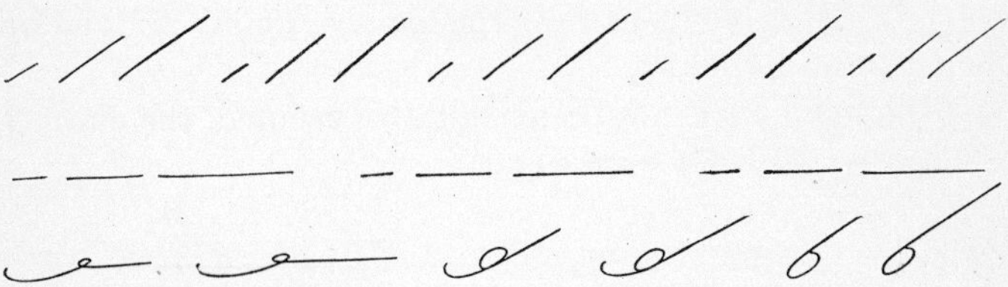

Key: it, would, did (repeated).
not, more, men (repeated).
limb, lemon, raid, rated, aid, aided.

10. Review Drill on Circle Joinings.

Words

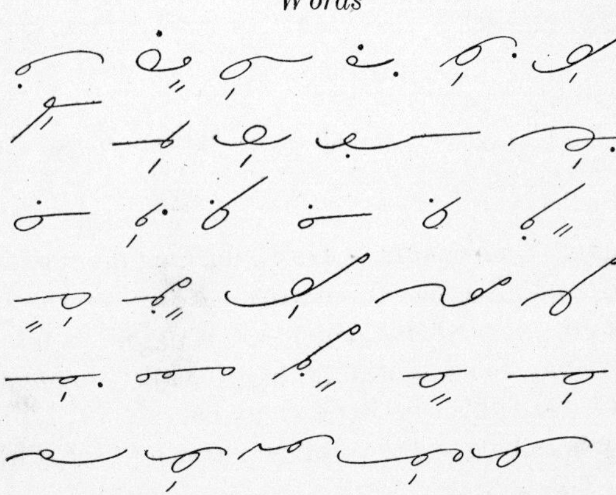

Key: egg, Harry, acre, hearing, taking, raid; deem, meat, rare, realm, gaining; ham, eating, had, him, hat, Ed; May, Nettie, lady, gritty, caddy; meaning, enemy, Teddy, Nan, main; kill, rake, trick, leaky, rag.

Sentences

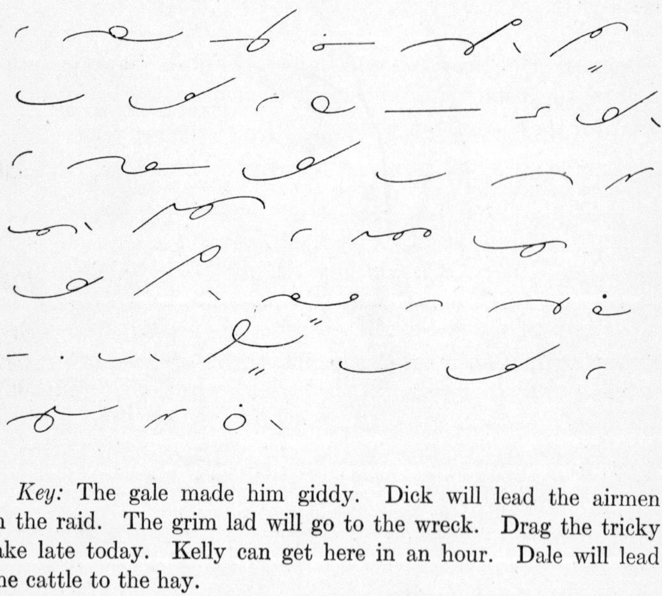

Key: The gale made him giddy. Dick will lead the airmen in the raid. The grim lad will go to the wreck. Drag the tricky lake late today. Kelly can get here in an hour. Dale will lead the cattle to the hay.

11. Methods of Learning Brief Forms for Common Words. About two hundred words constitute more than half the words used in spoken and written language. Brief shorthand forms for these words of high frequency have been developed. The following extract is taken from "Factors of Shorthand Speed," by David Wolfe Brown:

It is highly important that whatever the student undertakes to memorize should be memorized thoroughly. From half-recollection comes hesitation; and from hesitation comes loss of speed. Especially in the study of the wordsigns,* most students undertake to learn too many at once. It cannot be too often repeated that in shorthand whatever needs to be memorized at all needs to be so mastered that it may come instantly to the mind and fingers whenever wanted.

Bernard De Bear, a well-known English reporter and teacher, suggests the following method of learning the brief forms for these common words:

Take a double sheet of foolscap and fold it over into folds which will give about twelve divisions in all. Copy from the textbook neatly and carefully the signs you are about to learn, one on each line. Having thus filled the first column, close the book, and endeavor at once from memory to transcribe into longhand in column 2. The words having only just been copied, this should prove no difficult task; but any blanks should be filled in from the key and underlined, to denote that the signs were not remembered. This done, fold under column 1, so as to leave only the longhand words in column 2 visible, and transcribe those into shorthand in column 3, so nearly as the memory will allow. Gaps can now be filled in from column 1, which, however, should not be resorted to until the attempt has been made to work through the entire list. Then retranscribe the shorthand lines on column 4. And so on to the end—shorthand into longhand, and vice versa. It may be guaranteed that by the time the twelve columns have all been filled in the manner indicated, that particular set of words or phrases will have been almost thoroughly mastered.

*In previous editions of the Gregg Shorthand Manual, "brief forms for common words" were known as "wordsigns."

Plenty of dictation and reading practice is essential in learning the brief forms. Because of their simplicity, they are likely to be written more hurriedly, and consequently more carelessly, than the other characters, thereby losing their identity. Their execution should be practiced, therefore, until the student has thoroughly mastered each outline.

12. Elementary Phrase Writing. Phrase writing has been well described as an "art within an art." There is no doubt that a great saving of time and effort is effected by judicious phrase writing. The purpose of joining words is to eliminate the loss of time occasioned by lifting the pen and in passing from one shorthand form to another. The theory is that each pen lift is equal to a stroke, and therefore that every word joined saves the time equivalent to that used in writing a stroke.

Limitations of Phrase Writing. This theory, however, is true only where there is no *hesitancy in joining the words.* Furthermore, it is not true of very long phrases, because such phrases destroy the rhythm of shorthand writing.

The Kind of Phrases to Practice. Phrases are of three kinds: (1) those that have been memorized and can be written fluently without conscious attention; (2) those that are devised from well-understood principles; (3) those that are improvised on the spur of the moment.

As phrase writing is an art, only by much experience will the student gain a knowledge of just what words can be joined with safety and advantage, but this knowledge will be more quickly acquired through a close study of the examples given in the textbook than in any other way. At first it will be well to confine the phrasing to the common everyday phrases given in the Manual.

How to Practice Phrases. Phrases, like brief forms, are useful only if *thoroughly mastered.* The phrases illustrated on page 15 of the Manual are among the most common phrases of the language, and the student should devote sufficient practice to them to be able to execute them with great rapidity and accuracy. A point to be remembered in executing phrases is that ultimately a phrase is *one compact thing.* Think of it as one word and it will be executed in that way. There should be no stop at the joinings. By thinking of *each word* separately, there will be a tendency to stop at the end of each word, and facility in execution will thus be lost.

Practice each of the short pnrases, such as *it-is, of-the, to-the, with-the,* given in Chapter I of the Manual until it can be executed accurately at a very rapid speed. Read all the notes, repracticing any forms that are not well written. The elements of the short phrases need not be separated for practice, as they present no very great difficulties of execution.

The following additional phrases should be practiced:

Frequent-Phrase Drill

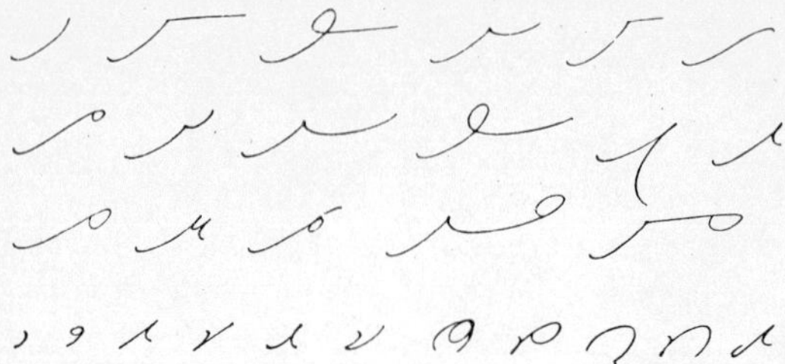

Key: of: of-the, of-it, of-our, of-their, of-his, of-that, of-them, of-this, of-your, of-all, of-those, of-what.

in: in-the, in-it, in-our, in-his, in-that, in-this, in-your, in-those.

be: can-be, would-be, could-be, may-be, will-be, to-be.

at: at-the, at-our, at-their, at-that, at-this, at-those.

and: and-am, and-I-am, and-are, and-not, and-the, and-they, and-their, and-will, and-I-will, and-be, and-is, and-that, and-was, and-with, and-like, and-may.

is: he-is, it-is, is-it, there-is, is-there, that-is, is-that, this-is, is-this, what-is.

13. READING AND DICTATION PRACTICE

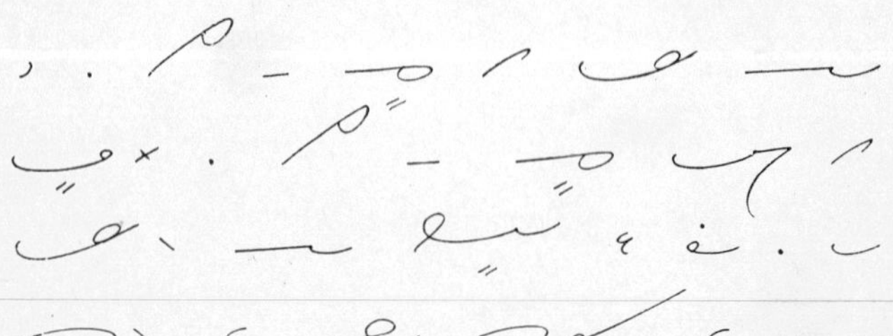

(125)

1.

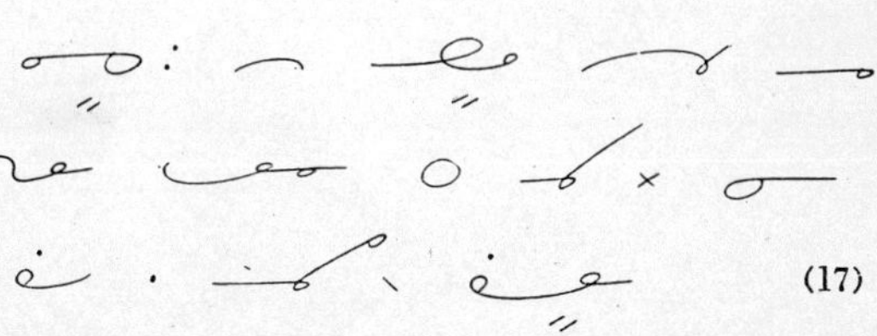

(17)

14. WRITING PRACTICE

1. Can you not take the limited train to Gary today?

2. He came here today to get the data to read, but it was not ready.

3. He lacked mental training, and his hearing was not good.

4. I am reading a tale of the air attack at Macon.

5. Will you get the training that you are in need of?

6. He dreaded the heat; it made him too ill to read.

7. The cricket game marked the end of the meet at Reading.

8. Take the rear gate to the lane; at the end of the lane a well-marked trail will lead you to the lake.

9. They will be ready by the end of May to take all the linen you can make.

10. He will take a late train to Lima.

11. I can be there at any hour that you will meet me.

12. Will you take me with you to Lynn?

13. I will take the money to the man by train.

14. They could not get all the money that was needed.

15. I could make little of that meeting.

16. It was more than I like to tackle at any time.

17. It will take time to get this acre graded.

18. By the time that you get there, they may be ready to go.

19. You may take this milk to the creamery when you are ready.

20. Take a little time to go into the data.

SPEED STUDY II

15. Down Strokes. Speed in the execution of the consonants presented in Chapter II of the Manual can be increased by combining muscular movement with a slight closing of the fingers with the downward sweep of the pen. Pass from one character to another in the most direct line, with the pen barely clearing the paper. Do not stop at the end of a character. Observe length carefully.

Drill

16. Circles Joined to Curves. In joining the two circles to the curves given in Chapter II, observe the same care in avoiding the retracing of the circle as you did in Chapter I.

Drill

Key: pay, bee, heap, about, fee, very, if, ever, half, I-have.

17. Straight Strokes. Because of their apparent simplicity, drill on the execution of the straight strokes is often neglected.

Note particularly in the following drill that the straight characters are really straight.

Drill

Right: 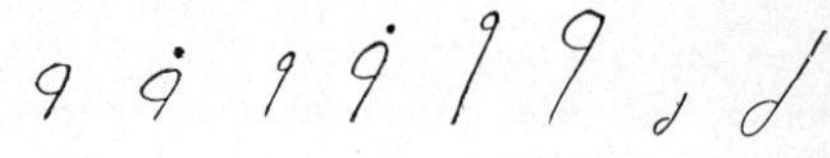

Key: I-shall, hash, each, hatch, edge, age, she, jay.

Wrong: 

18. Frequent Consonant Combinations. The combinations *pr*, *br*, *fr*, *pl*, *bl*, *fl* are of frequent occurrence, and special attention to the writing of them is essential. These frequently recurring combinations should be written with *one sweep of the pen.*

Right: 

Wrong: 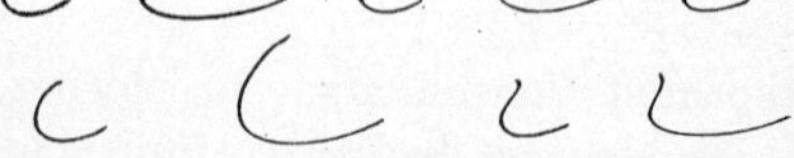

The following drill supplements the movement drills found in Paragraphs 37, 38, and 39 of the Manual:

Drill

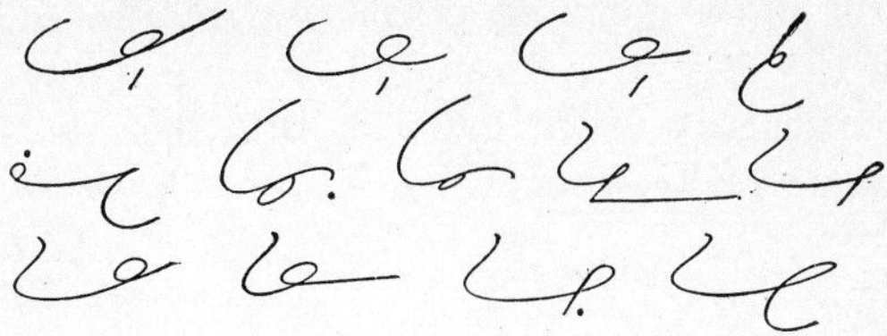

Key: played, player, plane, cheaper, helper, breaking, brick, freshmen, flesh, flat, frame, flashing, flapper.

In harmony with the *fr* and *fl* blends, the following combinations should be studied and practiced:

Key: keep, can-be.

19. Intervening Vowels. When a circle vowel intervenes between the *f* or *v* and a following *r* or *l*, and in similar joinings, the angle is restored and the circle placed outside, thus:

Key: fear, feel, fair, fail, vary, valley, avail.

20. Repeated Consonants. In placing a circle between repeated strokes, the distinctive form and slant of the consonants must be maintained.

By comparing the forms in the illustration on the next page, the importance of correct slant will be evident:

Right:

Wrong:

21. Facile Joinings. In the following joinings, observe how the distinctive form of each consonant is preserved.

In such joinings as *p-a-r*, for example, the circle should close up snugly.

Drill

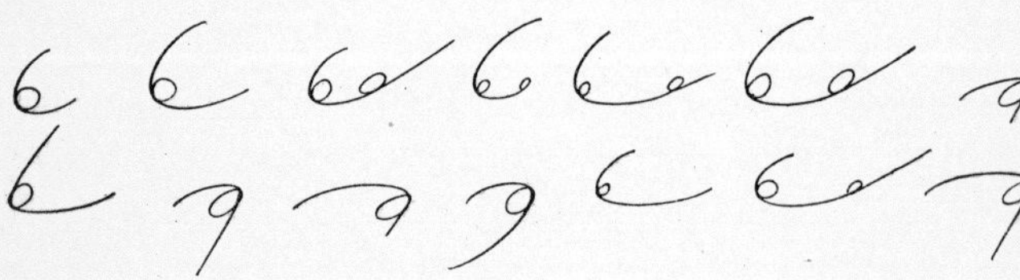

Key: par, bail, parade, berry, billet, ballad, cash, jail, cage, gash, cave, peel, pallid, gauge.

In such combinations as the following, a full curve produces a more facile joining:

Drill

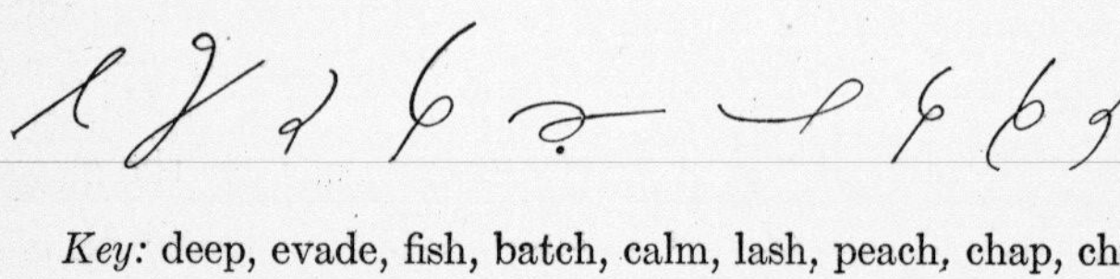

Key: deep, evade, fish, batch, calm, lash, peach, chap, chief.

22. Opposite Curves. In a few words the opposite curves introduced in this chapter are found in combination. The following illustrations should be practiced carefully:

Drill

Key: before, beef, pave, fib, bevy, peevish.

23. Modification of Circles. The mastery of the joinings illustrated in this drill is of importance. The circle is slightly flattened.

Drill

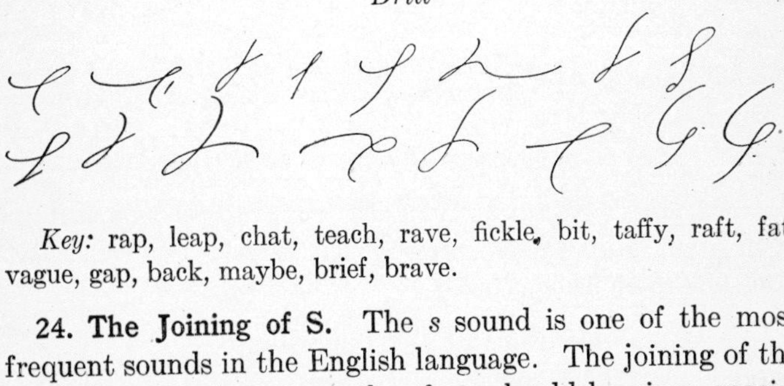

Key: rap, leap, chat, teach, rave, fickle, bit, taffy, raft, fat, vague, gap, back, maybe, brief, brave.

24. The Joining of S. The *s* sound is one of the most frequent sounds in the English language. The joining of the *s* to the other characters, therefore, should be given special drill.

The following drill is intended to develop skill in making a distinction in length between *s* and *p*, *b*; between *s* and *f*, *v*.

As you practice the strokes, repeat to yourself the words they represent—*put*, *be-but-by*, *is-his*, *for*, *have*, etc. Follow this silent reading method wherever practicable in your drills.

Drill

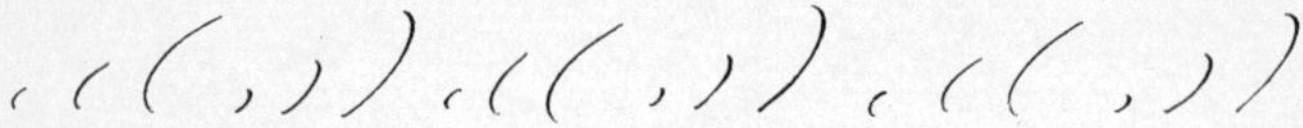

25. Joining S to Curves. When *s* is joined to a downward curve, it is important to get "around the corner" quickly. *Uniform slant* should be maintained. Give particular attention to the joining of *s* before *l*, and after *k*, *g*.

Drill

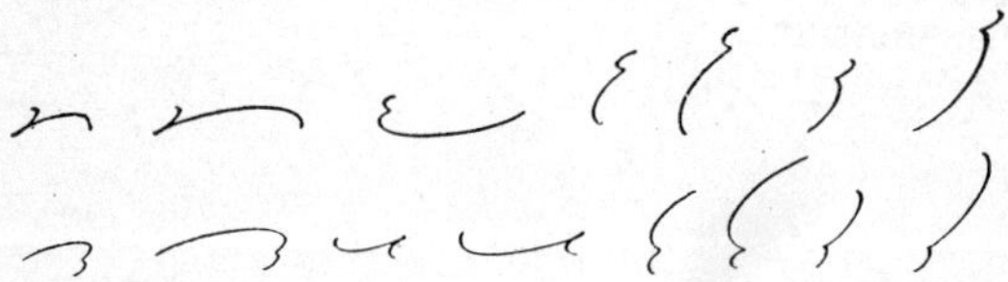

26. Joining S to Straight Lines. *S* joins to straight lines with a sharp angle, but there should be no pause at the joining.

Drill

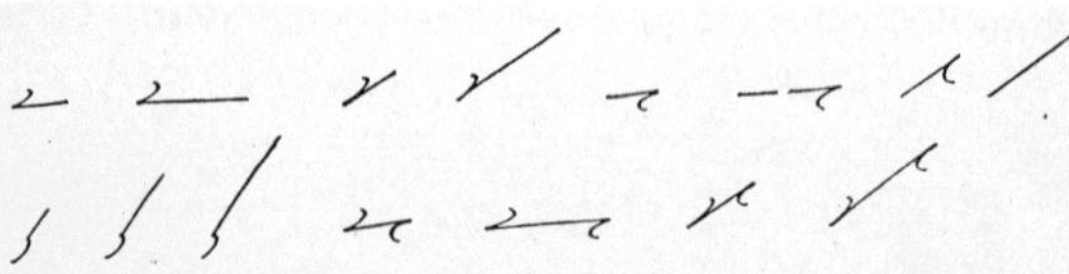

27. Intervening Circles. An intervening circle does not affect the rules for joining *s*.

Drill

Key: sick, sag, case, seal, race, lease, scene, same, said, days. teas, safe, face, sap, bees, sieve, vase, sash, siege, chase.

28. The Str Combination. *Str* is one of the most facile of forms when properly written. It should be executed without a stop. *T* should be written very *short* and with a rather vertical inclination.

Drill

Key: stray, strap, stretch, stream, streak, strain, stress.

29. The Ses Blends. These graceful, "wavelike" characters should not be given a very deep curvature. Compare

Right:

Wrong:

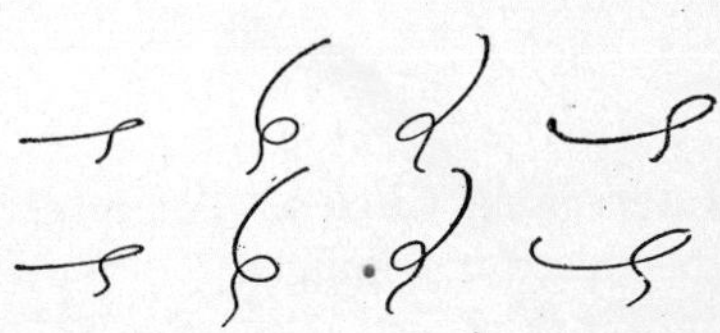

In joining *ses* after a circle vowel, following or preceding another consonant, the first *s* may be "lost" in forming part of the circle, thus:

Drill

Key: faces, masses, cases, races, places, teases, leases, guesses.

30. Brief-Form Plurals Drill.

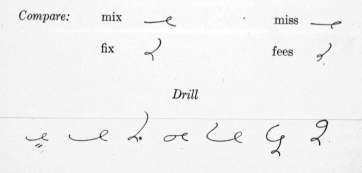

Key: hours, goods, ends, markets (Mrs.), countries, dates, comes, others, times, worlds, matters, systems, works, presents, desires.

31. Joining X. The character for *x* is written with a distinct downward-forward movement.

Compare: mix miss

fix  fees 

Drill

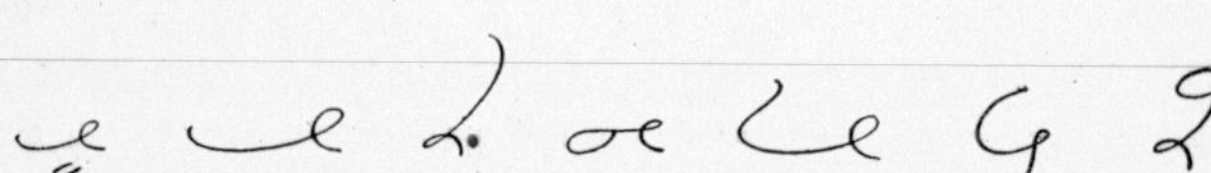

Key: Rex, lax, vex, annex, flax, prefix, affix.

32. The Xes Blends. In this blend the *s* following *x* takes the slant of *x*.

Drill

Key: prefixes, affixes, annexes, vexes.

33. Review Drill on Vowel Joinings.

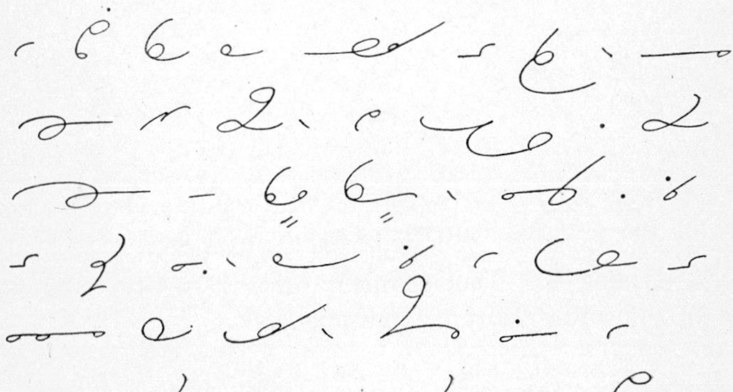

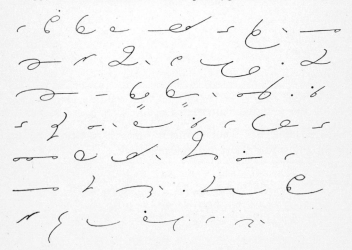

Key: The happy pair were married in the chapel. Many came to the affair. They will play a fair game in Perry Park. He made a hit in the fifth inning. He will hit the plane in the enemy air raid. I have given him the money for the goods. A formal appeal to the public will help the cause.

34. Frequent-Phrase Drill.

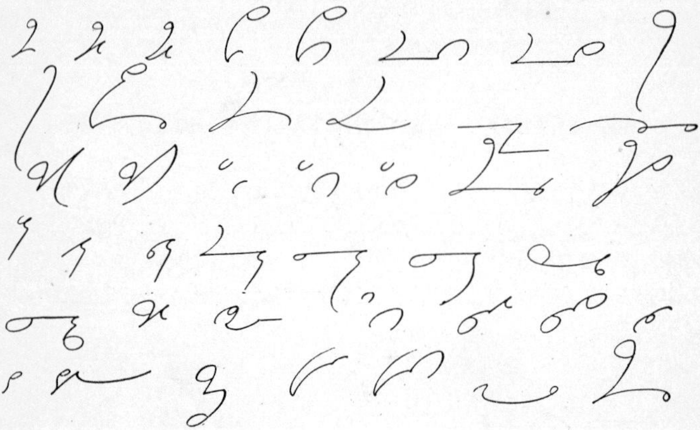

Key: if-the, if-it-is, if-there-is, about-the, about-this, from-this, from-that, I-have-been, you-have-been, has-been-given, very-good, very-well, much-more, give-me, I-should-be, I-should-have, over-the, over-this, over-that, every-minute, every-day, of-such, to-such, with-such, from-such, he-must-be, I-must-have, I-will-see, I-must-say, as-it-is, these-are-not, under-this, I think-it-is, I-think-that, they-think, he-says, he-says-it-will, I-shall-not-favor, between-the, between-this, your-letter, I-have-given.

35. Abbreviations. A simple statement of the abbreviating principle appears on page 10, Paragraph 23, of the Manual. In the shorthand-transcription plates of this and following Speed Studies, the abbreviating principle will be applied to common geographical names, the days of the week and the months of the year. The principle is extended in this way so that the dictation material in the early part of the training may be made as practical and as interesting as the principles illustrated will permit.

36. READING AND DICTATION PRACTICE

2.

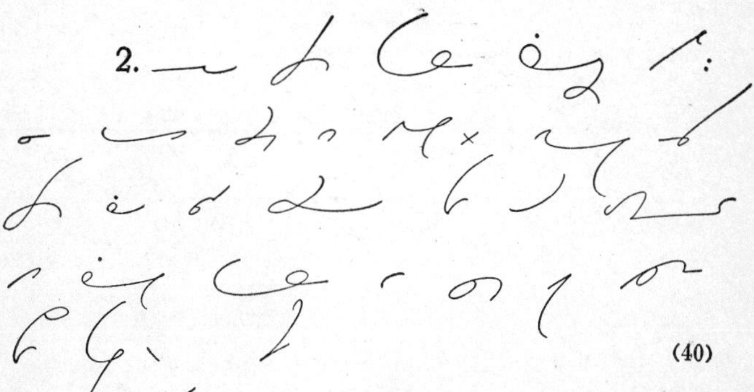

(40)

3.

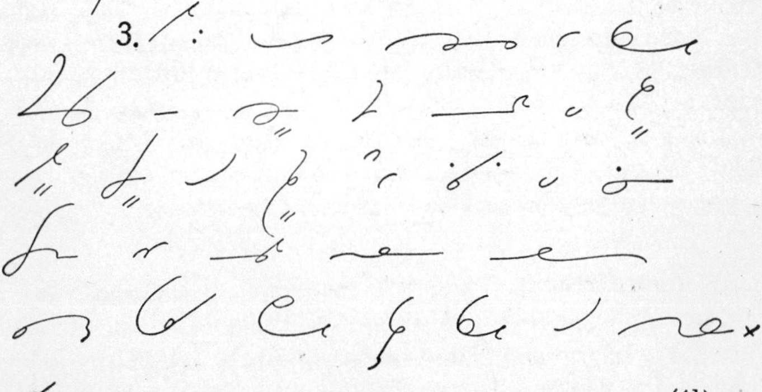

(41)

4.

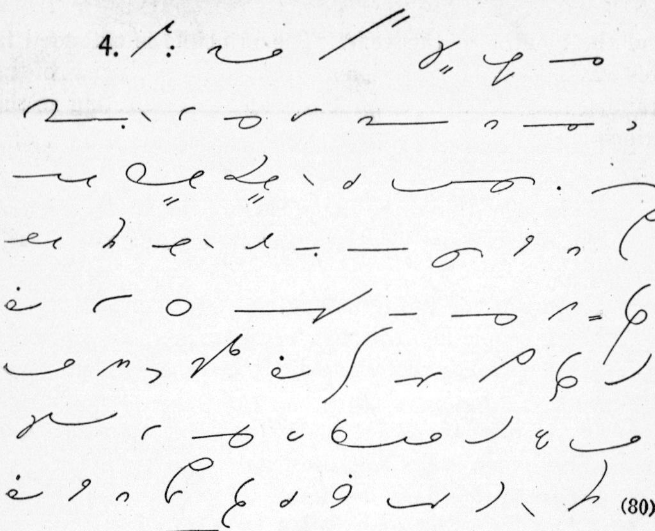

(80)

5.

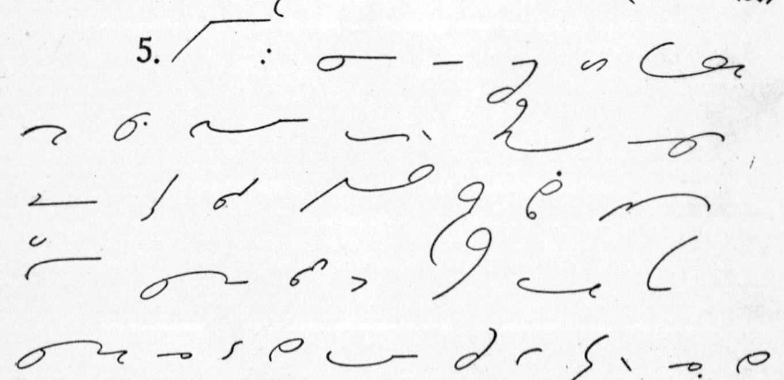

(77)

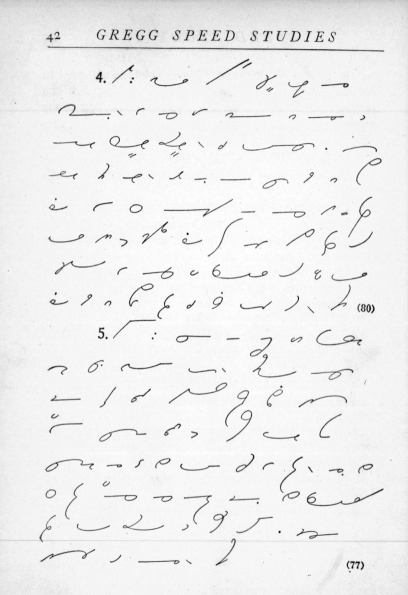

37. WRITING PRACTICE

1. Such business matters as these take much work and planning before they are ready for action by the staff.
2. I cannot leave for my vacation until this session about taxes is over.
3. He is eager to see the range back of the Black Hills.
4. She will be busy for days making an analysis of the census.
5. When will you finish making my red felt hat?
6. Many people favor part-time work.
7. These changes will have little bearing on businesses like yours.
8. Our staff needs all the money you can spare to study thoroughly every one of the cases.
9. I must settle my affairs first.
10. The missing papers have not been traced.
11. Change your plans before anything more is said about them.
12. The chief is busy at his desk and will not be free to go over business matters with you this morning.
13. You may read what he said in the minutes of our meeting.
14. He felt that the rich gifts would make his guests happy.
15. Many came to the dress sales today.
16. You may publish in the press what you will about our scheme.
17. I have a chance to visit in the country.

SPEED STUDY III

38. O-Hook. The *o*-hook should be made small, narrow, and deep.

Observe the comparative sizes of the three characters of this related group—*o, r, l.* Say the words *of, our, will* as you write the outlines.

Drill

39. O-Hook Joined. The joining of the *o*-hook to other characters should receive close attention. Observe carefully the initial and final joinings of the *o*-hook in the following drill, after which practice each until it can be written with facility and accuracy.

Drill

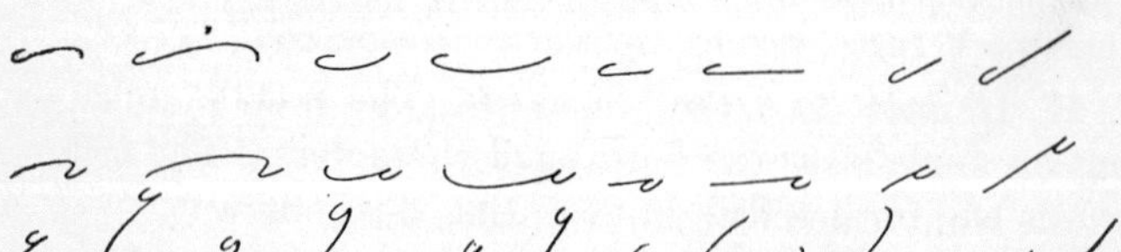

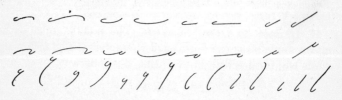

40. The Three Sounds. In this drill note particularly the variety of spellings for the medium sound—*aw* as in *law*, *ou* as in *ought*, *au* as in *caught.*

Drill

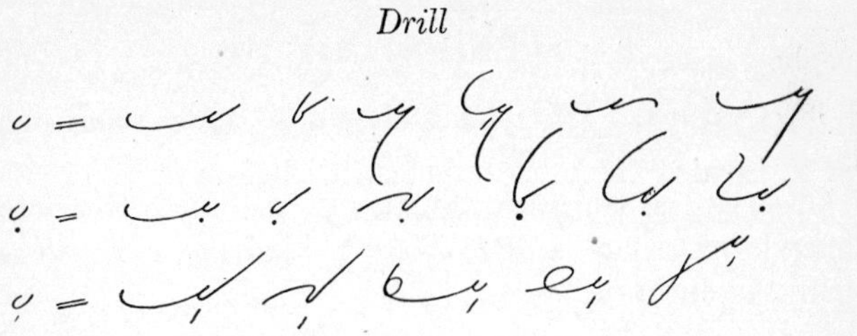

Key: lot, shot, rob, probe, rock, lodge, law, ought, caught, bought, brought, fraught, load, code, shallow, narrow, shadow.

In the majority of cases the *o*-hook joins naturally without an angle. In joining the *o*-hook after *k* and *g*, the movement is similar to that in writing *gr*—there should be no stop.

Drill

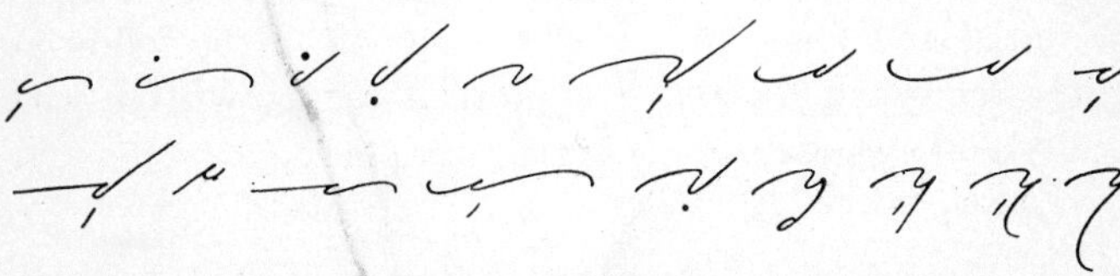

Key: oak, hog, hot, awed, call, goad, wrought, lot, note, mode, told, mock, rogue, caught, coffee, coach, cope, cob.

41. O-Hook to Down Strokes. The *o*-hook joins without an angle after the downward characters. The following words will furnish drill in executing this joining:

Drill

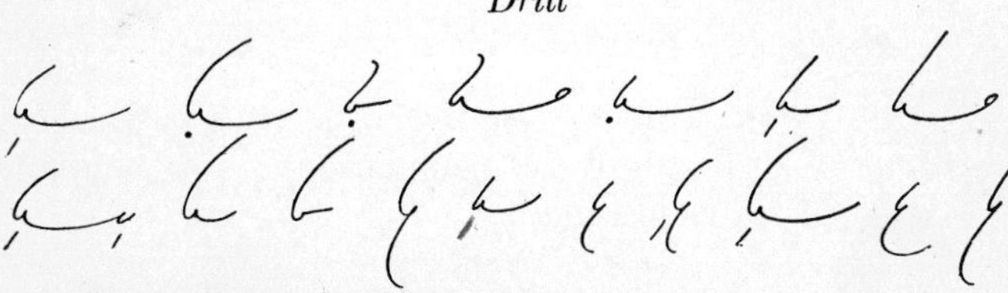

Key: pole, ball, fawn, folly, shawl, chore, jolly, polo, bore, bone, bob, shore, shop, pope, bowl, chopper, job.

42. O-Hook on Side. The following words will furnish drill in turning the *o*-hook on its side before *n*, *m*, *r*, *l*, when not preceded by a down stroke.

Drill

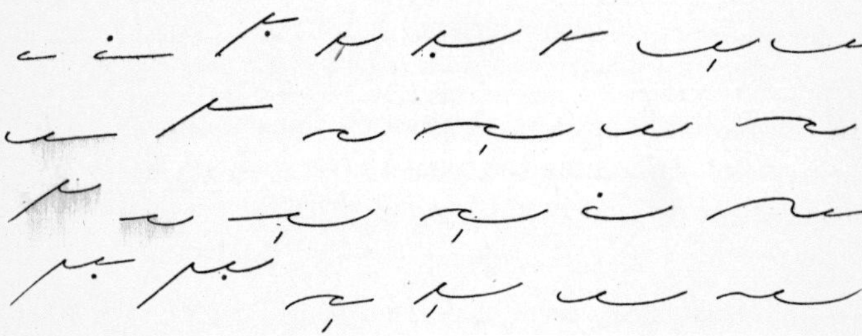

Key: on, home, dawn, tore, tall, tone, lower, loan, roam, dome, core, goal, roar, gore, door, nor, mole, coal, hall, grown, drawn, drawer, cone, toll, roll, crawl.

43. O-Hook Blend. Between *s*, *f*, *v*, *p*, *b* and a following *k* or *g*, the *o*-hook is indicated by rounding the angle, thus:

Drill

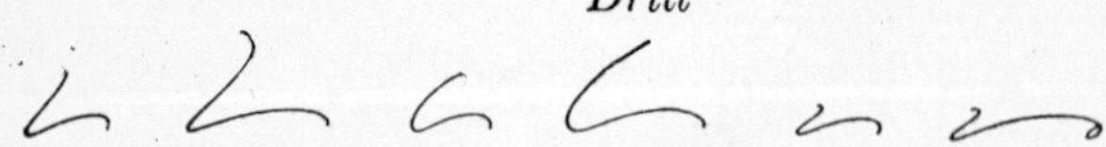

Key: folk, vogue, poke, bog, soak, soggy.

44. The Combination So. In words beginning with *so* the right *s* is used, in accordance with the rule regarding initial *s* given in Paragraph 49 of the Manual. The *so* combination is similar in form to the *fr* blend, and should be practiced until it can be executed rapidly as one movement of the pen.

Drill

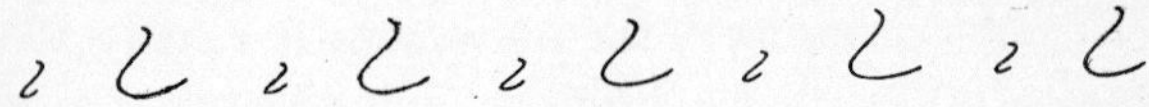

Drill

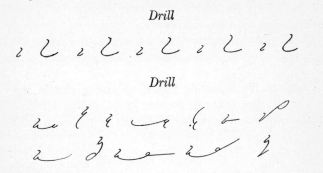

Key: sorrow, soap, sauce, loss-laws, pause, sown, soda, soul, sofa, solemn, solid, soft.

45. Obscure-Vowel Drill. (Illustrating Paragraph 16 of the Manual.)

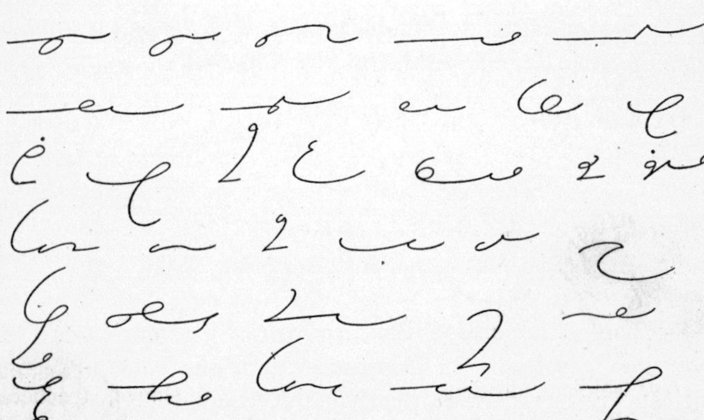

Key: maker, acre, eager, memory, mental, mineral, metal, error, prayer, wrapper, happen, labor, even, spell, salary, season, history, broken, occur, often, lower, author, compel, bravery, analysis, formal, convention, career, recipes, machinery, brokers, moral, magic.

46. R. In expressing *r*, the movement is exactly the reverse of that ordinarily employed in joining a circle to straight lines.

Compare the following forms, observing closely the direction the pen takes in making each joining, after which practice the movements until they can be made with facility:

Comparative Word Drill

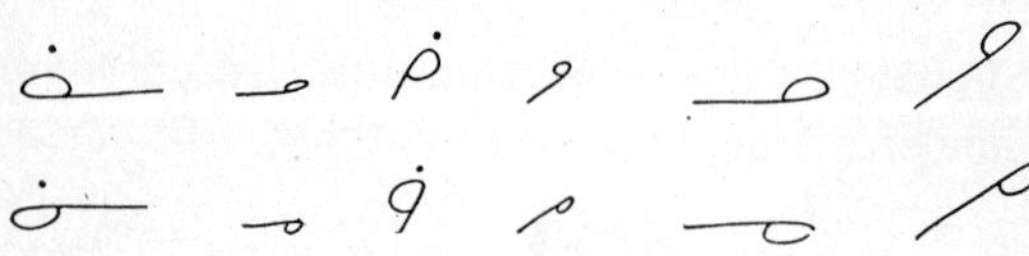

Key: harm, near, harsh, tear, mar, dare.
ham, any, hash, tea, may, day.

47. Ers Drill.

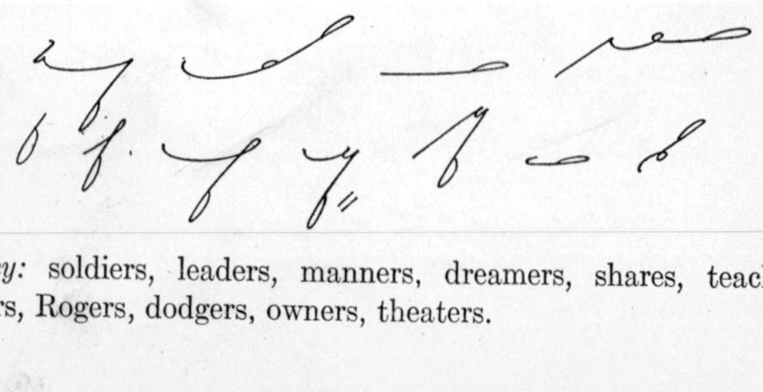

Key: soldiers, leaders, manners, dreamers, shares, teachers, ledgers, Rogers, dodgers, owners, theaters.

48. Brief-Form Derivative Drill—Er, Or. (Supplementing Paragraph 76 of the Manual.)

Key: dealer, giver, sender, speaker, officer, timer, shipper, publisher, thinker, teller, believer, keeper, lover, complainer, weaker, nearer, collector, receiver, bigger, employer.

49. Th Joinings. These two small upward curves should leave the line of writing immediately, thus:

Right: 

Wrong: 

Left-Motion Th Drill

Before *o, r, l:*

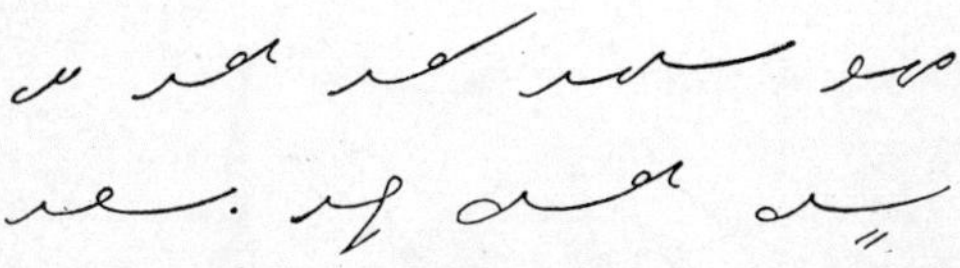

Key: although, threats, thread, throttle, thirsty, thrilling, thrift, athletes, Ethel.

After *o, r, l:*

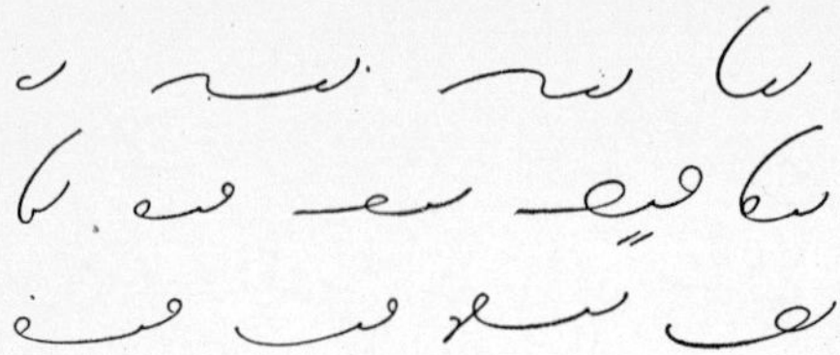

Key: oath, clothing, growth, broth, both, earthly, mirth, Martha, berth, healthy, wealthy, stealth, lath.

Right-Motion Th Drill

Initial:

Key: the, they, that, this, these, those, then, them, with, within, other, thing, thicker, thickly; ethics, thief, thieves, theme, thinner, thatched.

Final:

Key: Smith, Edith, death, faith, seethe, breadth.

50. Frequent-Phrase Drill.

The:

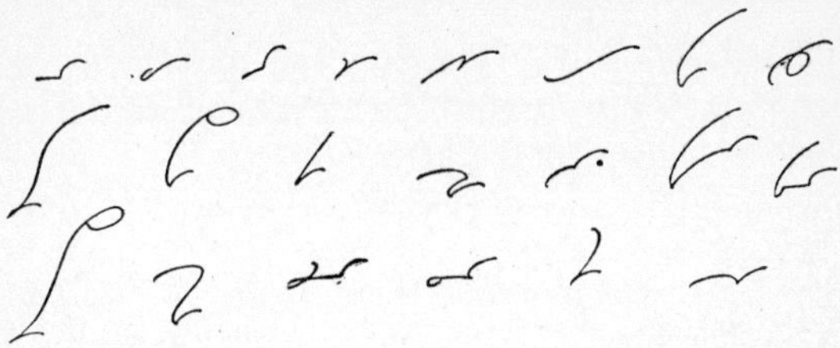

Key: in-the, of-the, at-the, is-the, to-the, and-the, by-the, that-the, before-the, about-the, which-the, because-the, the-thing, between-the, upon-the, above-the, keep-the, send-the, when-the, for-the, can-the.

There:

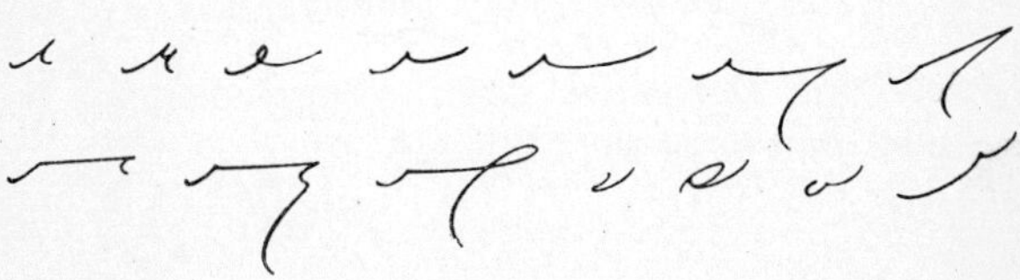

Key: there-is, there-was, there-were, there-are, there-will, there-will-be, there-would-be, there-must, there-must-be, there-may-be, is-there, that-there, of-their, and-there.

They:

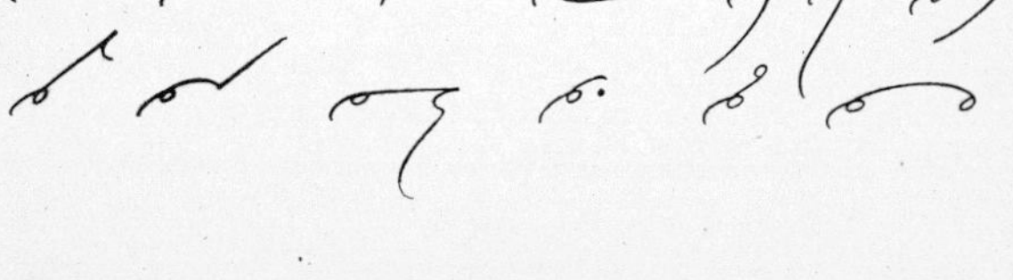

Key: they-can, they-go, they-are, they-will, they-have, they-have-been, they-would-have, they-desire, they-could, they-must-be, they-think, they-tell, they-give.

51. Suffixes Ily, Ally. Compare the movement in writing the loop for this suffix with the movement used in making the *ly* circle as shown by the arrows:

Comparative Word Drill

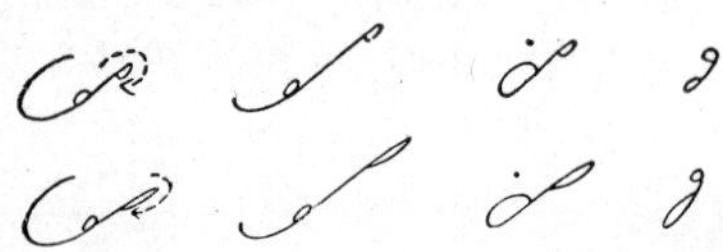

Key: pretty, ready, hearty, easy.
prettily, readily, heartily, easily.

52. Brief-Form Derivative Drill. (Supplementing Paragraphs 80, 82, and 83 of the Manual.)

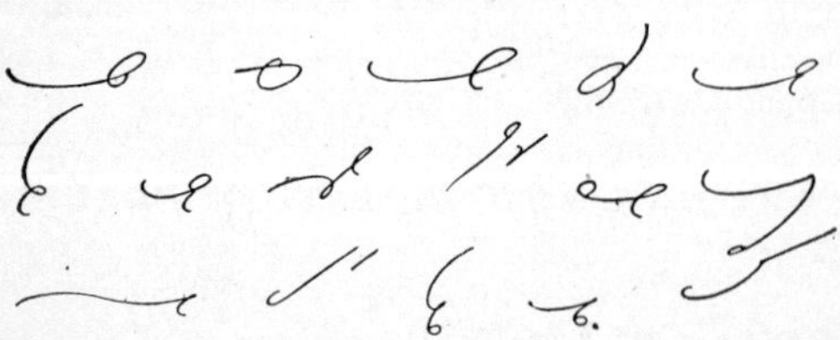

Key: likely, namely, likes, favors, letters, believes, regards, committees, dearest, earliest, lovely, girls, ordered, possibly, receiving, wanted.

53. Frequent-Phrase Drill. a. *To* not abbreviated:

Key: to-call, to-come, to-give-you, to-his, to-it, to-their, to-send, to-send-him, to-talk, to-tell, to-take, to-them, to-these, to-think.

b. *To* abbreviated to *t:*

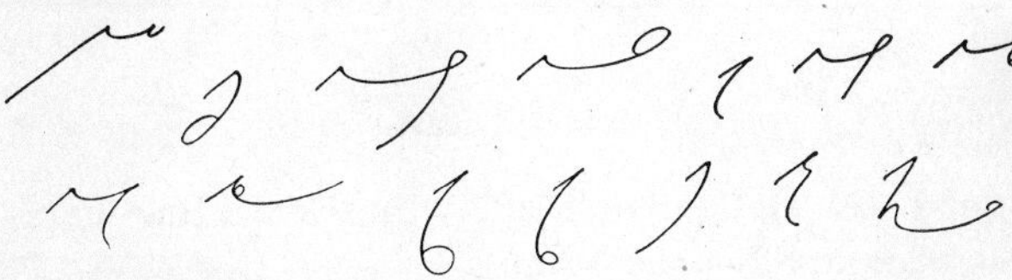

Key: to-draw, to-favor, to-leave, to-like, to-put, to-reach, to-receive, to-represent, to-sell, to-be-able, to-believe, to-have, to-speak, to-which-your-letter.

54. READING AND DICTATION PRACTICE

6.

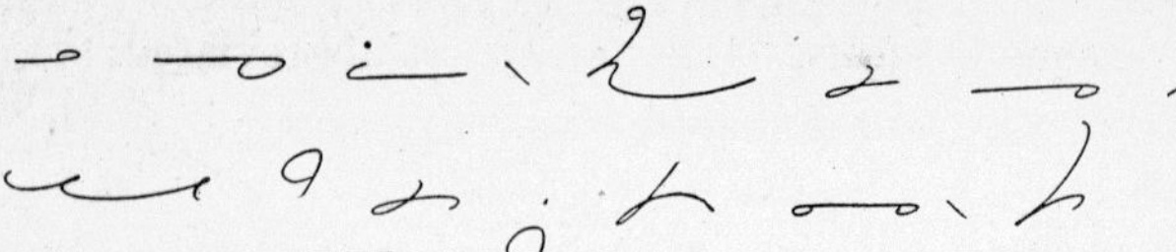

(45)

7.

(63)

8.

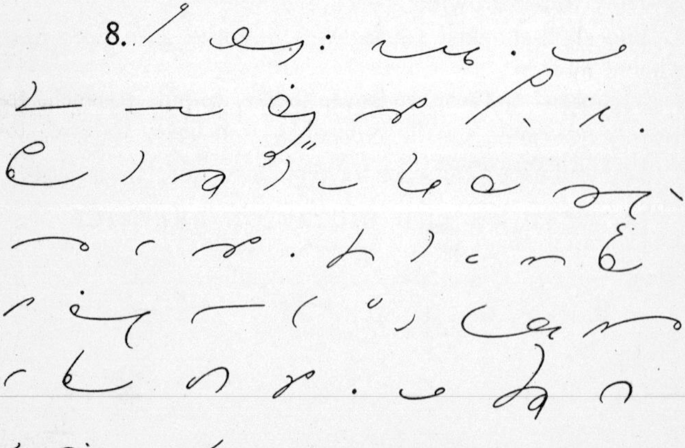

(54)

55. WRITING PRACTICE

1. What was your golf score Saturday, John?
2. He broke the bottles with a brick.
3. It is cheaper to borrow the money on a sixty-day note from the dealer than to take it from our business.
4. There is no lack of laws in this country.
5. When it is raining I read on the porch.
6. The mills ordered heavy scales placed near their incoming tracks.
7. He complained that the stove smoked and needed cleaning.
8. As summer approaches, working people get the holiday fever.
9. We sell a great many Easter eggs.
10. The door was locked and the guests hammered with the brass knocker.
11. Will you take a snapshot of that ocean steamer?
12. They were throwing stones at the horses.
13. The shell-shocked soldier was honored as a hero and a leader of men.
14. I heartily favor my daughter's eager desire to earn money.
15. The cashier of the grocery company put the ledger in the inner vault.
16. The auctioneer gave the rare armchair to the hermit collector.

SPEED STUDY IV

56. O͞O-Hook. The observations made on page 44 with regard to the formation of the *o*-hook apply with equal accuracy to the *o͞o*-hook.

Study the comparative sizes of the three characters of this related group, *o͞o*, *k*, *g*. Say the words *you*, *can*, *go*, as you write them.

Drill

57. O͞O-Hook Joined. The following drill will furnish practice in the joining of the *o͞o*-hook initially and finally to all consonants:

Drill

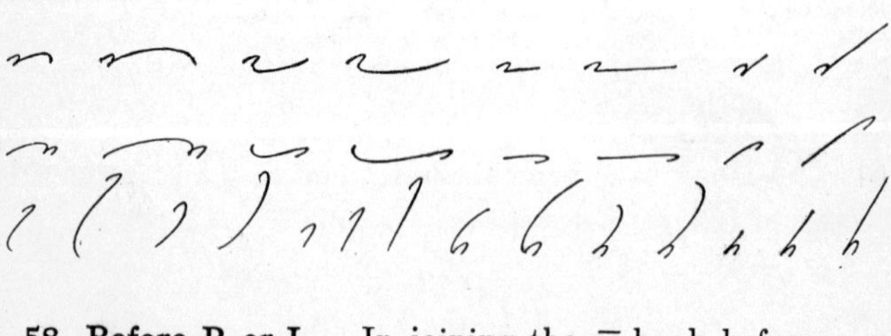

58. Before R or L. In joining the *o͞o*-hook before *r* or *l*, the movement is similar to that used in writing *kl:*

Drill

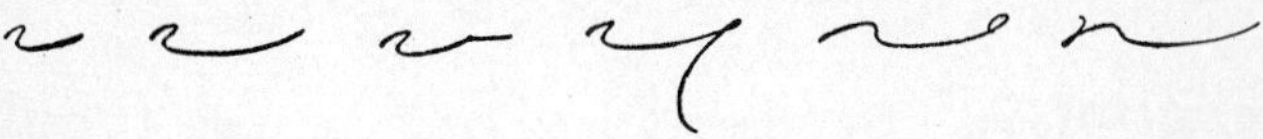

Key: you-are, you-will, you-are-not, you-will-be, clear, skill.

59. $\overline{\text{OO}}$-Hook Blend. When *r* or *l* is followed by *p* or *b*, the hook is shown by rounding the angle, thus:

Drill

Key: rub, droop, group, troop, drub, loop.

60. $\overline{\text{OO}}$-Hook on Side. Turning the *o͞o*-hook on its side forms an important study in execution.

Drill

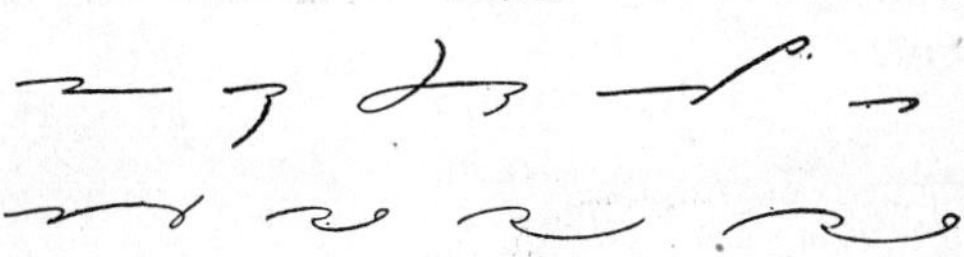

Key: number, enough, famous, muddy, knew, nugget, curry, cull, gully.

61. $\overline{\text{OO}}$-Hook to Down Strokes. The *o͞o*-hook frequently precedes or follows a downward stroke.

Drill

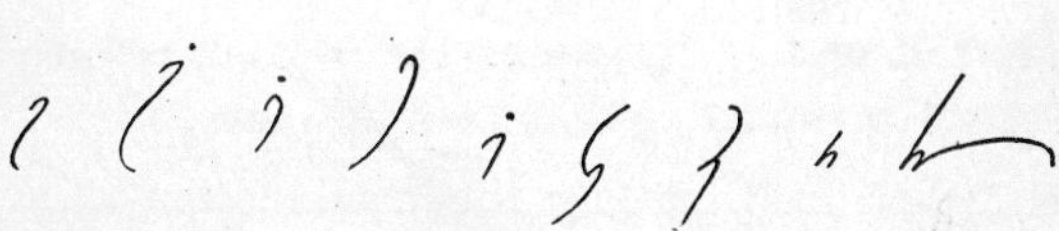

Key: up, hub, hoof, you-have, hush, puff, fudge, shoe, jug.

62. Us-Blend Drill. a. At the beginning of words:

Key: us, whose, hustle, husky.

b. Following a down stroke:

Key: shoes, campus, gracious, choose, issues, cautious, vicious.

c. Following *k* or *g*:

Key: cousin, goose, gust.

63. Obscure-Vowel Drill.

Key: upper, supper, dozen, oven, rubber.

64. W. When the *o͞o*-hook is followed by a vowel, it is always *w*. It will aid you greatly in acquiring facility in writing words containing *w* if you will begin by drilling on joining *w* to all the vowel signs. Practice writing *w* with a small circle or loop, calling the combination *wĭ, wĕ, we͞e*;

with a large circle or loop, calling the combination *wă*, *way*; with the *o*-hook, calling the combination *wŏ*, *waw*, *woe*; with the *ōō*-hook, calling the combination *wŏŏ*, *wōō*. Whenever you have any word beginning with *w*, you will then think of its form in *combination* with the vowel that follows it and be able to write it easily. Practice the following:

Drill

Key: win, wet, weave; wag, wade; wash, wall, wove; wool.

65. W to Circles. When a circle or a loop follows *w*, it should not interfere with the characteristic form of the hook.

Right: 

Note particularly that the circles or loops come entirely outside the hook. If care is not exercised, the hooks may degenerate into the following inartistic and awkward forms:

Wrong: 

Drill

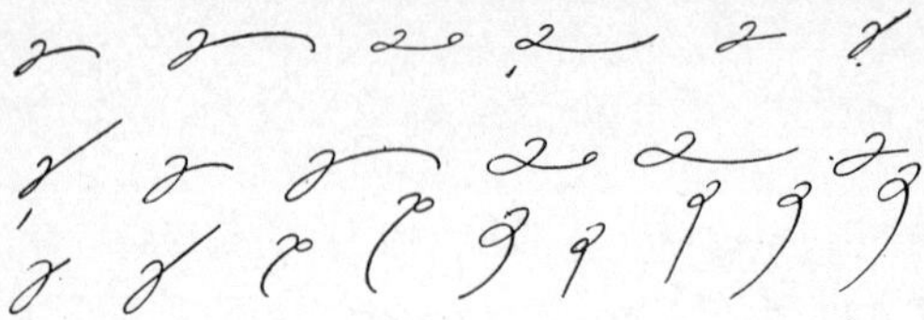

Key: wick, wig, weary, weal, win, wet, weed, wake, wag, wary, wail, wane, wait, wade, weep, web, waif, witch, wedge, weave, wave.

66. Hooks Joined. Observe how consecutive hooks are joined:

Drill

Key: woe, woo, walk, wall, wool, wash, woof, wove, woke.

67. Dash for W. When the dash is used to express *w* within a word, it should be placed under the vowel following *w:*

Drill

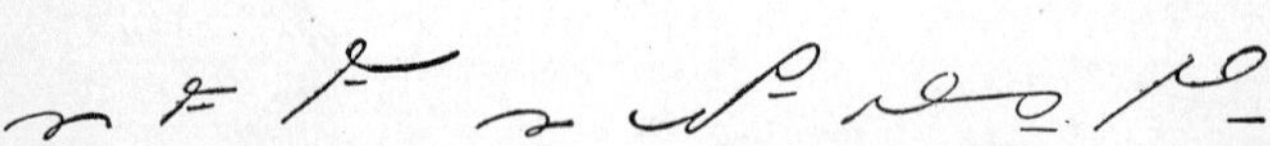

Key: quick, twin, dwell, queen, roadway, tramway, doorway.

68. Wh Combination. In *wh*, the dot for *h* should be made first:

Drill

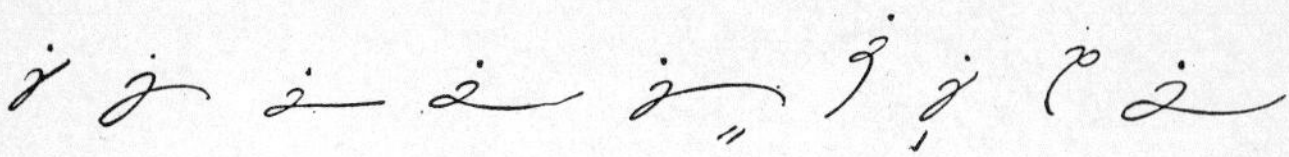

Key: whit, whack, whim, wheel, Whig, whiff, wheat, whip, whale.

69. Ye and Ya Loops. The execution of the *ye* and *ya* loops, as distinguished from joined circles, should be carefully analyzed and practiced:

Drill

Key: yam, yak, year, yell, Yale, yet, yelp.

70. Ng and Ing. Practice the following comparative group of words in order to remove all hesitancy in deciding whether to use the lowered *n* or the *ing* dot. With the exception of the brief forms for *thing*, *think*, *thank*, the dot is invariably used for the suffix *ing*.

Drill

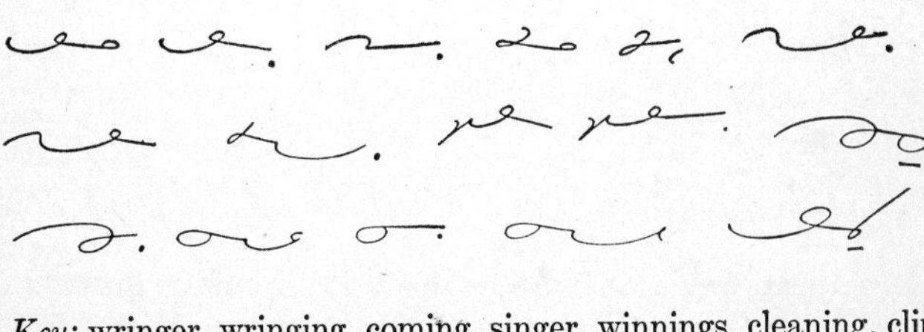

Key: wringer, wringing, coming, singer, winnings, cleaning, cling, shingling, string, streaming, gangway, gaining, angry, aiming, angles, languid.

71. Prefix Drill.

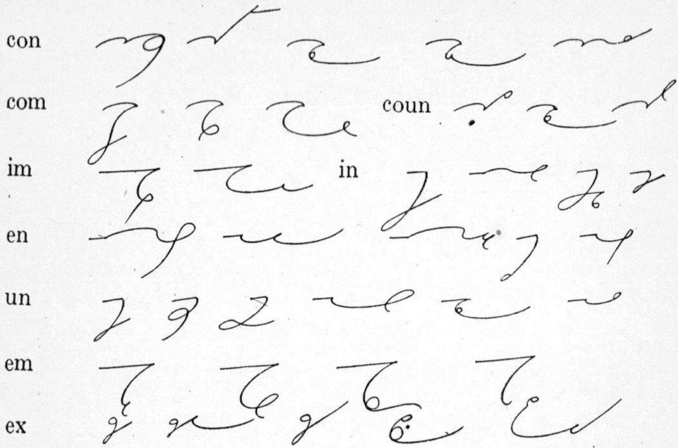

Key: con: concave, condone, conceal, console, concrete; *com:* combat, compass, complex; *coun:* county, counsel, counties; *im:* impeach, implore; *in:* invade, increase, infancy, inset; *en:* engrave, enroll, engross, envy, enrich; *un:* unfit, unsafe, unfair, unlace, unseal, unreal; *em:* emboss, embrace, embark, embody; *ex:* exit, extol, exceed, exhale, explode.

72. Brief-Form Derivative Drill—Ing, Ings, Thing, Ingly. (Supplementing Paragraph 106 of the Manual.)

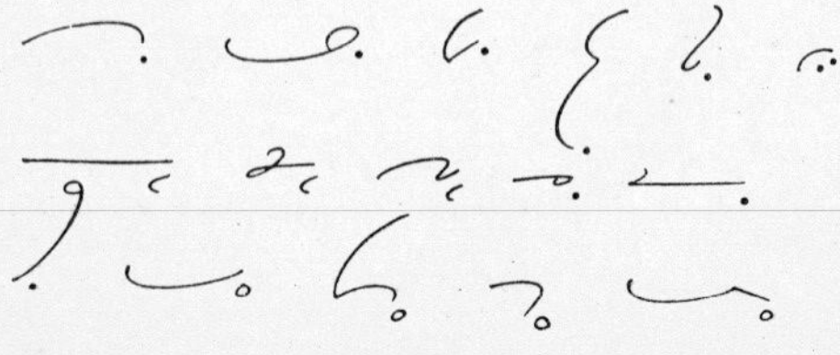

Key: going, liking, parting, publishing, following, thinking, mornings, winnings, callings, anything, something, everything, willingly, becomingly, questioningly, longingly.

73. The 1,000 Commonest Words—Words 1 to 50.

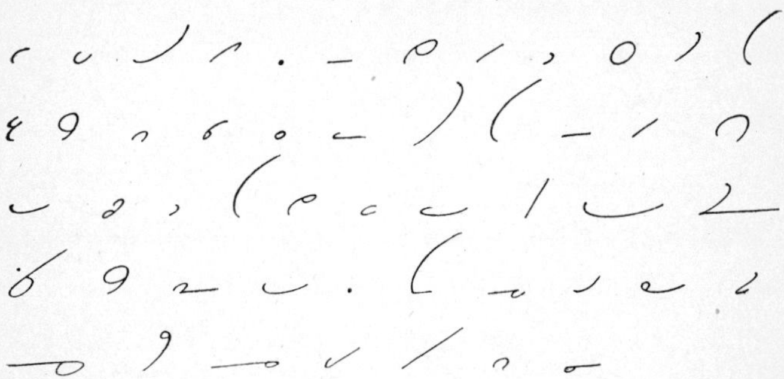

Key: the, of, and, to, a, in, that, it, is, I, for, be, was, as, you, with, he, on, have, by, not, at, this, are, we, his, but, they, all, or, which, will, from, had, has, one, our, an, been, no, there, were, so, my, if, me, what, would, you, when.

74. Brief-Form Derivative Drill. (Supplementing Paragraphs 95, 102, and 109 of the Manual.)

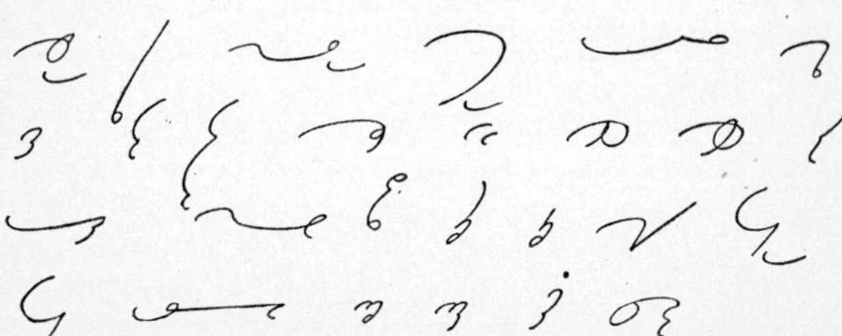

Key: carrier, charger, clearer, governor, longer, questioner, yours, puts, publishes, gives, things, cares, carries, forces, looks, clears, especially, fully, surely, questioned, purchaser, purchased, remembers, worldly, worlds, houses, accepts.

75. Frequent-Phrase Drill.

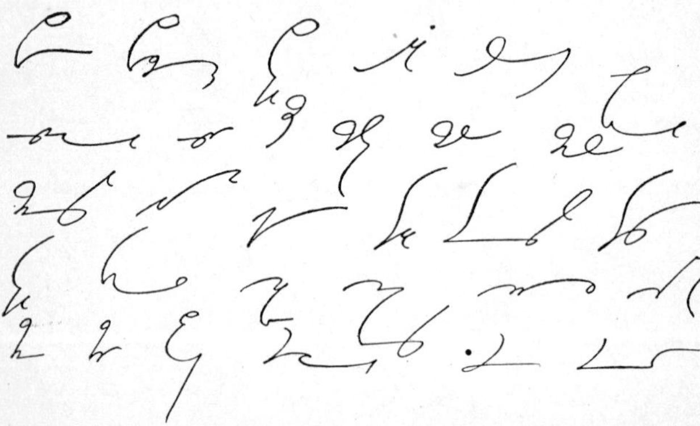

Key: about-them, about-these-goods, about-which-it-is, and-hope, and-I-will-have, anybody-else, anyone-else, any-other, as-if, as-it-has-been, as-there-were, as-you-are-aware, as-you-may-desire, at-all-times, at-which-time, before-it-was, before-many-days, before-that-time, by-which-it-is, by-your-letter, call-upon, cannot-be-made, can-you-give, could-not-be, each-one, each-other, express-charge, for-collection, for-him, for-more-than.

Note: In the phrase *did-not*, a circle is inserted to make a positive distinction between this phrase and *would-not*. Compare and practice the following phrases:

76. READING AND DICTATION PRACTICE

9. THE TALE OF A LOG MILL

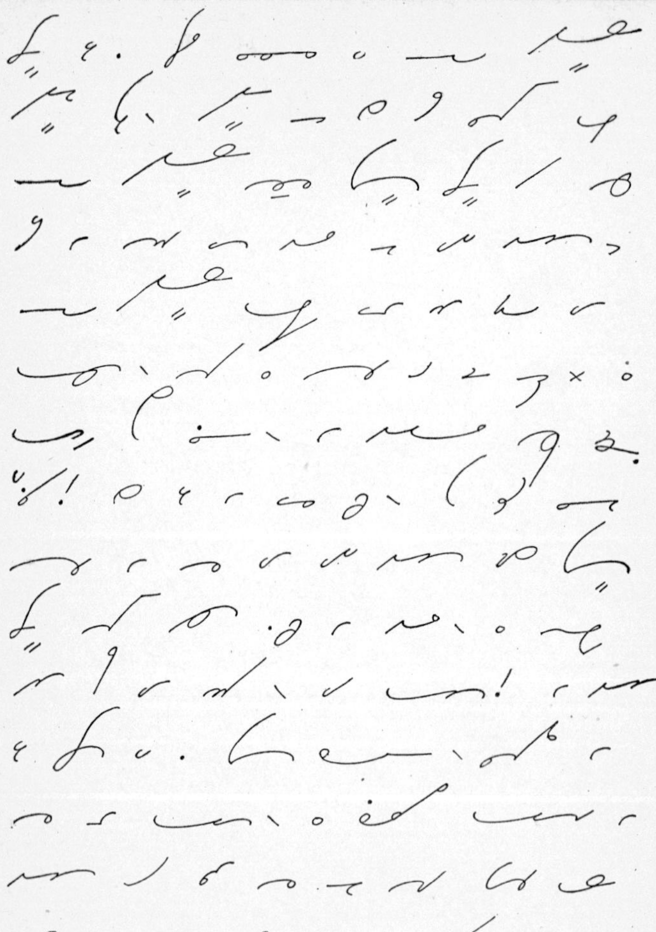

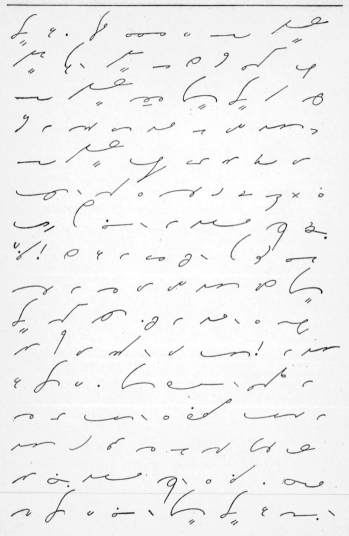

Ethel M. Brown (411)

77. WRITING PRACTICE

1. He billed all the charges during the afternoon.
2. I have been thanking your friends for the loan of their cars.
3. In answer to the question he quoted the remarks of a noted author.
4. They walked slowly through the woods to the swimming pool.
5. Make a loose loop with this piece of string.
6. Shut the valve to the water tank quickly.
7. The pinks and other flowers along the walks in our yard are in full bloom.
8. Shut and lock the ballot boxes.
9. Take the tools upstairs to the washroom.
10. The judges gave three medals to the star athlete who threw the weights.
11. He won the shot-put, the hammer-throw, and the discus.
12. We watched the wrecking crew tow the coupé away from the scene.
13. The cook cut her finger cutting the butter for the noon meal.
14. The cousins wished each other a happy farewell.
15. He hung the drinking cup on the hook in the wall by the water cooler.
16. I watched them weighing the youngster.
17. Do not lose the ticket.
18. Send all our rugs to the cleaner.
19. He could not eat much of the honey; it was too sweet.
20. She sang a song about a cruel and jealous lover.

78. Formation of the Diphthongs. In writing the signs for *u*, *ow*, and *oi*, place the circle so that it does not interfere with the correct form of the hook:

Right:

Wrong:

Drill

Key: he, you, use, I, your, how-out, of, he, point-appoint. use, how-out, point-appoint (repeated).

79. Diphthong = Vowel + Vowel. The following word drill illustrates the statement given in Paragraph 112 of the Manual: "A pure diphthong is the union in one syllable of two simple vowel sounds uttered in rapid succession."

Drill

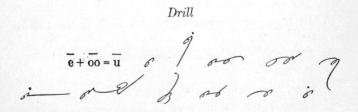

$\bar{e} + \bar{oo} = \bar{u}$

Key: use, huge, unique, acute, cube, human, utilized, views, unit, cue, hue.

ä + o͞o = ow

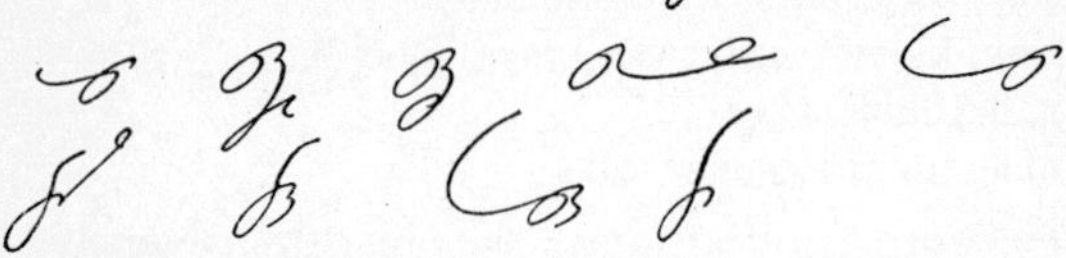

Key: out, voucher, spout, shower, row, outfits, outside, outline, plow, powder, powers, blouse, bough.

aw + ē = oi

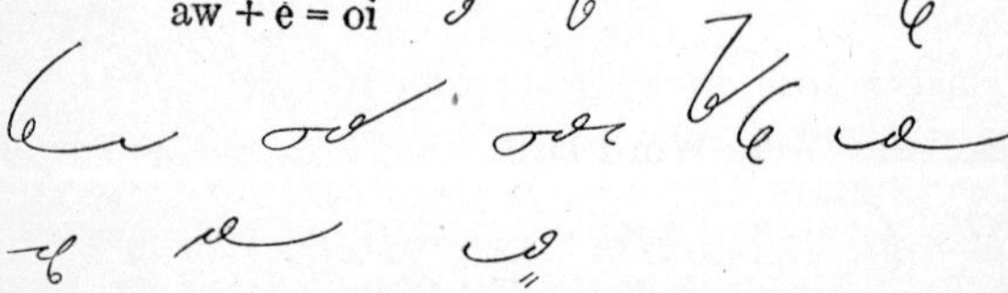

Key: point, joy, enjoyed, boys, boiler, annoyed, annoyance, poise, royal, noisy, toil, Roy.

80. Broken-Circle Joinings. An important point to remember in executing long *i* is that it is a *circle*, even though broken, hence the rules for joining circles apply to it also.

Drill

Inside Curves:

Outside Angles:

Opposite Curves:

Straight Lines:

Key: hike, spry, pile, guy, kind, light.
tiny, knives, size, twice, wipe, pipe, fine.
guile, choir, fiber.
hide, necktie, miner, tides.

In a few words, initial long *i* is joined more easily, thus:

Key: higher, Irish, while, ice, hyphen, ivory.

81. Broken-Circle Word Drill.

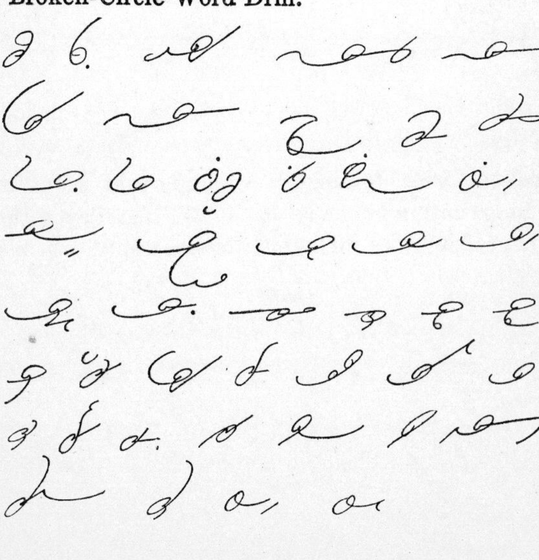

Key: aside, buying, authorized, climate, crime, bride, climb, compile, confine, finally, flying, fry, highway, height, high school, hired, Nile, library, lights, lighter, lighted, license, lightning, minor, nights, nicely, nicer, knife, oversight, prized, pine, retire, rides, rye, size, spite, shining, tight, tile, tires, triumph, vital, vice, wired, wires.

82. "Large Circle I" Brief Forms. The following frequent-phase drill illustrates the convenience of the unbroken *a* circle for the pronoun *I* and for the diphthong *i* in the brief forms given in Paragraph 114 of the Manual:

Frequent-Phrase Drill

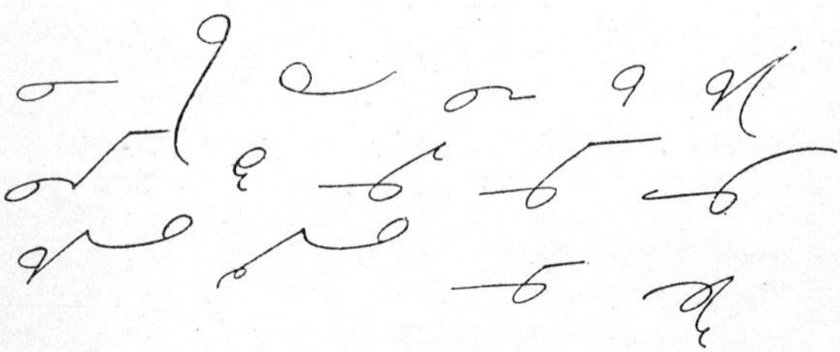

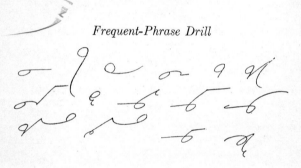

Key: I-am, I-have-been, I-will, I-cannot, I-shall, I-should-be, I-could-not, I-was, My-dear-Sir, My-dear-Madam, all-my-time, I-should-like, they-would-like, might-not, quite-possible.

83. Comparative Word Drill—Long $\bar{i}$+Any Vowel.

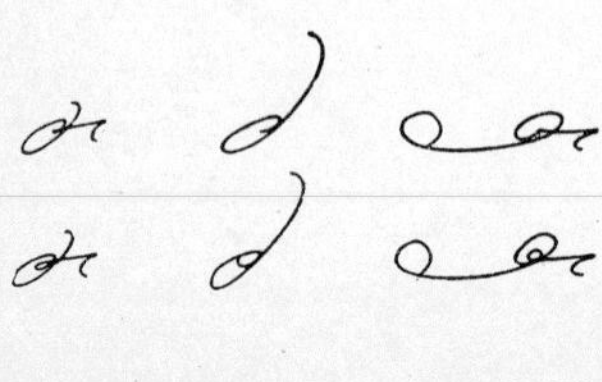

Key: signs, vie, aligns.
science, via, alliance.

84. Other Vowel-Combinations Drill.

ē + ō =
ō + a =
ō + e =
ā + o =
ĭ + a =
ē + a =

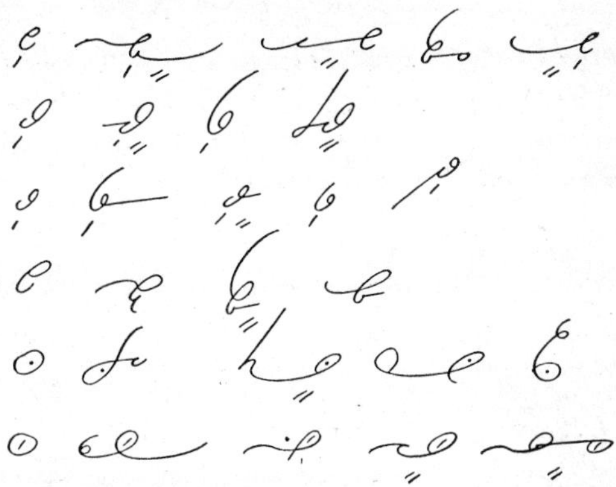

Key: creole, Romeo, peony, Leo.
Noah, boa, Genoa.
poem, Owen, showy, doughy.
chaos, Bayonne, rayon.
piano, Julia, alias, sepia.
cereal, creation, Korea, Crimea.

85. U Drill. (Supplementing Paragraph 121 of the Manual.)

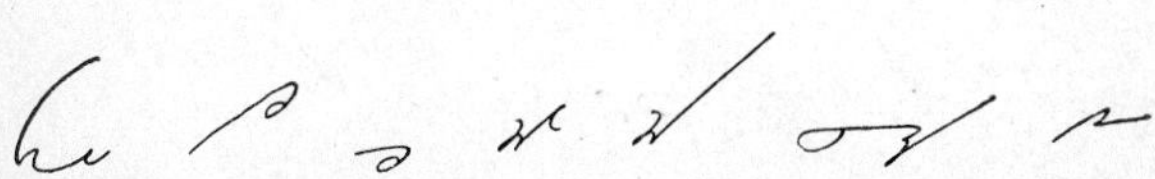

Key: bureau, duly, newly, suits, suited, amused, tune.

86. Brief-Form Derivative Drill.

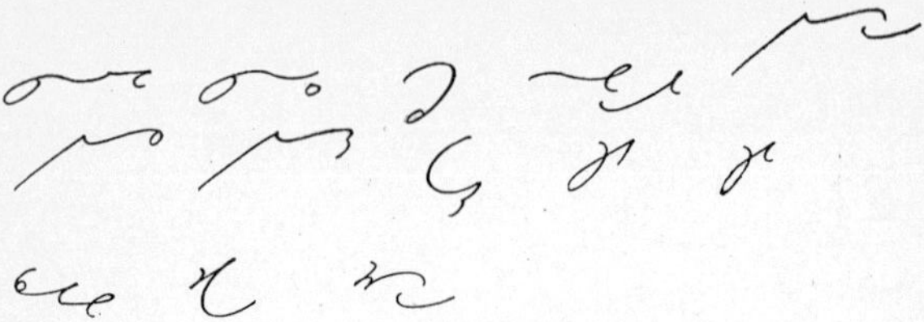

Key: accordance, accordingly, confidently, correspondents, director, directly, directs, persons, satisfaction, satisfies, seriousness, stopper, successor.

87. Frequent-Phrase Drill.

Key: I-can-find, I-cannot-find, he-will-find, find-enclosed, how-can, how-could, write-me, he-will-write, this-side, I-trust, in-respect, in-consideration, throughout-the, please-give, please-give-this-matter, please-let, please-remember, please-return, please-see, please-ship-the, please-wire, please-write, we-enclose, I-enclose, why-are, why-do, why-have, why-not, why-will, why-would.

88. Short U and Ow Drill. (Supplementing Paragraph 124 of the Manual.)

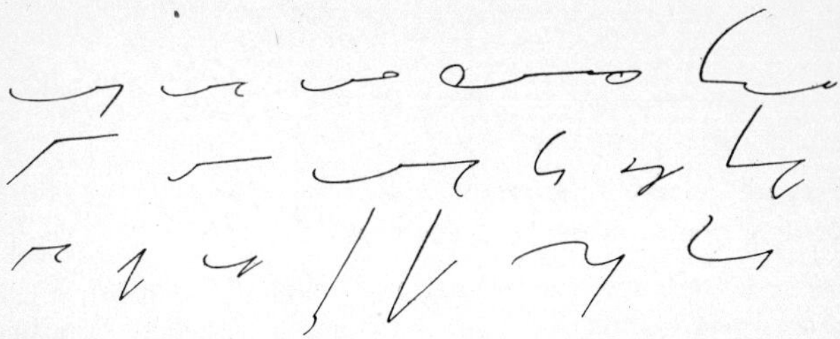

Key: lunch, runs, runner, alumni, bungalow, dumb, thumb, lump, punish, sunset, jumped, towns, touched, rushed, judges, judged, grudge, flush.

89. Sumption Drill. (Supplementing Paragraph 126 of the Manual.)

Key: assumption, resumption, consumption, presumption.

90. Ness Suffix Drill.

Key: fullness, littleness, gladness, sureness, kindness, clearness, likeness, nearness.

91. Pre Prefix. *Pre* is always written in full except in *presume* and its derivatives.

Comparative Word Drill

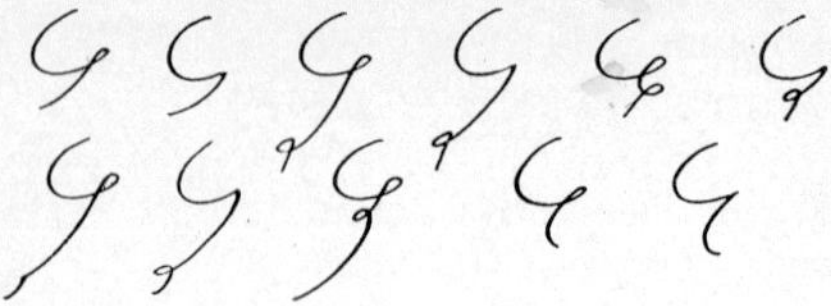

Key: prefer, proof, prevision, provision, precision, procession, previous, perverse, preserve, prepare, purpose.

Drill

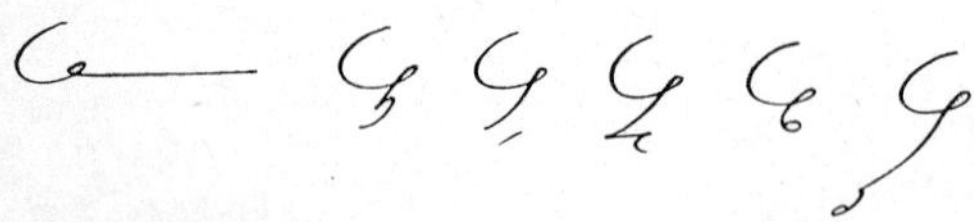

Key: premium, precious, preferred, preference, precede, previously.

92. Per, Pur Prefix Drill.

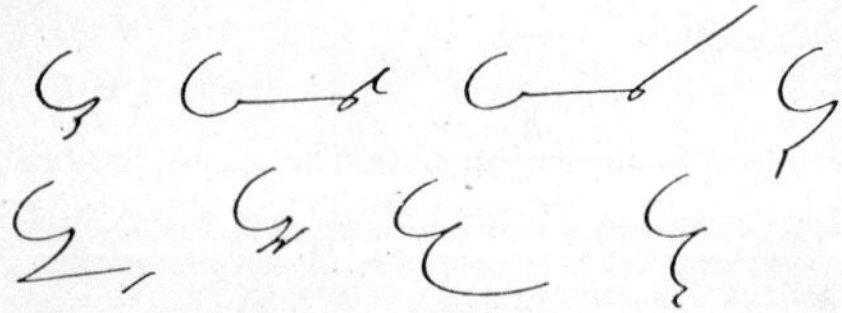

Key: persons, permits, permitted, perfection, performed, pursuit, purple, purposes.

93. Pro Prefix Drill.

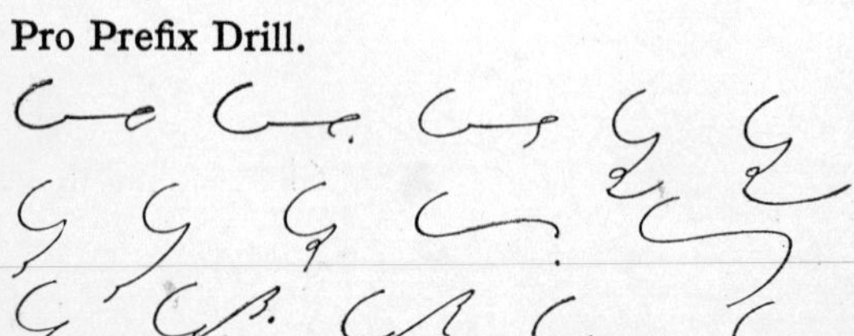

Key: promised, promising, promises, professor, professional, proofs, proves, procession, progressing, progressive, proposition, producing, produces, procure, procured.

94. Brief-Form Derivative Drill—Able, Ible. (Supplementing Paragraph 127 of the Manual.)

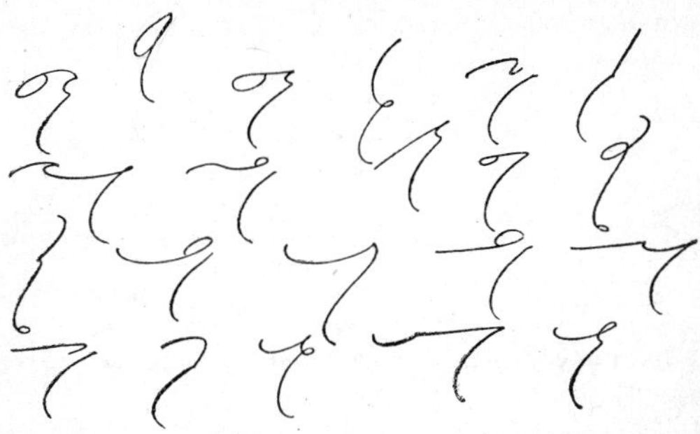

Key: acceptable, agreeable, answerable, believable, callable, changeable, collectible, creditable, desirable, enable, favorably, forcibly, likable, lovable, mailable, marketable, movable, questionable, receivable, remarkable, respectable.

95. Ment Suffix Drill.

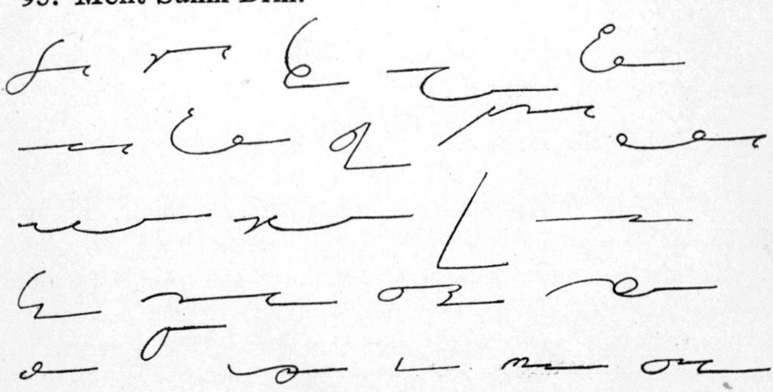

Key: payments, statements, basement, employment, experiment, moments, supplement, attachment, documents, elements, enrollment, installment, judgment, monument, punishment, commencement, amusement, garment, appointment, agreement, requirement, shipment, wonderment, announcement.

Note: The four words *cement, raiment, lament,* and *comment* are written in full.

96. Brief-Form Derivative Drill.

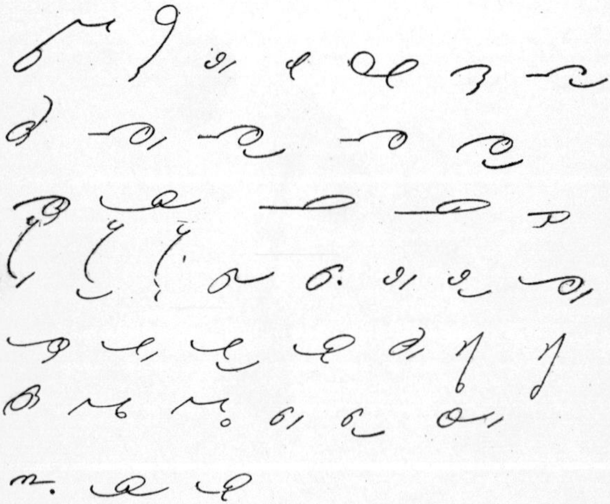

Key: addresses, advantages, appointed, appoints, arranges, considers, enclosure, finds, inquired, inquirer, inquiry, kinder, kinds, lighter, mails, miles, names, objected, objector, objects, outer, outing, pointed, pointer, required, requires, respected, respecter, rights, sided, stranger, strangely, thousands, trustee, trustingly, used, user, wired, wondering, writer, writes.

97. READING AND DICTATION PRACTICE

10.

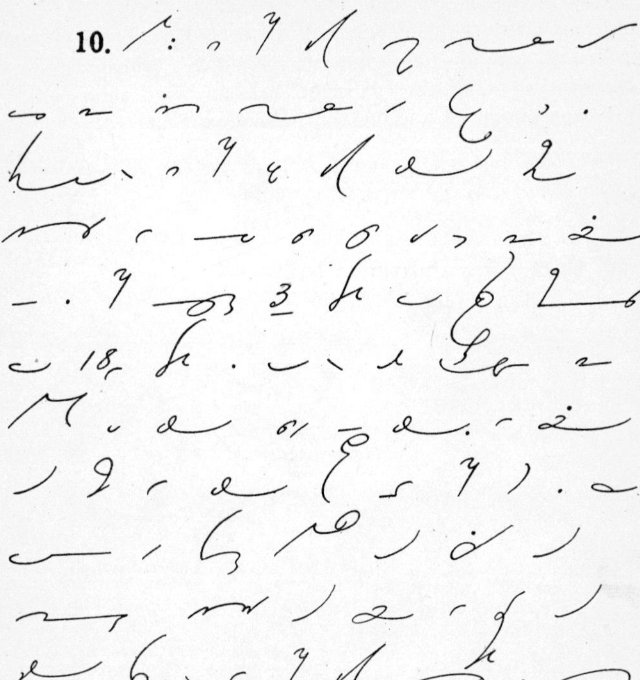

Note: Beginning with letter 10 a few outlines written in accordance with Paragraphs 136, 204, and 222 of the Manual will be given in the Reading and Dictation Practice.

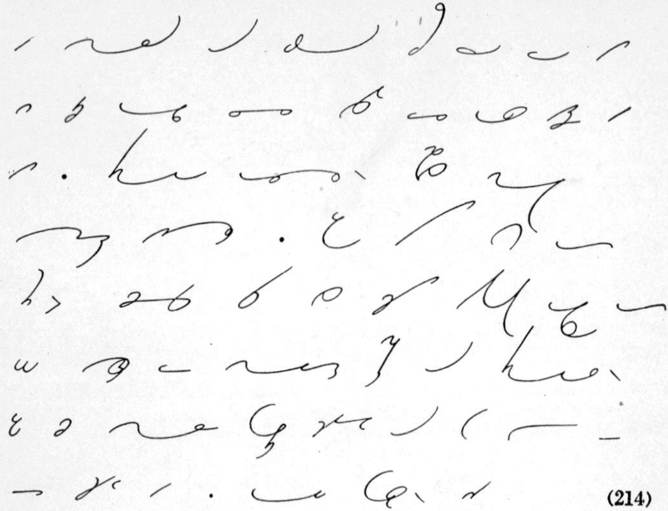

(214)

11. 

(52)

12. 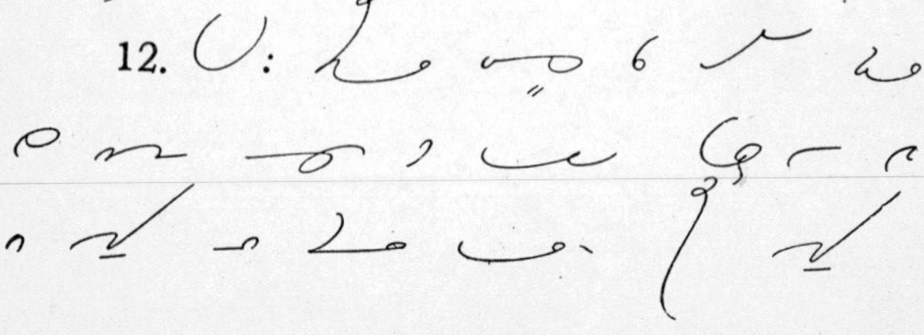

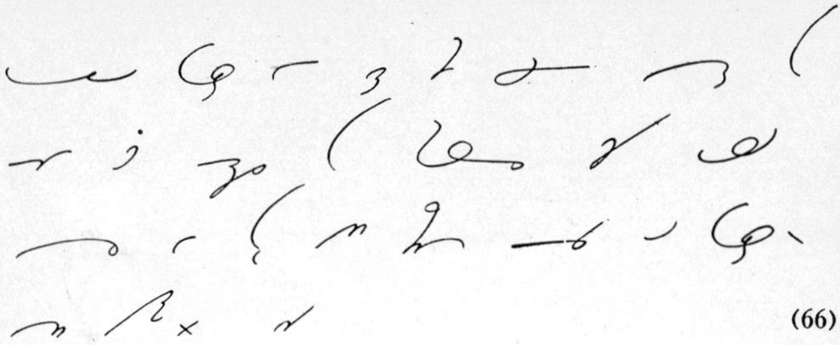

(66)

13.

(40)

14.

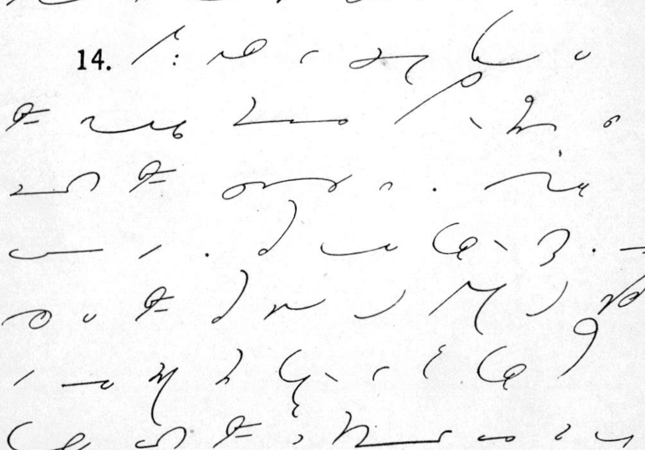

(82)

15.

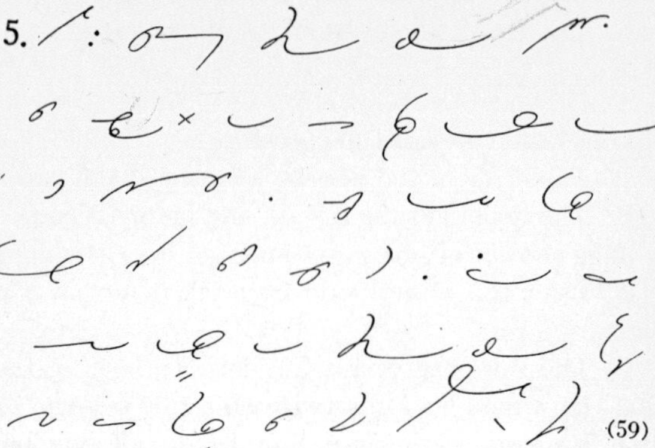

(59)

16.

(90)

98. WRITING PRACTICE

1. He bought several boxes of flashlight powder to use in taking inside views of his home.
2. The error in the vouchers annoyed the cashier.
3. The boiler sprung a leak, and before it could be stopped a huge shower of hot water spouted over the floor.
4. I saw the miner hide the sack of ore in a rusty water pipe.
5. The tides are very high at this season of the year.
6. He wiped his knife twice on a pile of rags.
7. I finally authorized him to do all our buying while abroad.
8. We are tired and retire early these hot nights.
9. Due to an oversight on the part of our cook, there was no ice in the cooler.
10. What is the height of that pine tree near the highway?
11. Science fights for the health of the nation.
12. She played an amusing tune on the piano.
13. Thousands of tons of cereal are marketed daily.
14. The runner reached his goal at sunset.
15. Here are permits for all the persons in your party.
16. I cannot produce the proofs I promised the judge.
17. He made an important announcement regarding the experiment.
18. The installment payments that we have agreed upon will begin May 15.

SPEED STUDY VI

99. The Blended Consonants. The blunt or obtuse angle is a great obstacle to shorthand speed, because, in order to make the angle distinct, it is necessary to pause abruptly—and each abrupt pause means a loss in speed. If the writer does not pause abruptly in order to make the angle clearly, the lines tend to blend into the form of a large curve.

In this system the letters have been so arranged that when the lines do blend they form a natural curve, and each curve represents a syllable.

From the artistic viewpoint, the blended consonants form one of the most attractive features of the system. The beauty of the blends is incidental, however. Their practical value as speed expedients and the frequency of their use demand that the student give special attention to their mastery.

Proportion Drill

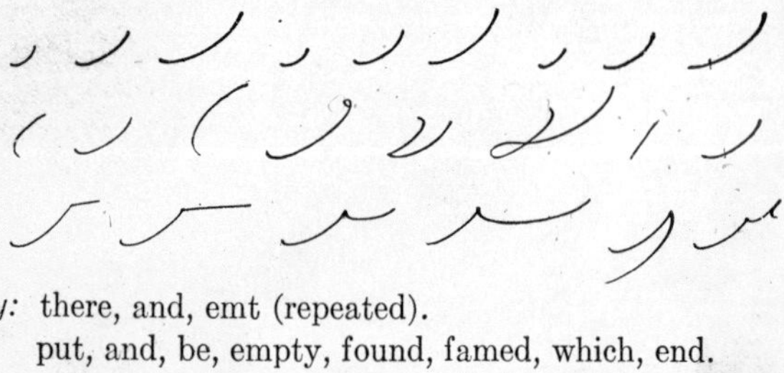

Key: there, and, emt (repeated).
put, and, be, empty, found, famed, which, end.
and-not, and-am, and-are, and-will, and-have, and-there-is.

100. Short U and Ow Drill. (Supplementing Paragraph 124 of the Manual.)

Key: around, refund, sounds, fund, ground, profound, stunt.

101. Ld Comparative Word Drill.

Key: fold, wild, child, gold, old.
foamed, wind, chimed, gaunt, owned.

102. Ld Derivative Drill.

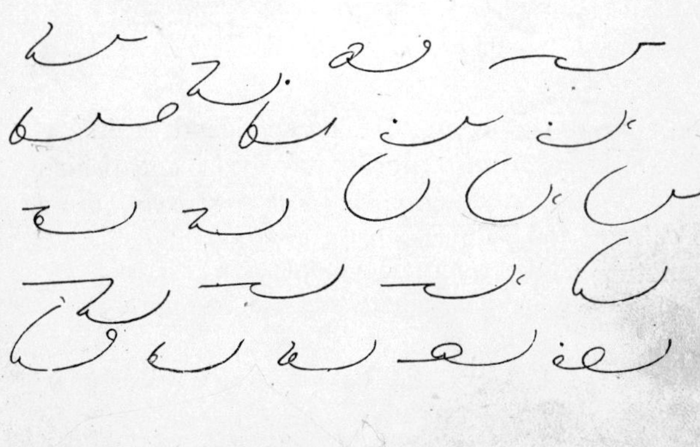

Key: folder, unfolding, wildly, golden, childlike, childish, holder, holdings, unsealed, unsold, build, buildings, builder, manifold, mould, mouldings, bold, boldly, shield, soiled, mild, herald.

103. "Morning," "Night," Phrase Drill.

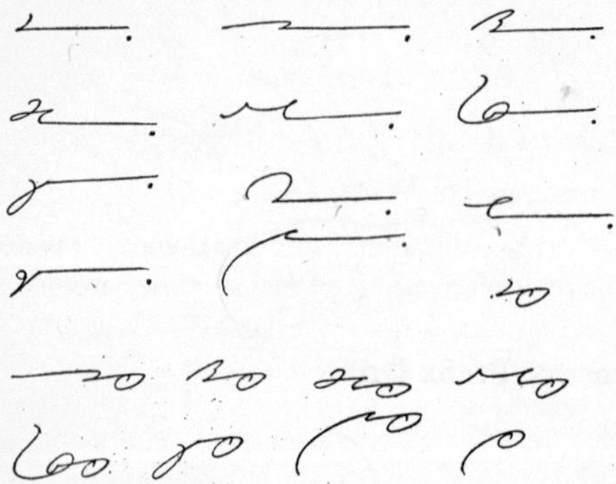

Key: Sunday morning, Monday morning, Tuesday morning, Wednesday morning, Thursday morning, Friday morning, Saturday morning, this morning, next morning, yesterday morning, tomorrow morning, Sunday night, Monday night, Tuesday night, Wednesday night, Thursday night, Friday night, Saturday night, tomorrow night, tonight.

104. Def-dev, Jent-jend. The *def* blend begins with *d*, hence it is written upward; the *jent-jend* blend begins with *j*, hence is written downward. *The first consonant in the blend determines its direction.* Study the following illustrations, noting particularly the size, formation, and slant:

this def-dev  jent-jend

These blends are often called egg-shaped characters. They should be narrow and should curve at the *beginning* and at the *end*, thus:

Proportion Drill

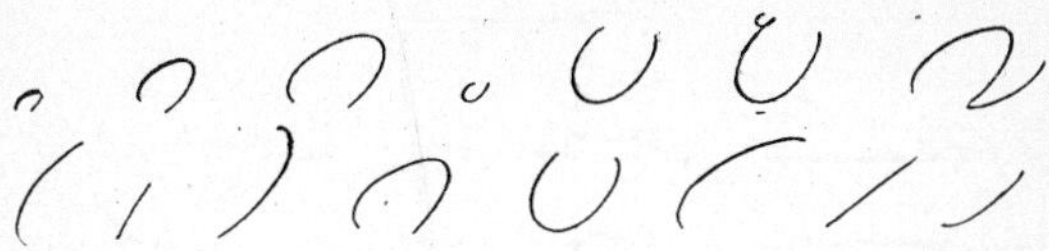

Key: you, this, different, of, gentlemen, opened, defend, be, which, have, difference, gentlemen, time, would, and.

105. Frequent-Prefix Drill.

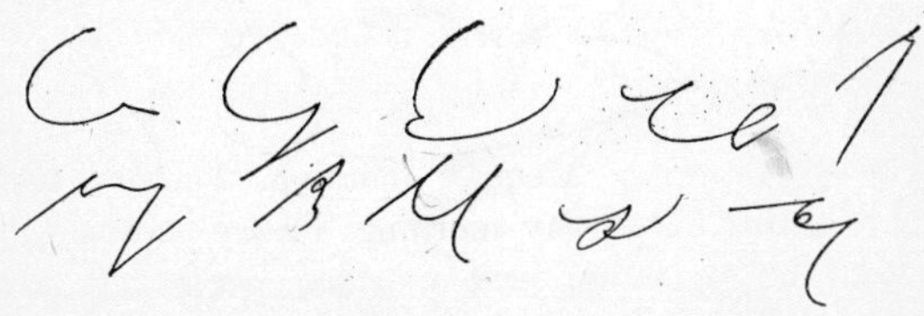

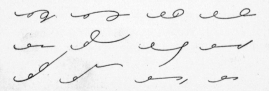

Key: belong, beloved, behold, replaced, discharge, discouraged, decisions, dependable, resigned, miserable.

106. Re Prefix Drill. (Supplementing Paragraph 147 of the Manual.)

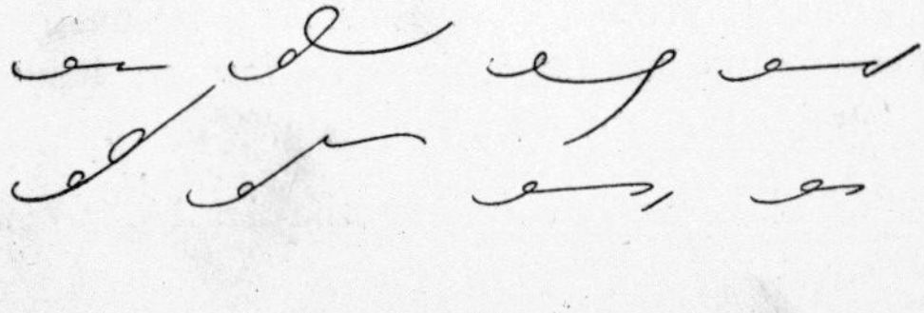

Key: recast, regain, rewrite, reline, renown, retail, relieve, remote, retard, redirect, removed, renew.

107. Contractions Drill. (Supplementing Paragraph 149 of the Manual.)

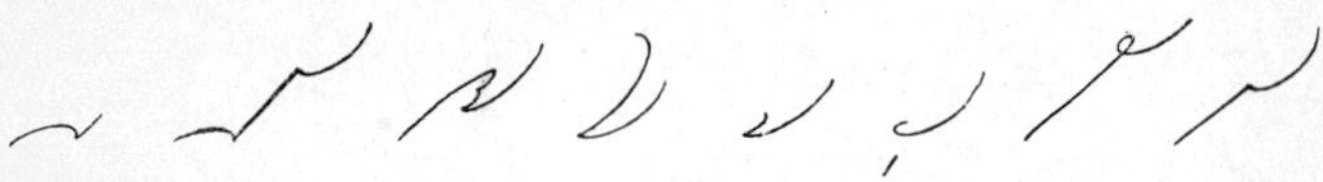

Key: can't, couldn't, doesn't, haven't, isn't, won't, didn't, wouldn't.

108. Brief-Form Derivative Drill.

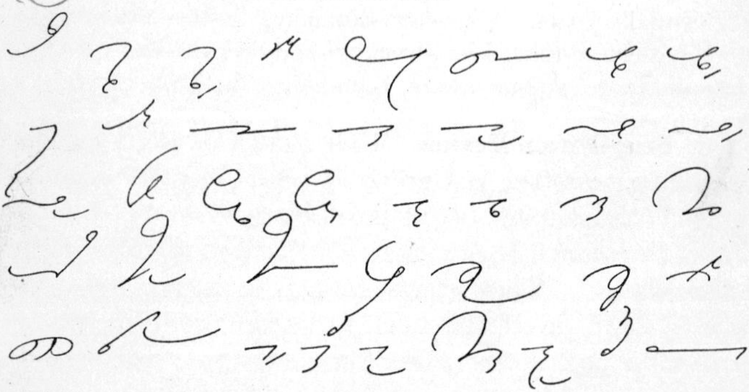

Key: entirely, copies, copied, stocks, allowable, acknowledgment, receipts, receipted, invoices, industries, movement, moves, mover, credits, credited, creditor, beauties, approximately, approximation, instances, instantly, qualities, definitely, recorder, advertiser, advertisement, previously, occasional, occasionally, quantities, acquaintances, educational, insured, insures, insurer, difficulties, inspector, sufficiently, determination.

Note: The *ses* blend is used in forming the plural of *invoice, course, force, office.*

109. Frequent-Phrase Drill.

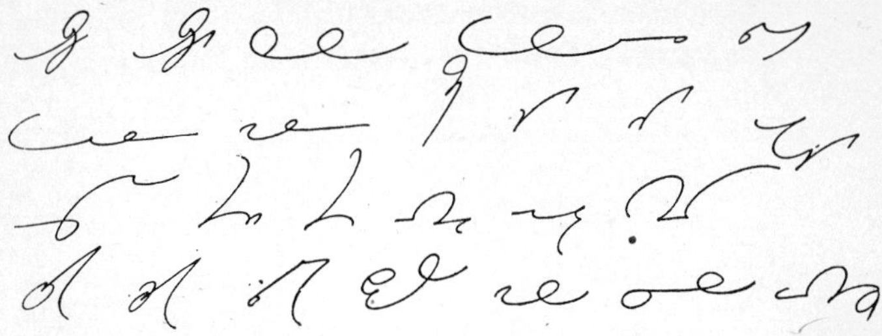

Key: entirely-satisfactory, entire-satisfaction, I-will-allow, please-allow-me, with-reference, please-remit, your-remittance, I-suggest, his-attention, your-attention, our-personal-attention, my-dear-Mr., Very-cordially-yours, Yours-very-cordially, in-this-instance, in-response, definite-time, I-had-been, we-had-been, he-had-not-been, I-was-not-aware, you-are-aware, I-am-aware, on-this-occasion.

110. Brief-Forms Review. Unit 18 of Chapter VI of the Manual contains the last group of brief forms for common words. The complete list of these words is arranged in the form of two charts, beginning on the inside of the front cover of the Manual. These charts should be studied for a few minutes daily, until the brief forms are indelibly photographed on your memory and flow from your pen without conscious thought.

111. READING AND DICTATION PRACTICE

Nearly all the brief forms in Chapters I to VI of the Manual are contained in the following sentences. Read the sentences in shorthand until your reading speed equals the speed with which you can read similar matter in type. Write the sentences until your accuracy is 100 per cent at a speed of 100 words a minute.

Sentences On Brief Forms

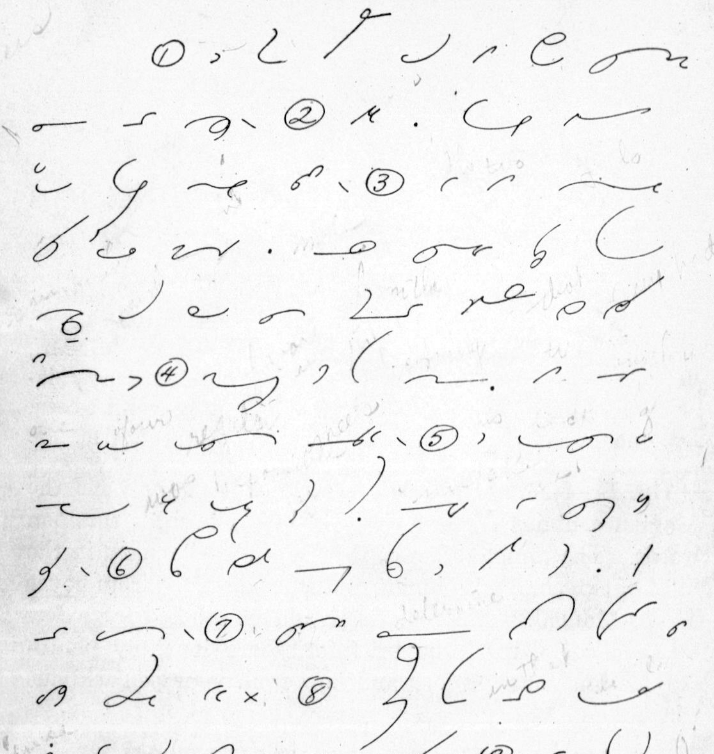

11
12
13
14
15
16
17
18
19
20
21

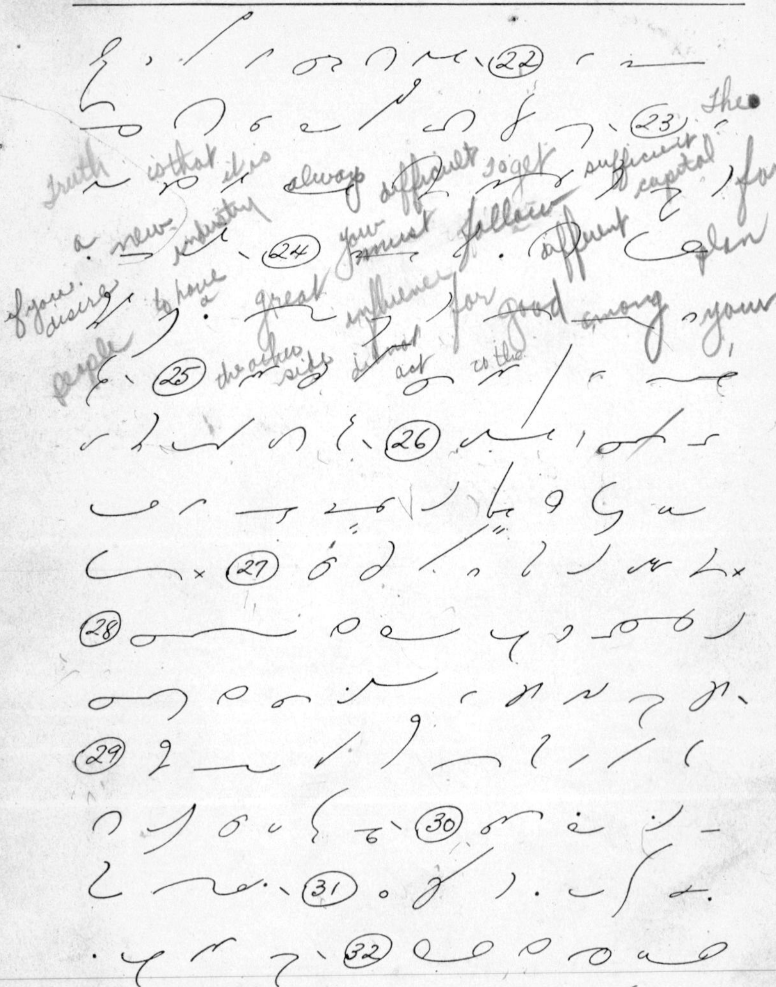

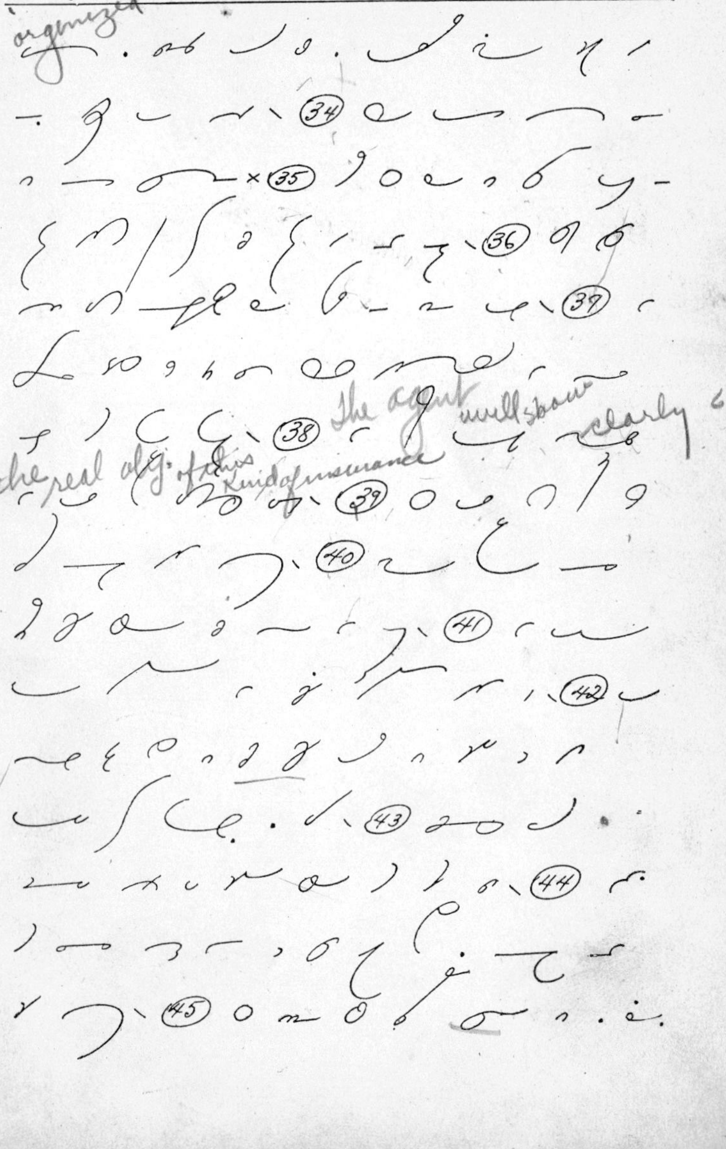
organized
34
35
36
37
The agent will show clearly
38
the real obj. of this kind of insurance
39
40
41
42
43
44
45

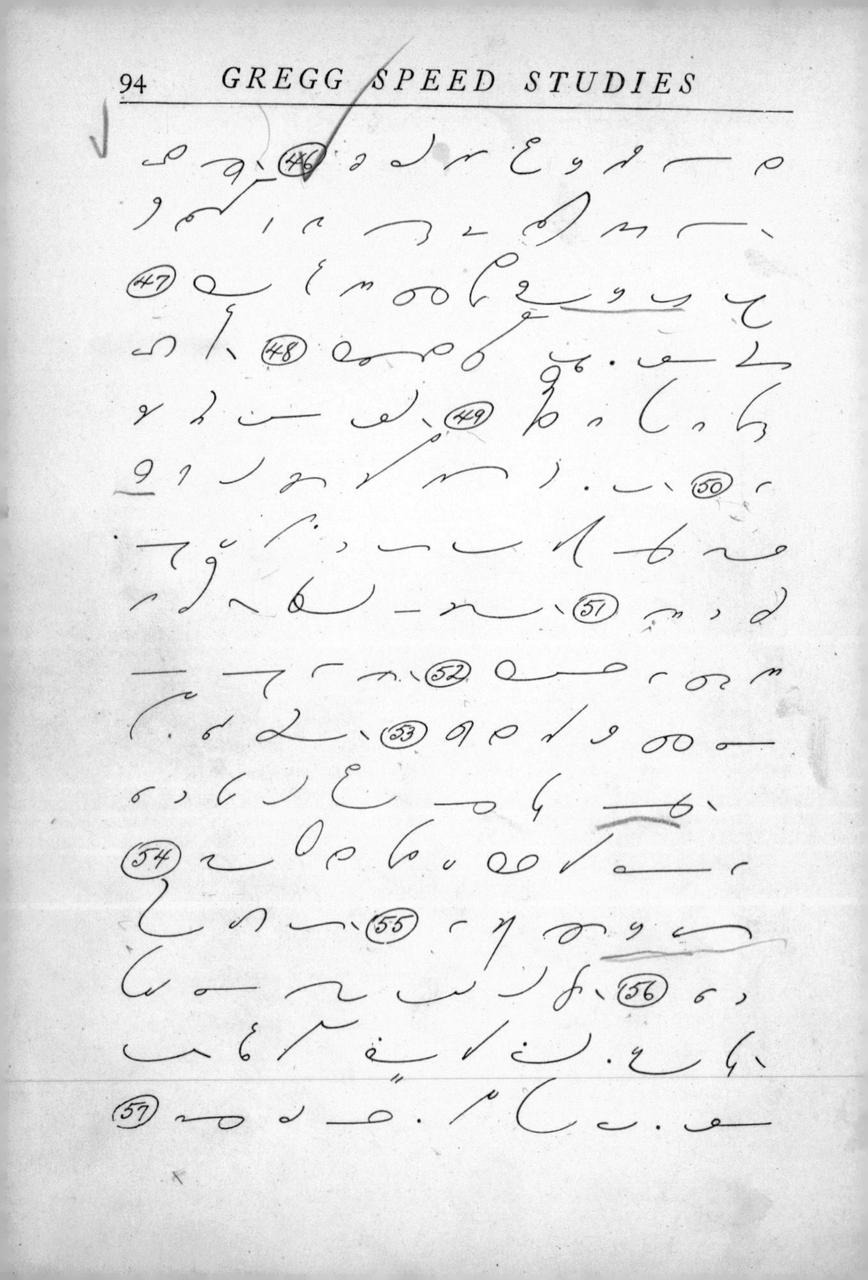

(46)

(47)

(48)

(49)

(50)

(51)

(52)

(53)

(54)

(55)

(56)

(57)

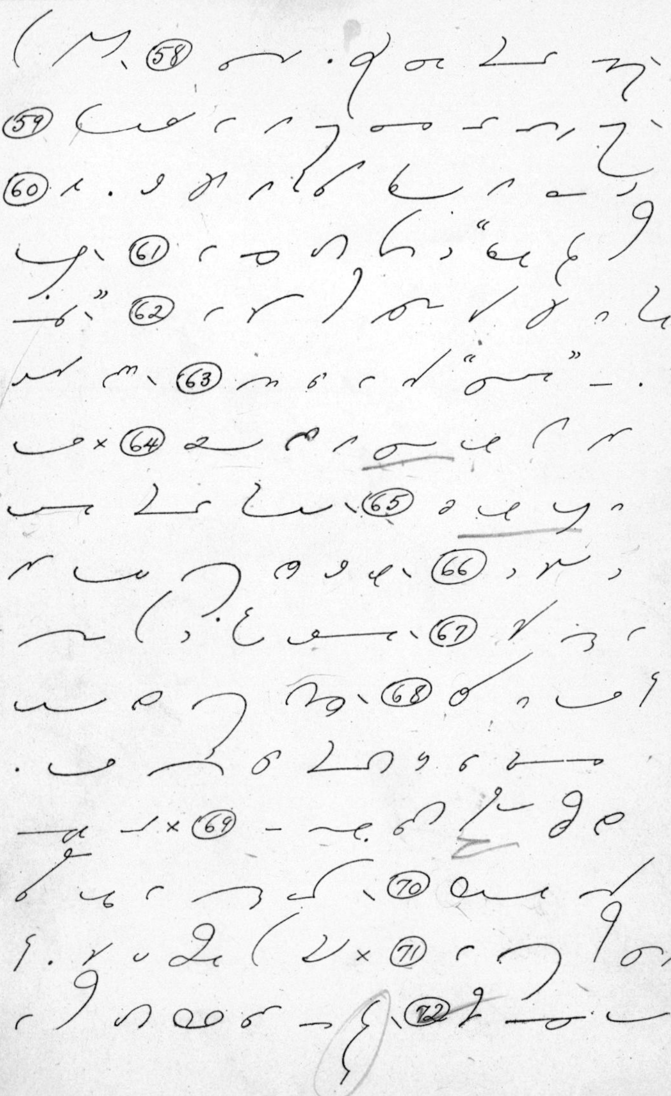
58
59
60
61
62
63
64
65
66
67
68
69
70
71
72

73
74
75
76
77
78
79
80
81
82
83

84
85
86
87
88
89
90
91
92
93
94

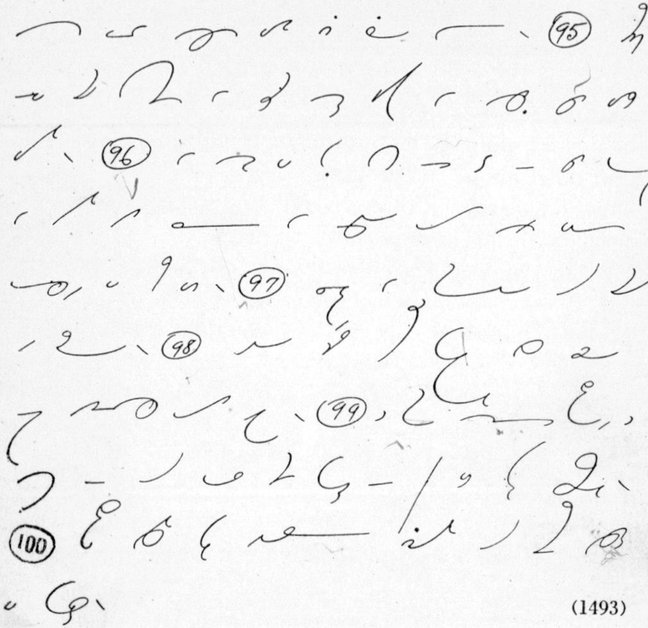

(1493)

112. WRITING PRACTICE

1. Without a question he gave the holder of the theater ticket a refund.

2. Mail these folders unsealed.

3. The clock chimed the hour of midnight, and there was profound quiet about the grounds.

4. The soldier was not discouraged and replaced his honorable discharge in his coat pocket.

5. He had removed his office to the top floor of the new building.

6. He could not see that his actions would retard the movement.

7. I have had copies of the valuable receipts made and filed in a fireproof safe.

8. The miner was killed in the gold rush.

9. I am unable to give my individual attention to the case that is on appeal.

10. We shall ask our agent to allow you more time to prepare this bill.

11. Will your friend help this committee in the publication of the new reference book on correspondence?

12. Most of his time after business hours was spent in work upon a course in marketing.

13. Please write the company fully about the advantage of advertising in our newspaper.

14. They looked out of the car window and saw the hills high above them.

15. Any date during the season will be satisfactory to Dr. Force.

113. The Ten-den, Tem-dem Blends. These two strokes take their upward direction from the *t* and the *d* and their comparative lengths from the *n* and the *m*.

Proportion Drill

Key: th, ten-den, tem-dem, th, ent-end, emt-emd.
timber, temple, temper, item, I-do-not.
to-me, at-any, at-any-time, they-do-not.

114. When the Blend Is Not Used. If a strongly stressed vowel occurs between the consonants *t-n*, *d-n*, *t-m*, and *d-m*, the blend is not used.

Drill

Key: dean, dine, team, tame, dome, dime, dawn.

115. Right-Motion Blend Drill.

Key: attended, suddenly, beaten, tonight, rotten, stencil, contented, dinners, obtained, eternal, maiden, tended, condemn, demurrage, maintain, costume.

116. Right-Motion Blend Drill. (Supplementing Paragraph 156 of the Manual.)

Key: intent, patent, sentence, attempt, attendance, content, extent, contempt, condemned, latent, straightened, pretend.

117. Rounding Angles. Curves predominate in this system, giving to the writing its fluency and similarity to longhand. Study a page of notes made by any expert writer and you will see that his notes contain almost no sharp angles.

Your notes may show exactness of form, but if the angles are positive, an absolute pause has taken place after each of them. When you have attained sufficient command over your hand to make the outlines rapidly and yet retain proportion of form, you will find that at the same time you have acquired skill in turning the corners—in other words, in eliminating the sharp points.

Practice the following drill on the blend phrases and other phrases in which the angle is eliminated in rapid writing.

Frequent-Phrase Drill

(Supplementing Paragraphs 157 and 158 of the Manual.)

Key: to-anyone, to-anyone-else, to-any-other, to-make-the, to-make-known, to-my-attention, to-my-credit, ought-to-know, it-might-be, it-may-not-be, at-any-date, at-any-day, at-any-future-time, it-must-be-done, it-must-have, would-have-been, would-have-been-able.

118. Er, Ar Drill. (Supplementing Paragraphs 162 to 164 of the Manual.)

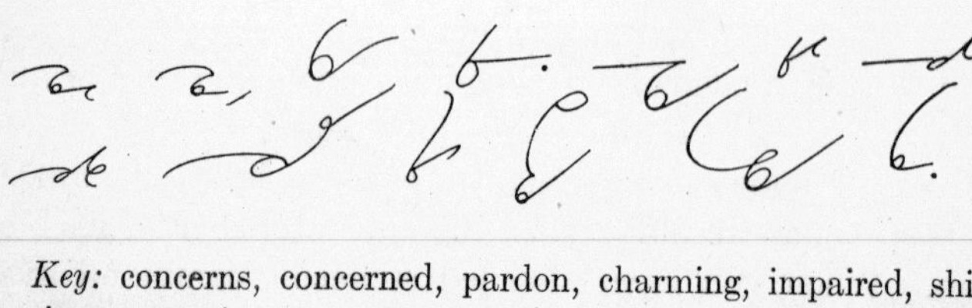

Key: concerns, concerned, pardon, charming, impaired, shirts, merits, courtesies, guaranteed, virtue, absurd, blizzard, burning.

119. "Omission of R" Drill—Er, Ar. (Supplementing Paragraph 165 of the Manual.)

Key: uncertain, cargo, largely, merchants, march, arguments, serving, reserved, deserve, servant, preserve, verse, verses, conversation, reservation, university, nerves, nervous.

120. "Omission of R" Drill—Or. (Supplementing Paragraph 165 of the Manual.)

Key: normal, enormity, mortal, dormitory, courts, sport, ports, resort, orderly, indorsed, organ, organizations, quarters, orchard, sorts, boarding, worried, worrying, worse, unworthy.

121. "Omission of R" Drill—Ern, Erm. (Supplementing Paragraph 165 of the Manual.)

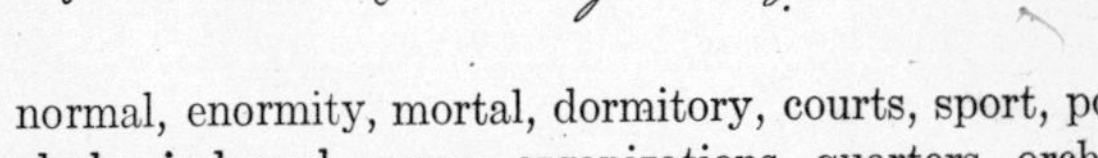

Key: term, learning, turning, turns, confirm, firmly.

122. Ther Drill. (Supplementing Paragraph 168 of the Manual.)

Key: brothers, mothers, fathers, gathered, bothered, farther.

123. Tain Suffix Drill. (Supplementing Paragraph 155 of the Manual.)

Key: contains, maintain-mountain, obtaining, attainable, sustained, pertaining, retainer.

124. Frequent-Phrase Drill.

were:

early:

year:

Key: we-were, you-were, they-were, we-were-not, you-were-not, they-were-not; at-an-early-date, at-an-early-day, by-early-mail, early-attention, early-information; year-or-two, year-or-two-ago.

125. Prefix For, Fore, Fur Drill.

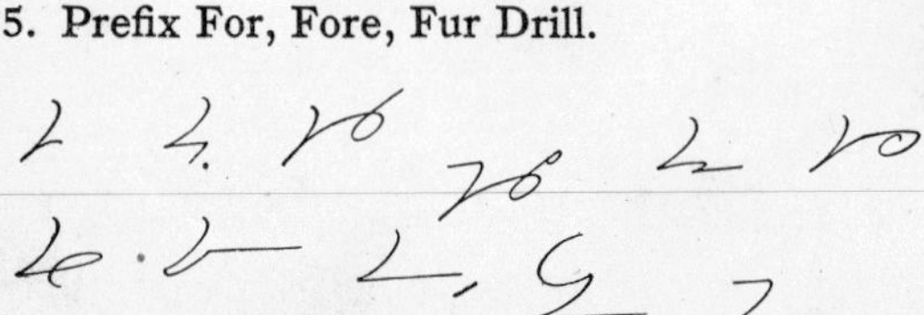

Key: forth, furnishing, fortunate, unfortunately, forenoon, fortnight, furnace, furthermore, formed, performed, informs.

126. Prefix For, Fore Drill. (Preceding a vowel.)

Key: forearm, forehead, forever, foreword, foreordain.

127. Age Suffix Drill.

Key: marriage, carriage, passage, message, discouraged, encourage, encouragement, managed, percentage, patronage, tonnage, luggage.

128. Brief-Form Derivative Drill—Ful Suffix.

Key: beautiful, careful, dutiful, forceful, grateful, regretfully, rightfully, skillful, successful, thankful, truthful, useful, wonderfully

129. Frequent-Phrase Drill.

him:

hope:

sorry:

want:

ago:

possible:

few:

sure.

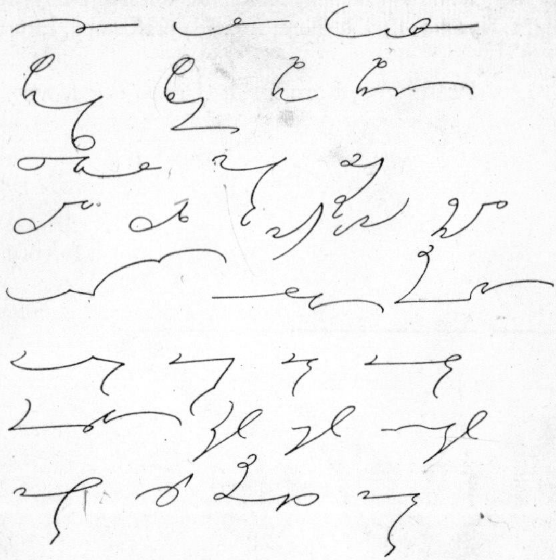

Key: him: give-him, let-him, please-write-him; *hope:* I-hope-you-will-be-able, I-hope-to-hear-from-you, we-hope-you-are, we-hope-you-can-go; *sorry:* I-am-sorry-to-learn, you-will-be-sorry, we-are-very-sorry; *want:* I-want-to-know, I-want-to-see, you-want-to-have, what-you-want, if-you-want-any; *ago:* long-time-ago, many-years-ago, several-months-ago; *possible:* as-long-as-possible, as-much-as-possible, as-soon-as-possible, as-many-as-possible; *few:* few-minutes-ago, for-a-few-days, in-a-few-days, in-the-course-of-a-few-days; *sure:* you-may-be-sure, quite-sure, we-feel-sure-that, you-must-be-sure.

Note: In the Reading and Dictation Practice from this point on, the student will find that a few outlines have been used that are written in accordance with the Manual, Paragraphs 195–198 and 220–222, and also some words listed in the Vocabulary of the Manual, pages 155–159.

130. READING AND DICTATION PRACTICE

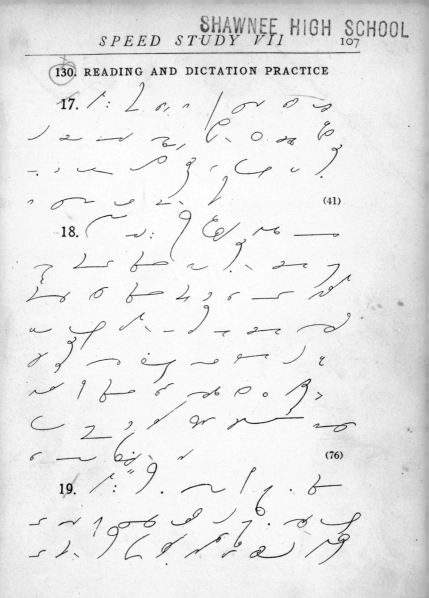

17.
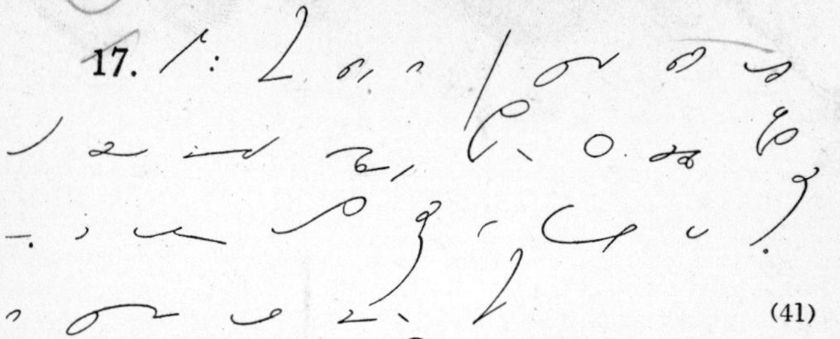
(41)

18.
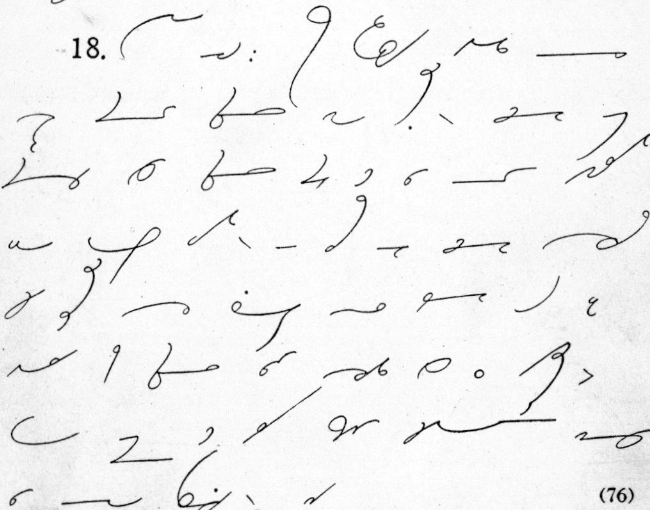
(76)

19.

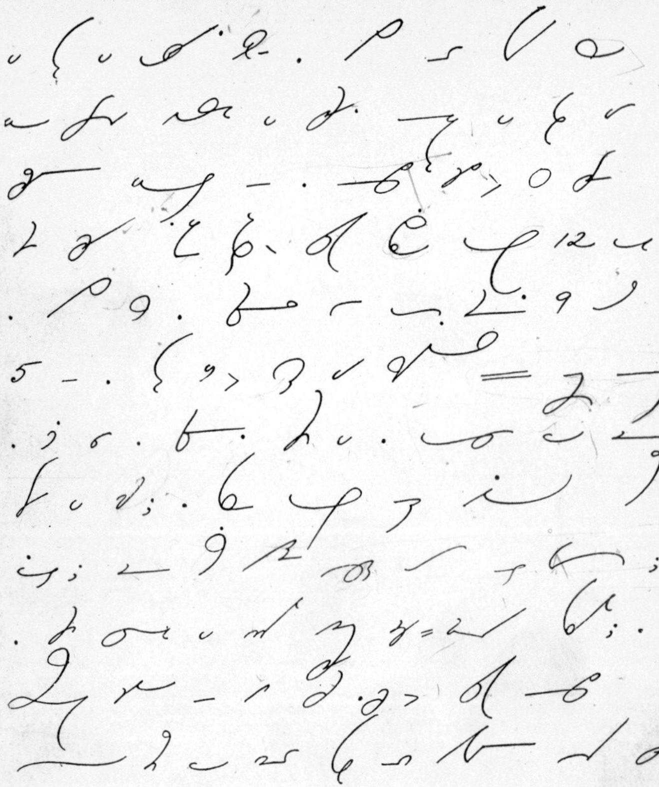

(178)

20.

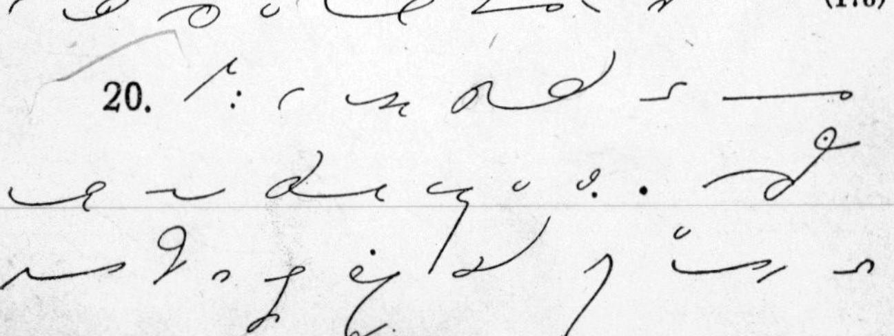

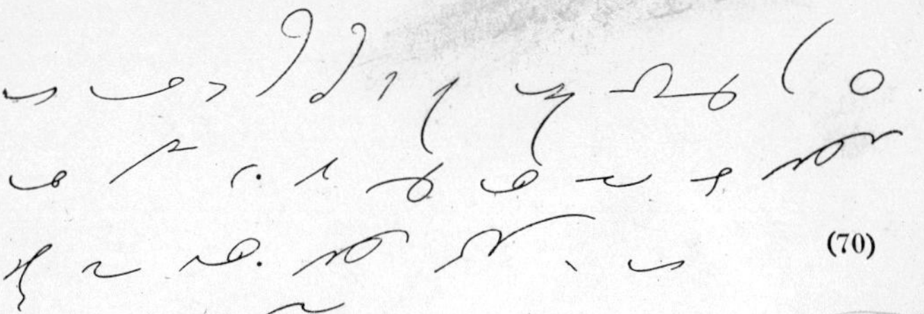

(70)

21.

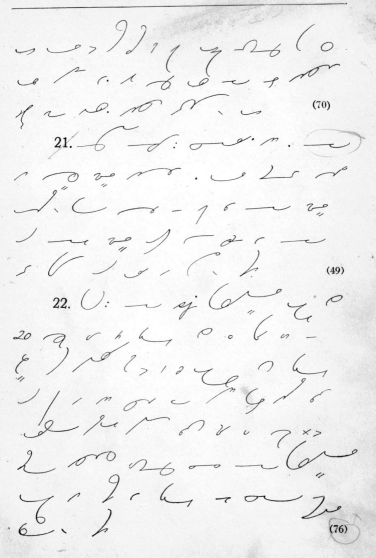

(49)

22.

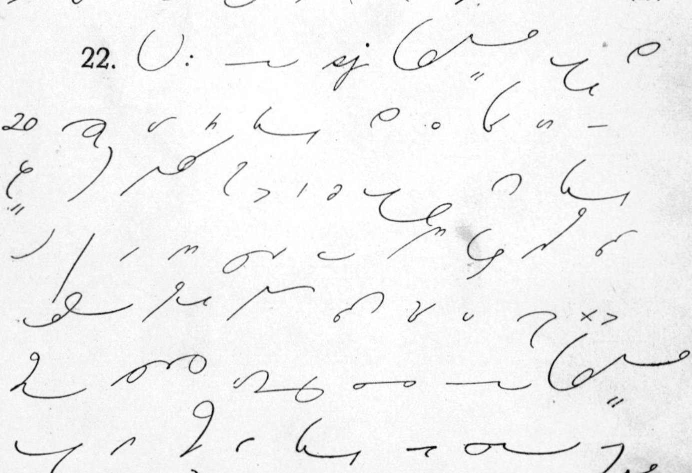

(76)

23. THE PRINTING PRESS

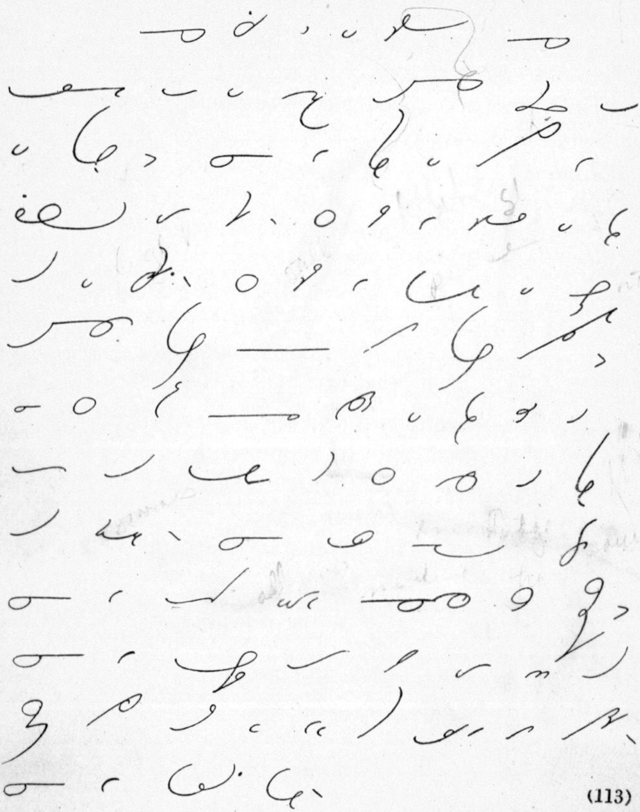

(113)

131. WRITING PRACTICE

1. The dean asked the student to dine with him.

2. Are you planning to attend the dinner in honor of the retiring officers?

3. He attempted to obtain a patent on a new kind of metal-stamping device.

4. I am sure that the boys are pretending to be frightened.

5. Have you a suitable costume for the dance tonight?

6. Thousands are wondering about the outcome of the inquiry.

7. They found it hard to choose a successor for the film director, who resigned suddenly because of his failing health.

8. Please wire him that it must be done now; he ought to know the seriousness of the matter.

9. The entire front of the plant is to be painted a dark brown, and the work is to be begun soon.

10. Do not forget to see the foreman at the printing plant about the envelopes we ordered.

11. I managed to get a passage to France on the "Southern Star."

12. A research will be made by the experts for the purpose of trying to reduce the cost of making this fluid.

13. The farmer tried to till the fertile soil of his farm according to the new theory of growing crops but without much success.

14. The meeting that was called to consider a new charter had to adjourn before action was taken on it.

SPEED STUDY VIII

132. The Termination Est. The termination *est* is expressed by *es* in words ending with a consonant, when the word is written *in full*.

Drill

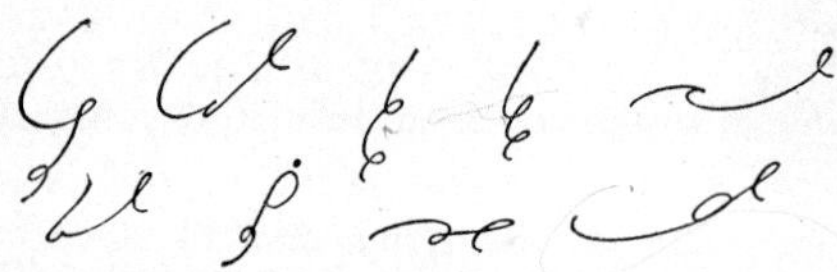

Key: briefest, broadest, cheapest, choicest, coldest, fondest, harshest, keenest, latest.

This applies also to brief forms or contractions when the *final consonant of the shorthand form* is also the *final consonant of the word.*

Drill

Key: longest, soonest, youngest, strangest.

The termination *est* is expressed by *st*, disjoined, in brief forms, abbreviated words, or words ending with a *vowel.*

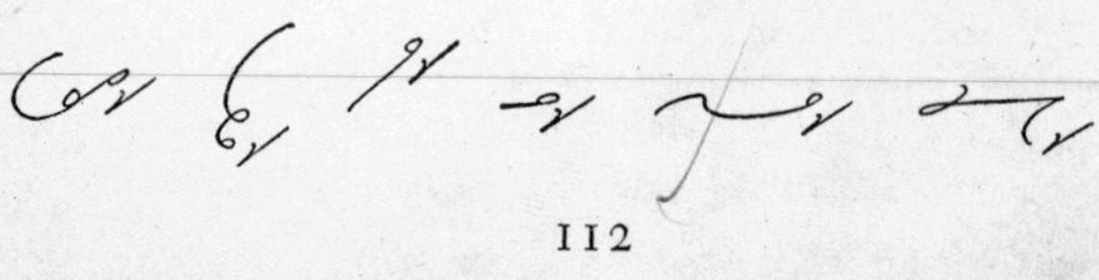

Key: prettiest, busiest, dearest, nearest, clearest, simplest.

When the form is distinctive, *st* may be joined:

Drill

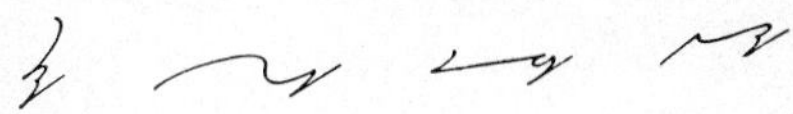

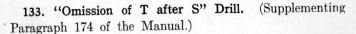

Key: fullest, greatest, smallest, truest.

For *earliest* and *highest* these brief forms are used:

Drill

133. "Omission of T after S" Drill. (Supplementing Paragraph 174 of the Manual.)

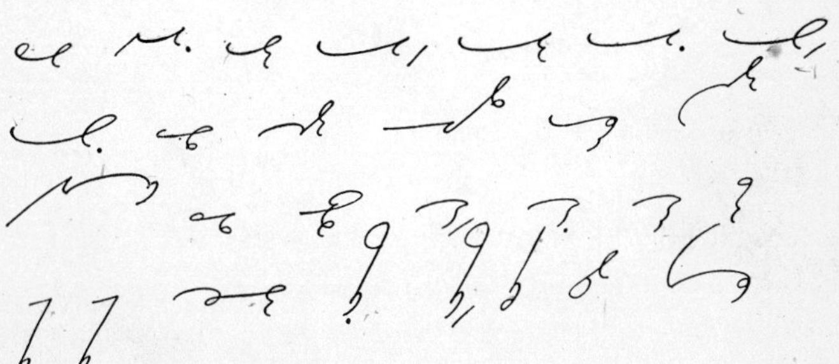

Key: earliest, trusting, respects, listed, lists, listing, lasted, lasting, honestly, contests, modesty, requests, dentists, disgust, earnestly, nicest, consisted, consisting, consists, exists, unjust, injustice, chemists, adjusting, adjusted, justly, attest, biggest.

134. "Omission of T after K" Drill.

Key: deducting, deducts, deduction, conducts, directions, directs, directors, elects, election, selection, enacts, acting, actions, acts, actionable, sections, strictness, strictly, attraction, convictions.

135. "Omission of T after P" Drill.

Key: excepting, adapts, adaptable, adapted, abruptness, concept, adopted.

136. "Omission of D" Drill.

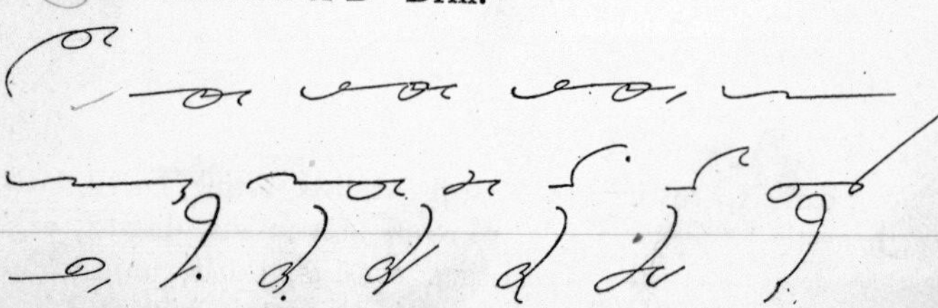

Key: demands, minds, reminds, reminded, recommend, recommendations, commands, sends, intending, intends, admitted, admired, advertising, advising, advised, advises, advanced, advantages.

137. Brief-Form Derivative Drill—Less.

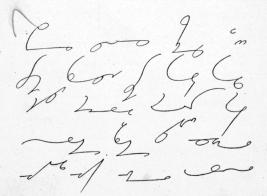

Key: endless, useless, friendless, groundless, nameless, nevertheless, numberless, powerless, regardless, effortless, listless, valueless, wireless, formless, unless.

138. Frequent-Phrase Drill. (Supplementing Paragraph 189 of the Manual.)

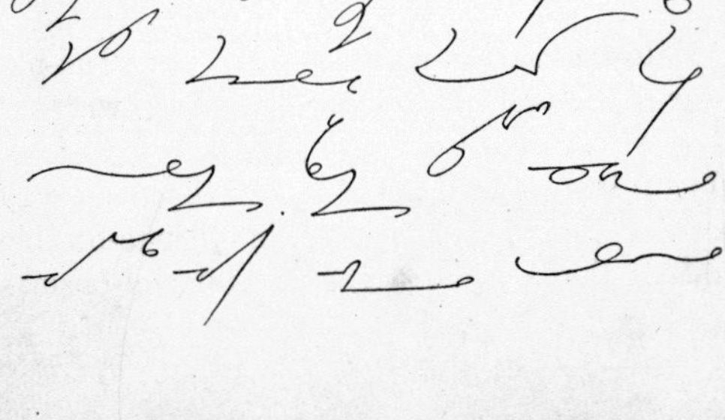

Key: about-how-many, according-to-my, adjust-the-matter, all-over-the-world, back-and-forth, balance-of-account, before-and-after, bill-of-exchange, bill-of-sale, for-a-day-or-two, for-a-number-of-years, for-a-long-time, free-of-charge, glad-to-hear-from-you, hope-to-hear-from-you, I-desire-to-thank-you, in-answer-to-your-letter, in-order-to-receive, in-order-to-judge, in-the-usual-manner, line-of-credit.

139. Frequent-Phrase Drill. (Supplementing Paragraph 189 of the Manual.)

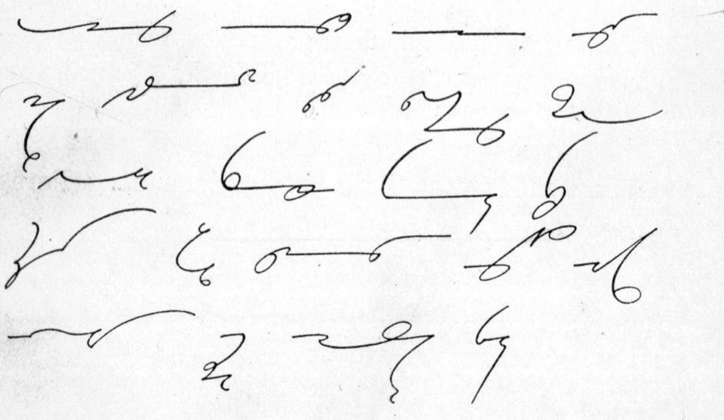

Key: look-into-the-matter, many-of-these, more-and-more, now-and-then, one-of-the-best, two-or-three-months, with-or-without, with-reference-to-the-matter, as-a-rule, at-a-loss, bear-in-mind, by-means-of-which, by-the-way, for-a-certain-time, hope-to-receive, how-many-of-them, in-addition-to-that, in-order-to-be-able, in-the-course-of-time, in-the-first-instance, in-your-line-of-business, upon-the-subject.

140. READING AND DICTATION PRACTICE

24.

(80)

25.

(40)

26.

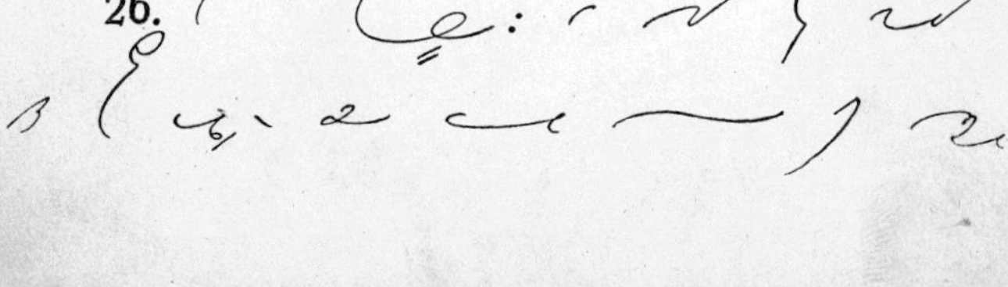

(125)

27.

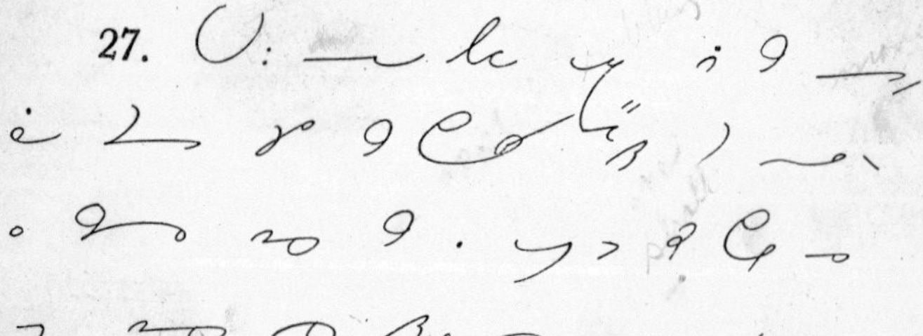

(53)

28.

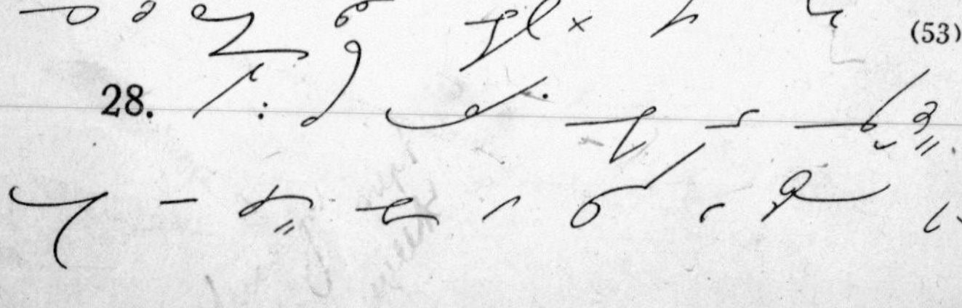

(103)

29.

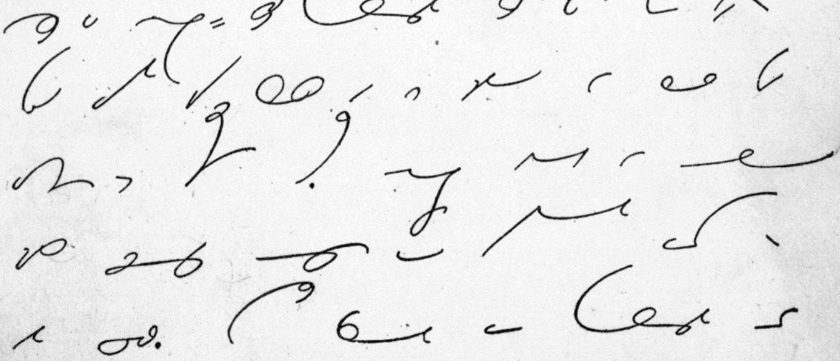

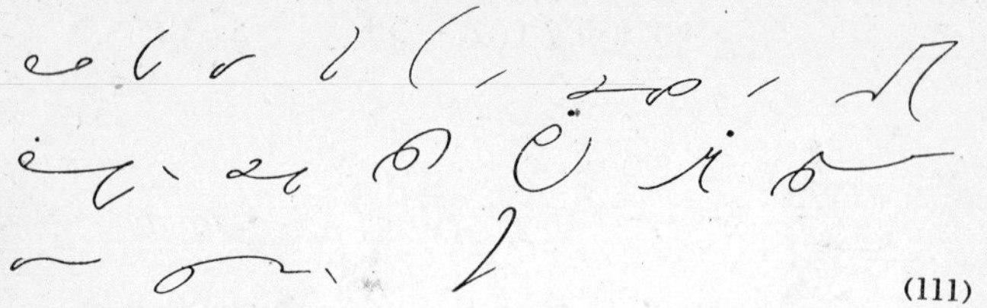

(111)

30.

(62)

31.

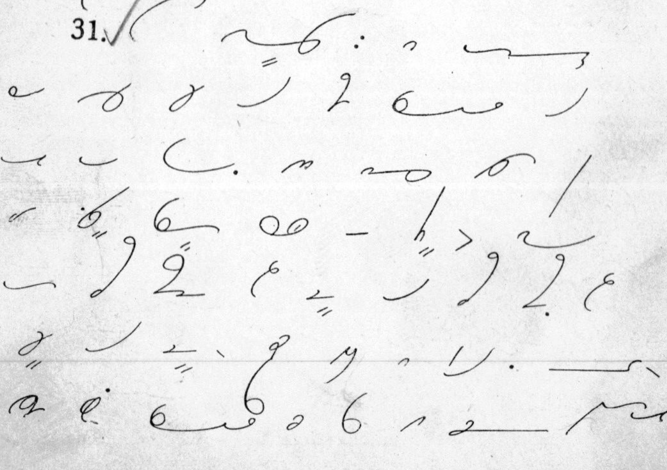

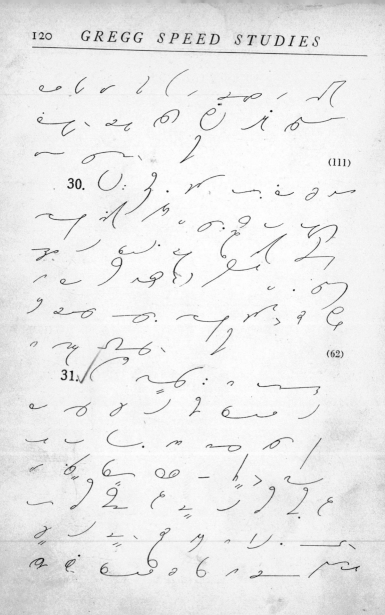

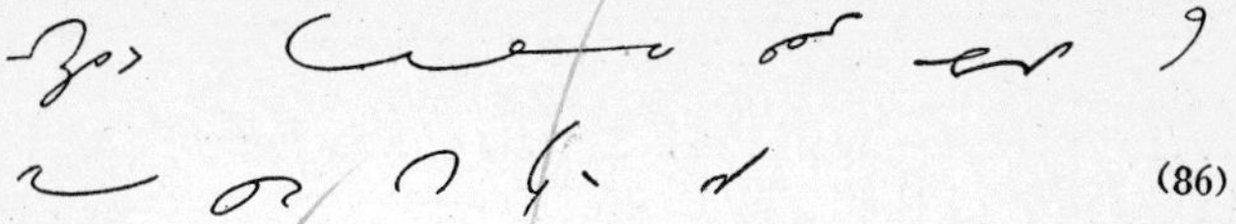

(86)

32.

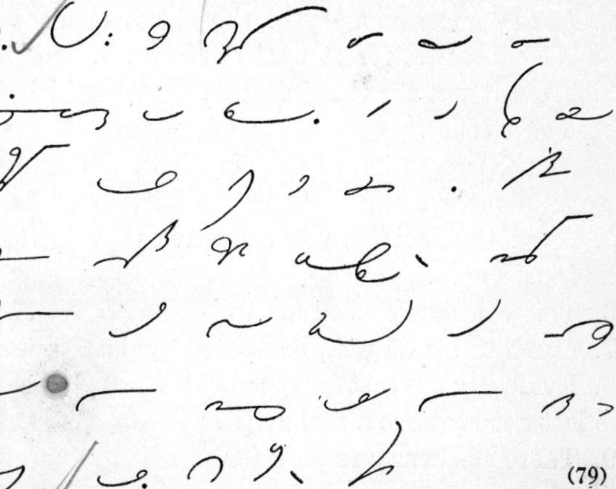

(79)

33.

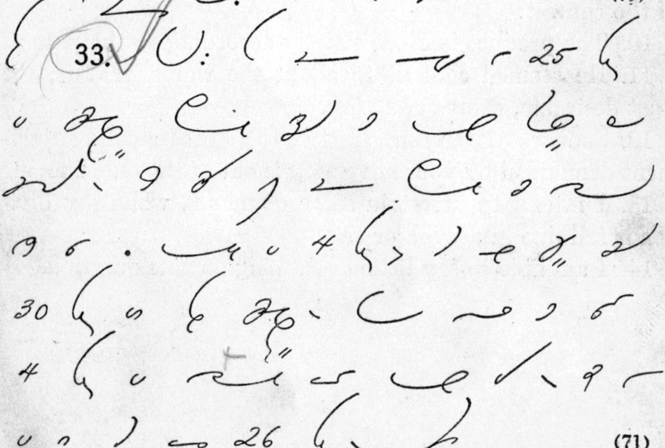

(71)

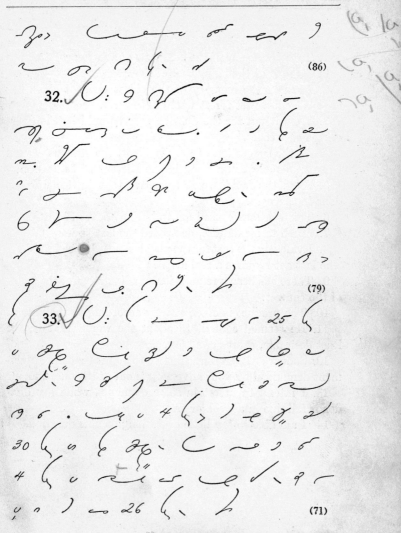

141. WRITING PRACTICE

1. This will be one of the best tests of how honest a person is in the face of the rising cost of living.

2. Even in the memory of the oldest resident there has always been a vast forest west of the farm.

3. Were it not for the dust this road would be the finest on the east coast.

4. At the suggestion of the president, the student elected five periods of work a week in the History of Education.

5. From the facts, we feel positive that justice was not done in this case.

6. This cold has caused me to lose my sense of taste.

7. Much to his disgust, he missed the last train.

8. Evidently the cast for the play has not yet been selected. The last act requires a real artist.

9. There has been a request for an adjustment of the terms of the contest.

10. The product is made strictly according to the patent.

11. He seemed content to adopt the worst, that is, the least desirable, course of action.

12. Sooner or later you will have to admit that the adjustment demanded by your adversary is out of the question.

13. I intend to invest in some diamonds when my dividends fall due in a week or two.

14. I am able to say little or nothing on this question.

SPEED STUDY IX

142. Abbreviated-Word Drill. (Supplementing Paragraph 193 of the Manual.)

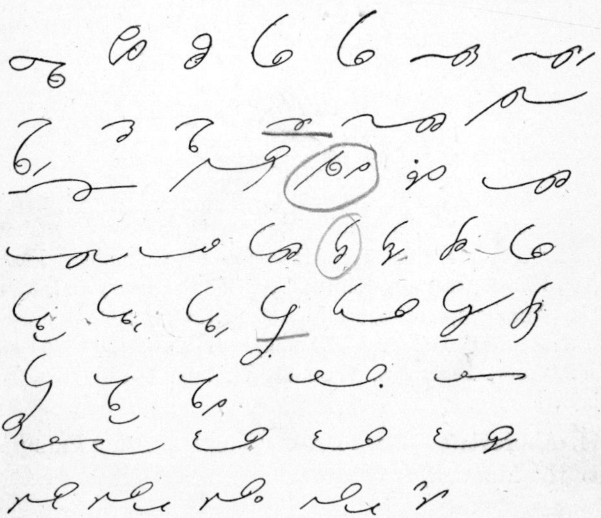

Key: anxiety, appetite, aside, bright, brightly, crowds, crowded, combined, conceive, compete, cure-curious, cloudy, doubtless, engagement, delightful, decidedly, hesitate, loudly, louder, loyal, proudly, poorly, poorest, purely, privately, procedure, proceedings, proceeded-perceived, prevailing, politely, persuade, powerful, provides, repeater, repeatedly, relating, remove, removal, slight, slightly, slightest, strikes, strikers, strikingly, traders, understood.

143. Abbreviation Drill. (Supplementing Paragraph 195 of the Manual.)

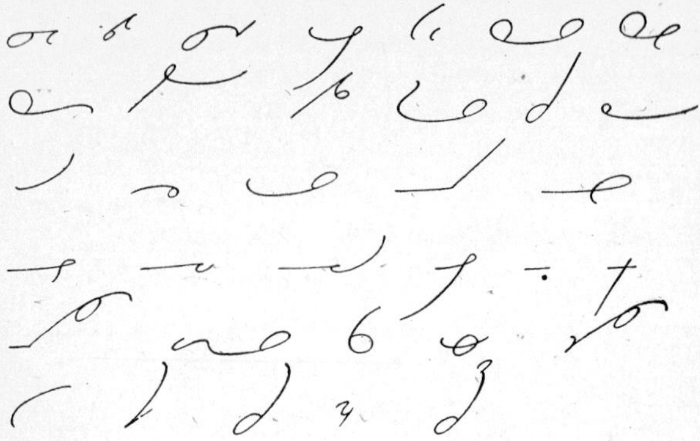

Key: answer, etc., account, Reverend, postscript, Alabama, Arizona, Arkansas, Delaware, District of Columbia, Florida, Georgia, Illinois, Indiana, Kentucky, Louisiana, Maryland, Massachusetts, Mississippi, Missouri, Montana, Nevada, New Hampshire, New Jersey, North Dakota, Oklahoma, Pennsylvania, Rhode Island, South Dakota, Tennessee, Vermont, Virginia, Washington, West Virginia.

144. Abbreviated-Word Drill. (Supplementing Paragraph 196 of the Manual.)

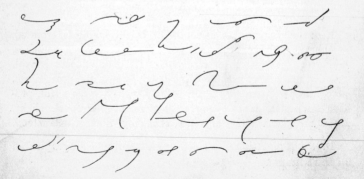

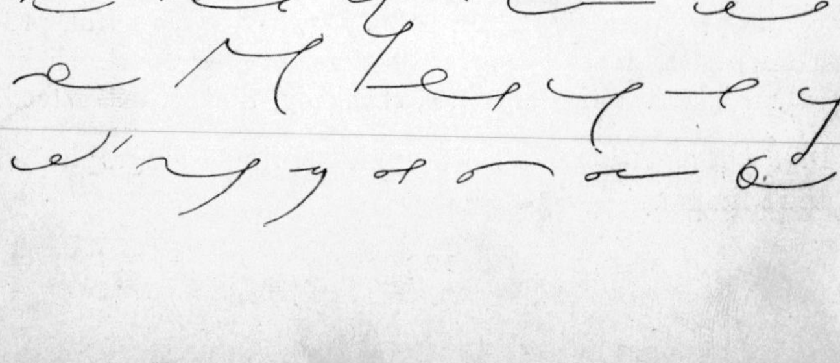

Key: illustrations, gratitude, involved, legal, moderate, philosophy, preliminary, ridiculous, trifle, unanimous, vulgar, colors, refrigerate, development, relatively, calculate, deliberate, malicious, liberty, master, originally, rendered, clever, novel, initial, ignorant, enormous, silence.

145. Abbreviated-Word Drill—Miscellaneous.

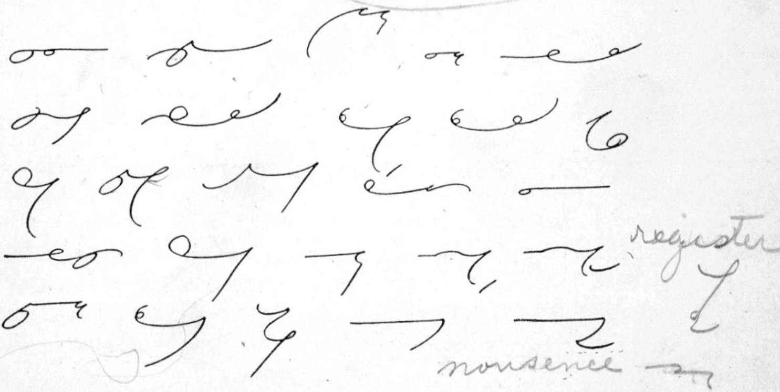

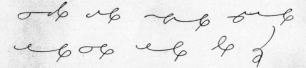

Key: animal, catalogue, demonstration, innocent-ce, military, sacrifice, calendar, celebrated, cylinder, typewrite-r, arbitrary, attribute, indulgence, eloquent-ce, eminent, miraculous, algebra, mischief, incorporated, incorporator, atmosphere, silver, refrigerate, manufacture, manufacturer.

146. Ization, Axation Drill.

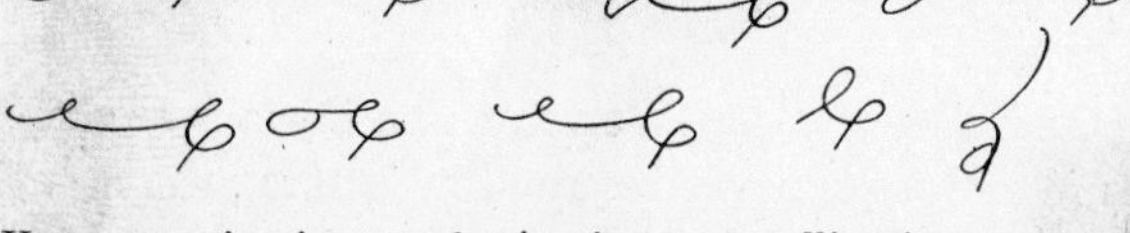

Key: amortization, authorization, crystallization, naturalization, realization. annexation, relaxation, taxation, vexation.

147. "Dollar" Standing Alone. When standing alone, *dollar* is expressed by *d-o.* With *k* beneath, it expresses *dollar and a quarter;* with *f*, *dollar and a half;* with the *cents* sign (above the line), *dollars and cents.*

Drill

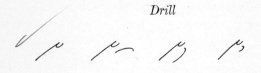

Key: dollar, dollar and a quarter, dollar and a half, dollars and cents.

148. Figures and Measurements Drill. (Supplementing Paragraph 204 of the Manual.)

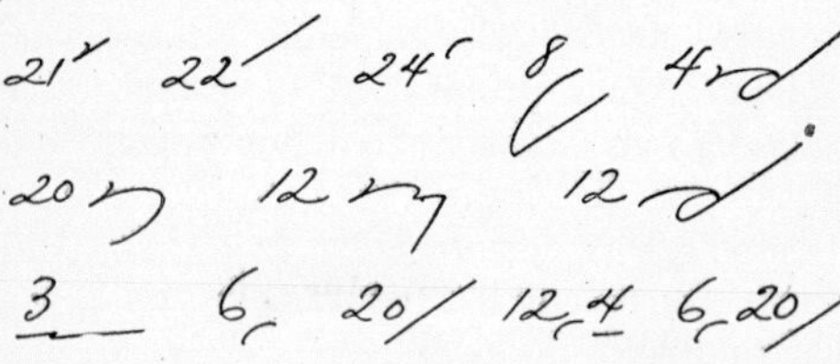

Key: twenty-first, twenty-second, twenty-fourth, \$8,000,000,000, 4 square yards, 20 square feet, 12 square inches, 12 cubic yards, 300,000,000, 6,000, \$20, 12,400, \$6,020.

149. Omission of Initial Vowel. The initial vowel in the prefixes *in* and *un* is never required in forming the negatives of derivatives of brief forms, or in forming the compound prefixes.

Drill

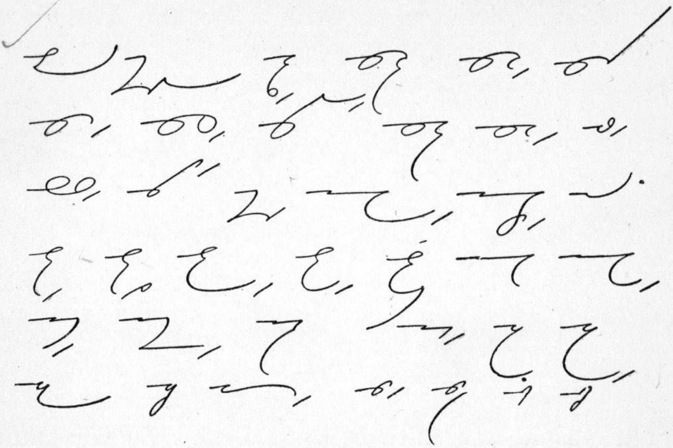

Key: unexcelled, ineffectual, inexperienced, unacceptable, unaccepted, unaccounted, unacknowledged, unacquainted, unaddressed, unanswerable, unanswered, unappointed, unarranged, uneducated, uneffected, unemployed, unempowered, unending, unexpected, unexpectedly, unexplained, unexpressed, unexpressive, unimportant, unimproved, uninfluenced, uninformed, uninsurable, uninsured, unobliging, unobliged, unofficial, unofficially, unorganized, unused, unusable, unusual, unusually.

150. READING AND DICTATION PRACTICE

34.

(49)

35.

(98)

36.

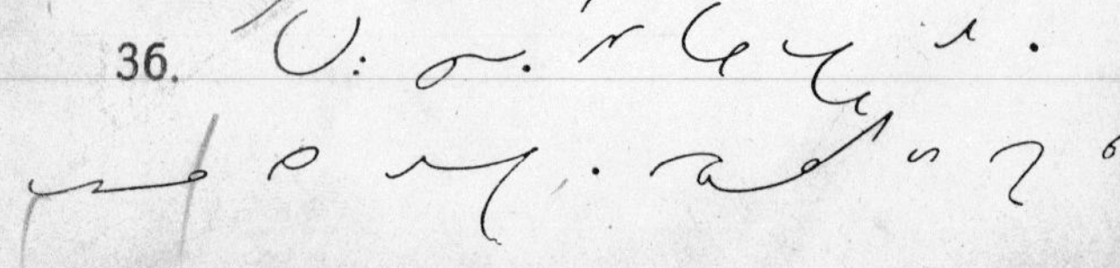

(34)

37.

(133)

38.

(166)

89.

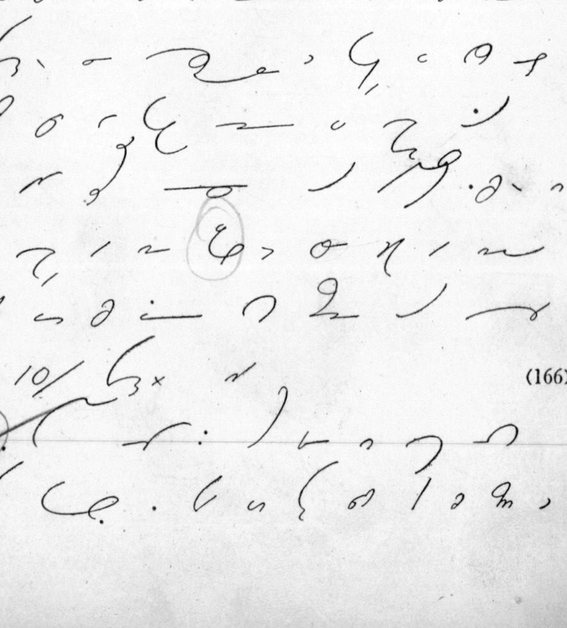

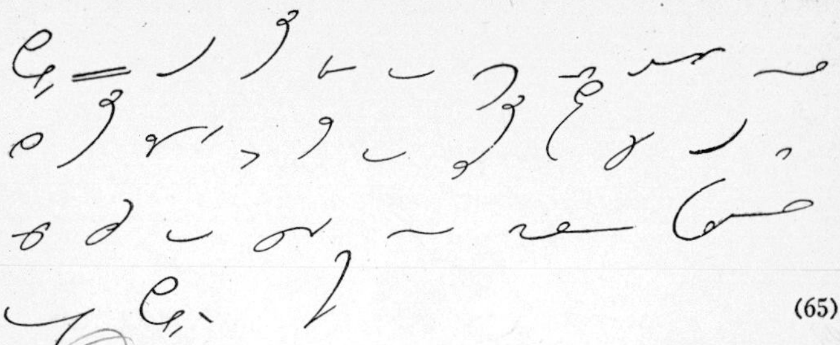

(65)

40.

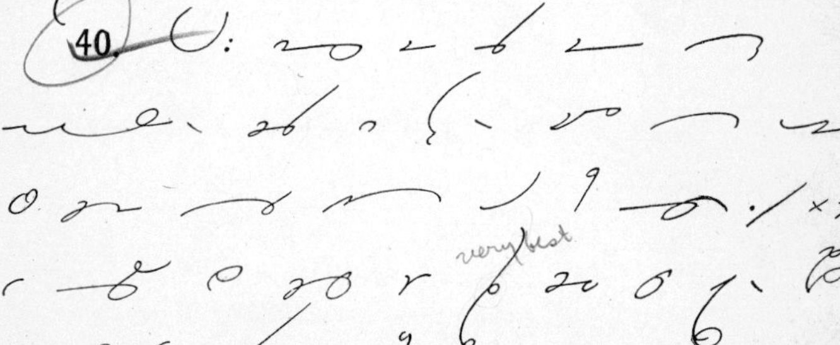

(55)

41.

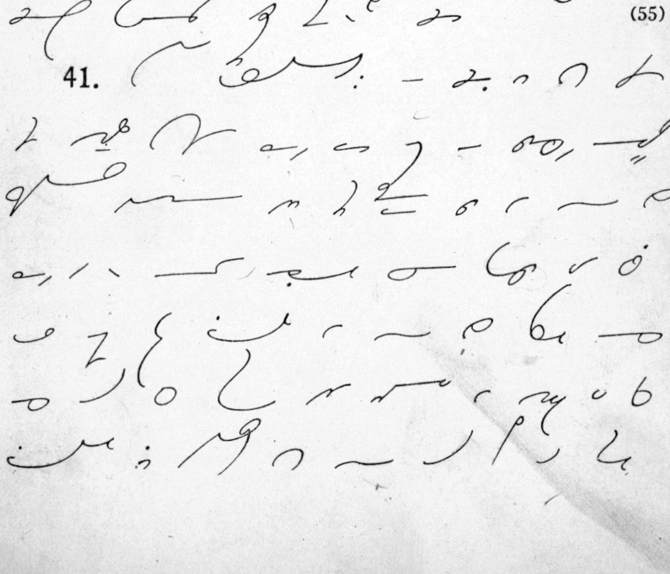

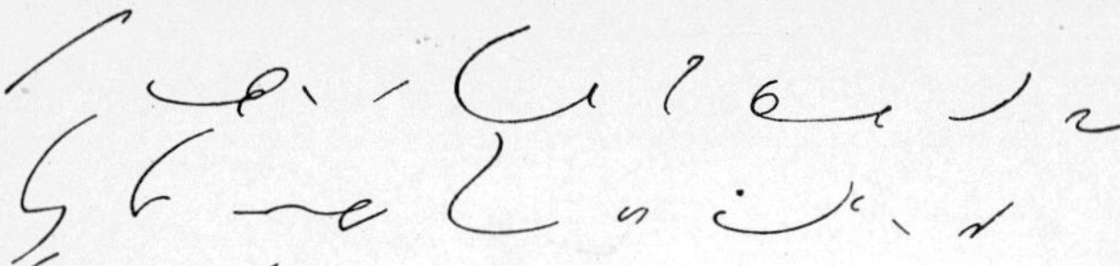

(95)

42.

(51)

43.

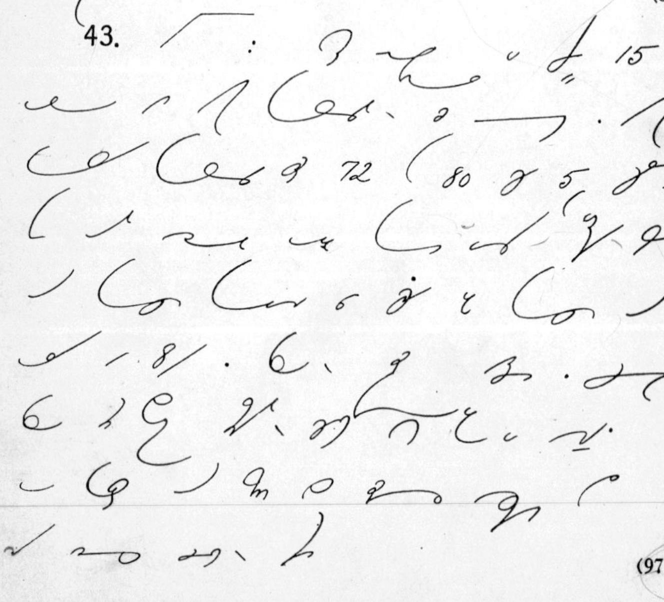

(97)

44.

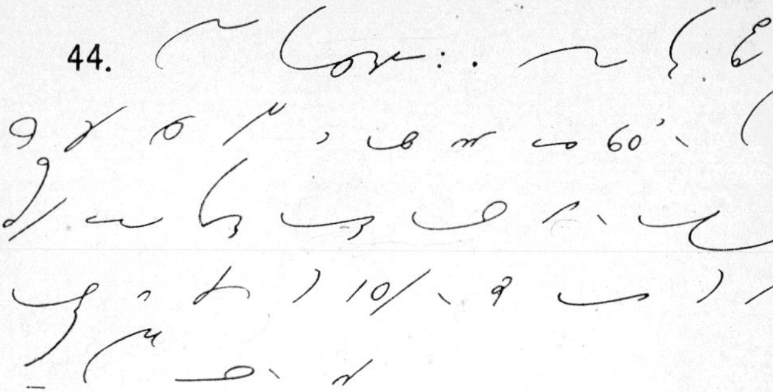

(48)

45.

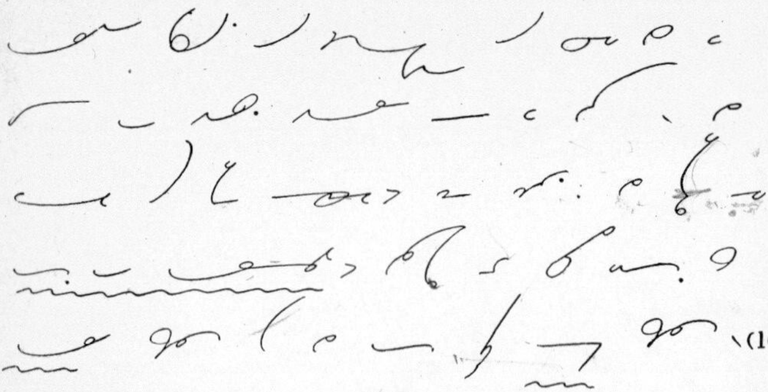

(164)

46. THE LITTLE THINGS

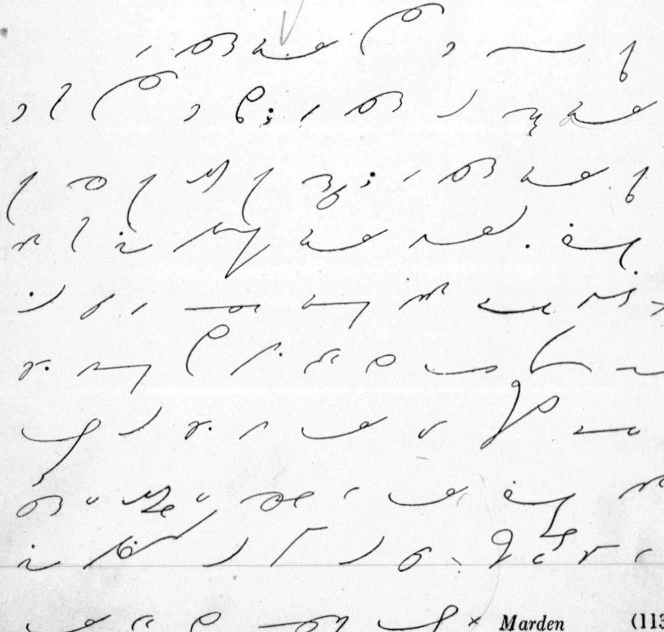

Marden (113)

47. HOW TO TAKE LIFE

Mark Twain (147)

151. WRITING PRACTICE

1. The duplicate as well as the original copy of the certificate is required.

2. "Pure high-grade food products always on sale at popular prices" is the policy of the new manager.

3. Travel removes prejudice, awakens the imagination, and develops one's knowledge of foreign languages.

4. This financial magazine, issued in England, contains many striking illustrations of the decided changes that have taken place in the balance of trade.

5. You are invited to attend a private showing of rare copies of original paintings.

6. Put aside all prejudice and cooperate with us in establishing a new policy that will benefit all of us.

7. The union called a strike and proceeded to argue at length about their apparent grievances.

8. Thank you for your splendid enthusiasm and appreciation of what I have tried to accomplish for the local association this year. Such an attitude is essential if all are to benefit from our endeavors.

9. He dictated a notation of numerous additions to be made in the revised edition of his book on the social history of his country.

10. The keen competition between the two salesmen indicated that their commissions were liberal.

11. In the future no freight will be received at this station unless it is separated according to destination. This rule will enable us to render you better service.

12. Somebody told me that his income included several hundred dollars a year derived from gilt-edged bonds, which paid him an average of 5 per cent per annum.

SPEED STUDY X

152. Disjoined-Prefix Drill.

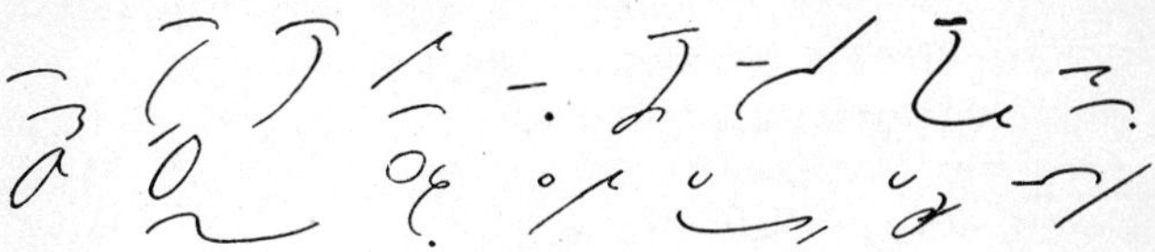

Key: contracts, contributed, contrive, district, entering, interview, entertained, intervals, instructing, agrees, agricultural, anticipating, includes, overlooked, oversight, encountered.

153. Done Phrases.

Key: we-have-done, may-be-done, what-has-been-done, can-be-done, to-be-done, could-be-done.

154. Than Phrases.

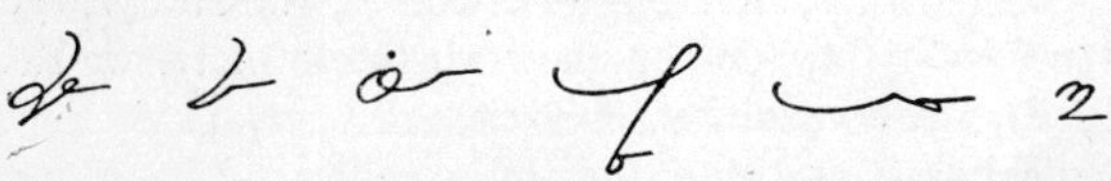

Key: faster-than, further-than, higher-than, larger-than, longer-than, worse-than.

155. Us Phrases.

Key: gave-us, wire-us, allow-us, told-us, favor-us, regard-us.

156. Department Phrases.

Key: banking department, receiving department, repair department, grocery department, shoe department, furniture department.

157. Frequent-Phrase Drill. (Supplementing Paragraph 224 of the Manual.)

Key: of-course-it-was, as-a-matter-of-course, we-always, you-always, ten-days'-sight, do-you-know-whether-or-not, we-have-your-order, first-class-condition, first-class-manner, sometime-or-other, as-quickly-as-possible, out-of-stock, so-far-as-I-know, to-a-large-extent, we-take-pleasure, your-immediate-attention, for-your-convenience, at-your-earliest-convenience, long-past-due.

158. READING AND DICTATION PRACTICE

48.

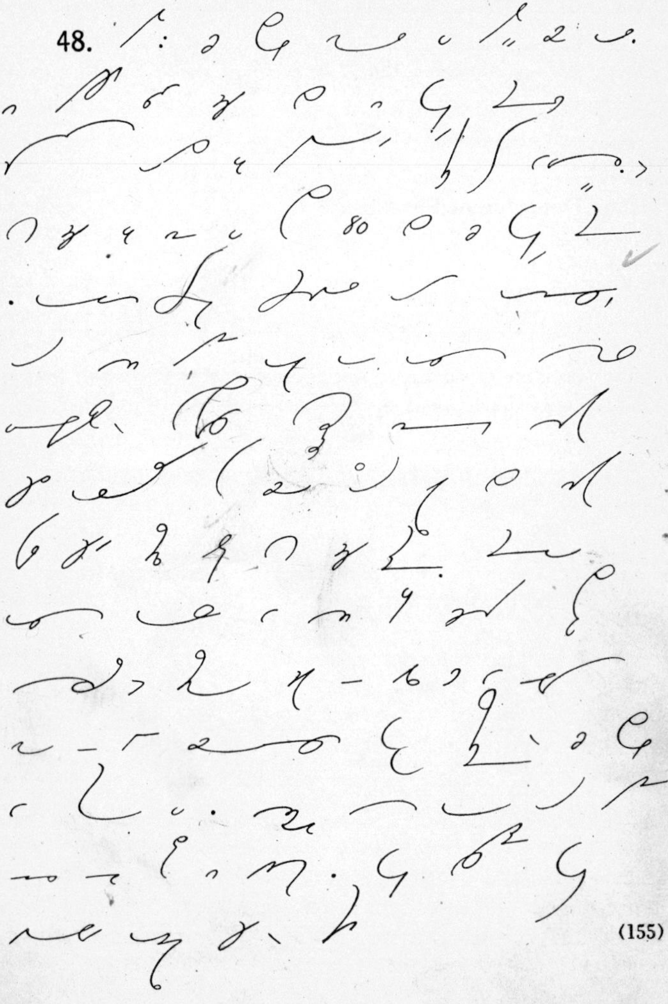

(155)

49.

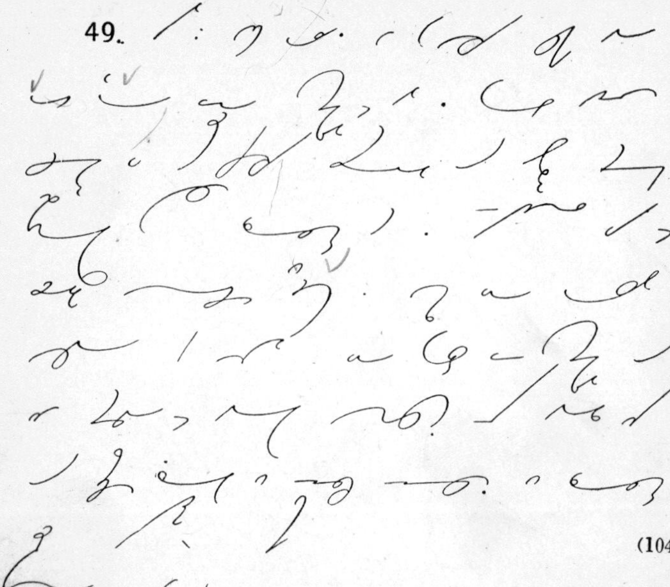

(104)

50.

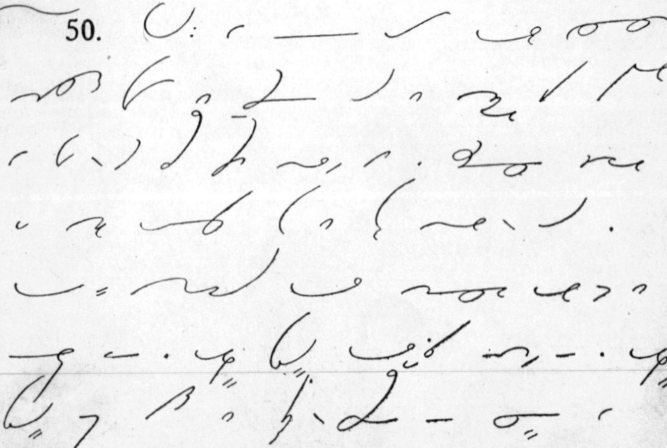

Jacquard

(116)

51.

75/

10 70/

(95)

52.

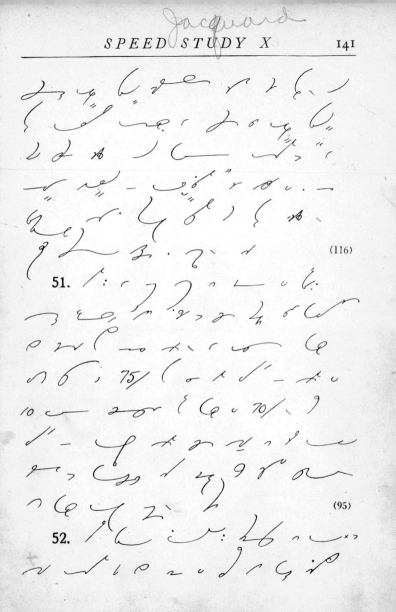

(151)

53.

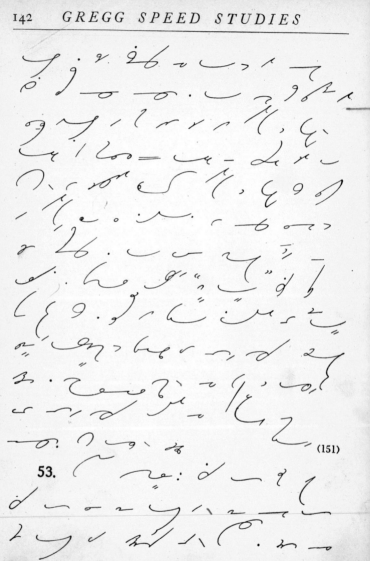

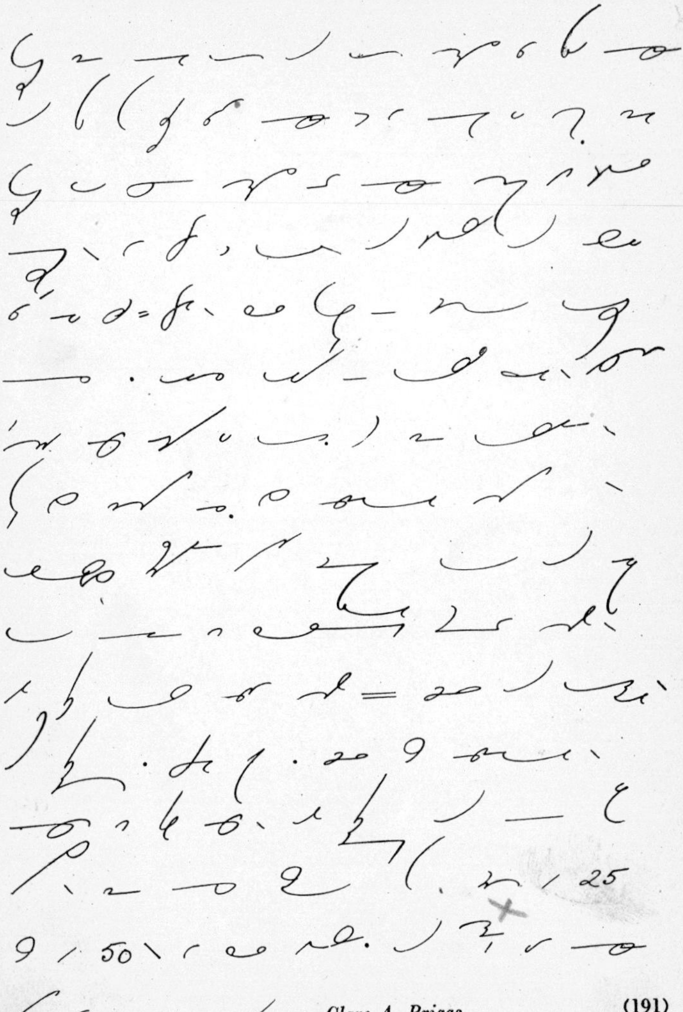

Clare A. Briggs (191)

54.

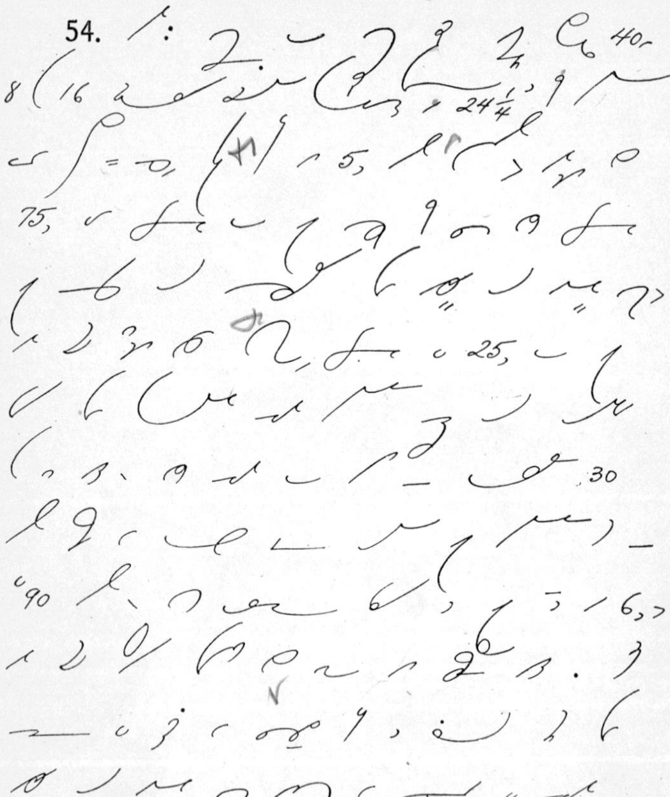

(205)

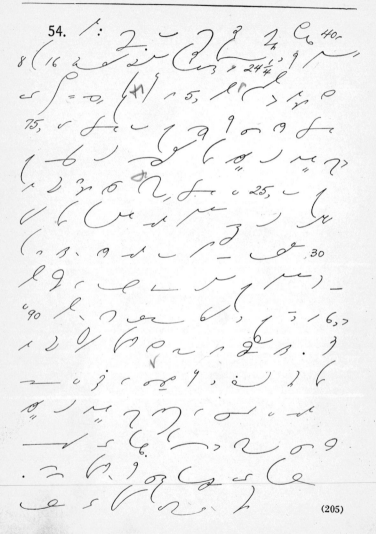

55.

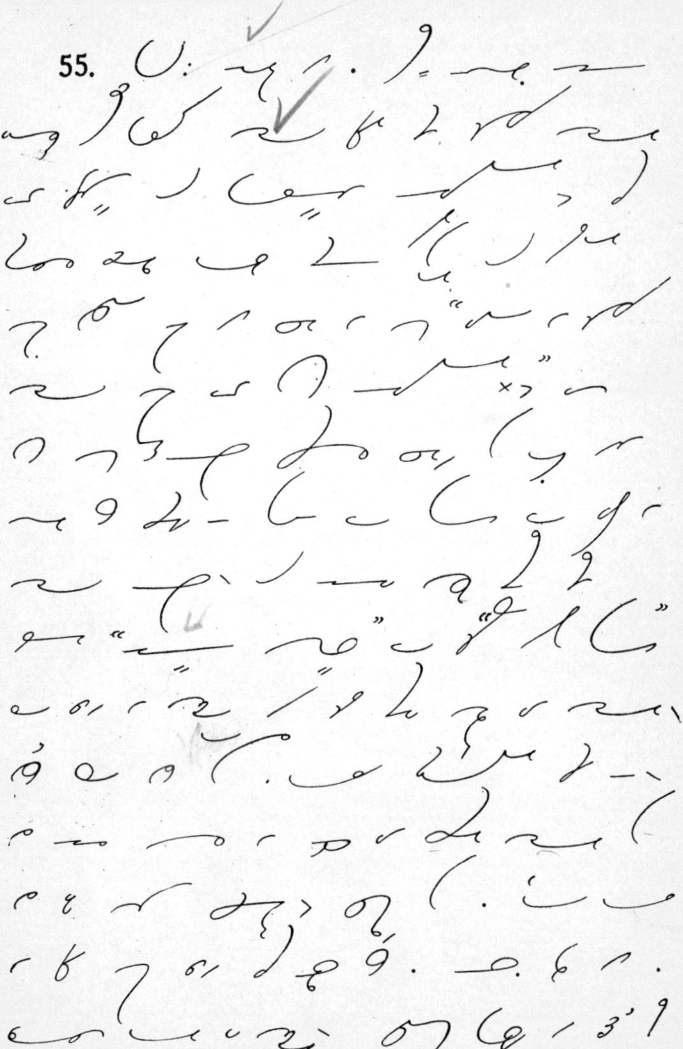

(185)

56.

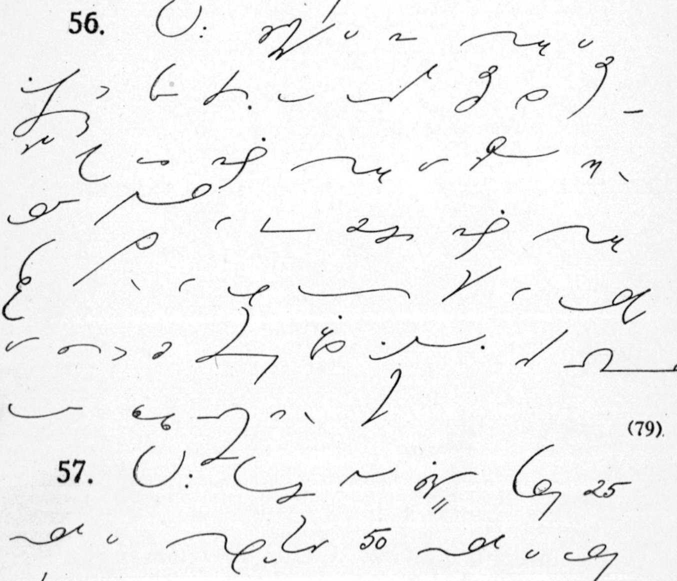

(79)

57.

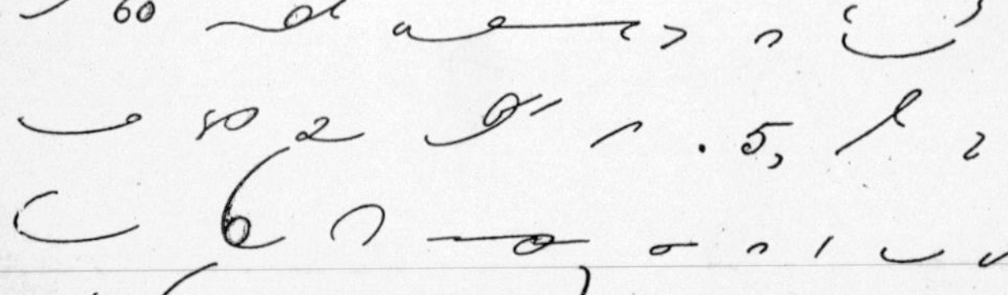

(52)

58. 

(63)

59. 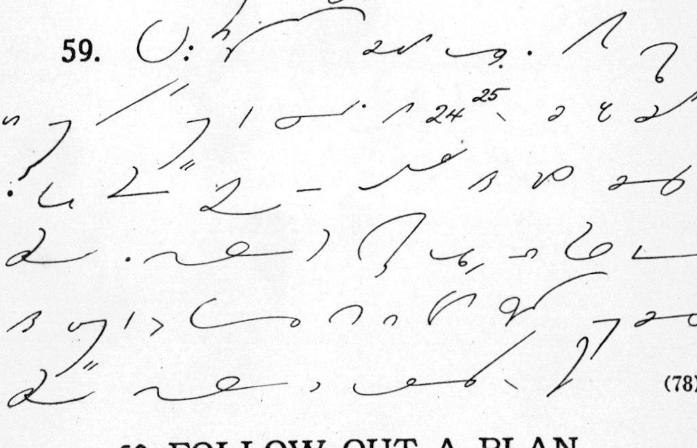

(78)

60. FOLLOW OUT A PLAN

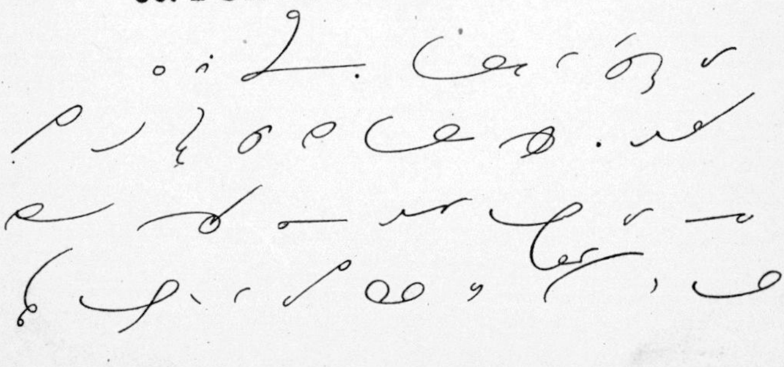

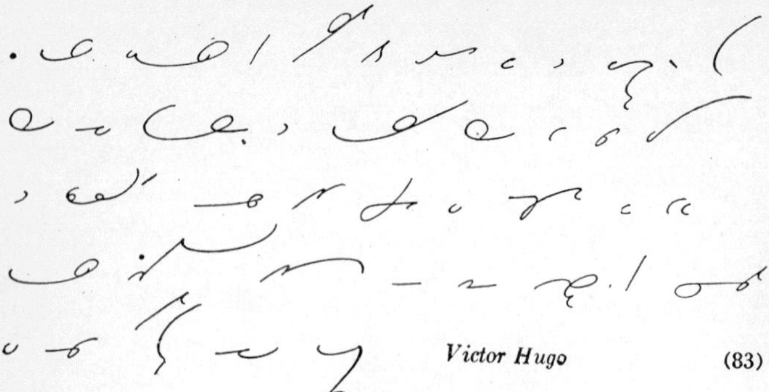

Victor Hugo (83)

61. AN ARTIST

Elbert Hubbard (56)

62. RELAX!

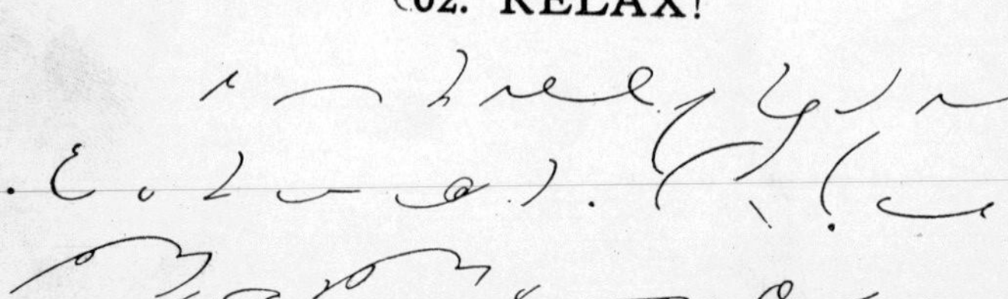

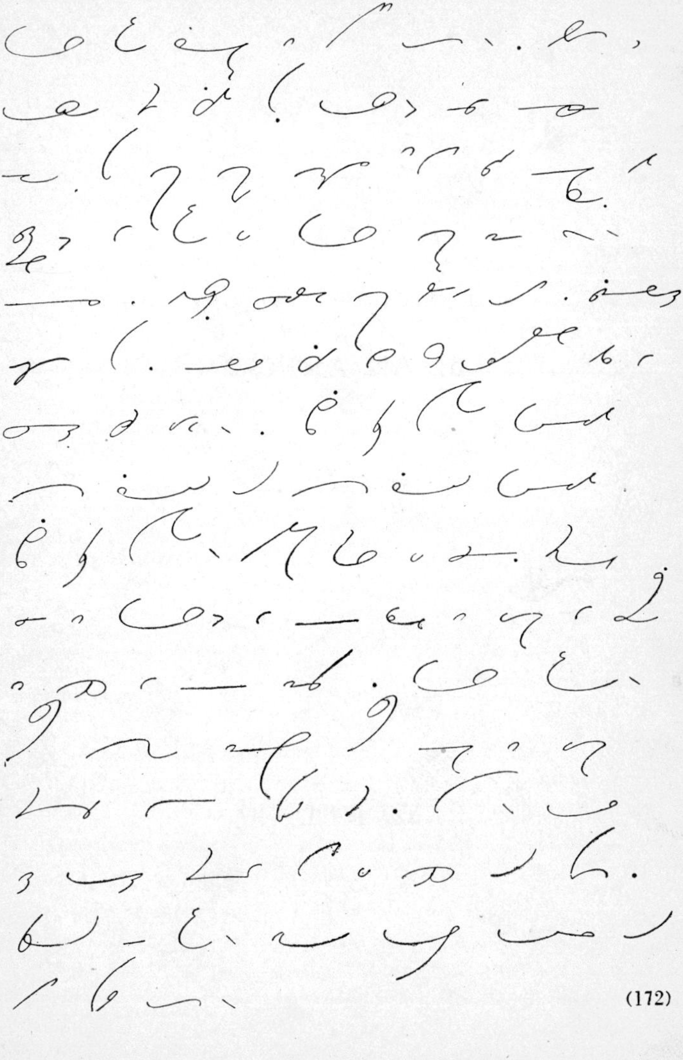

(172)

159. WRITING PRACTICE

1. The engineer signed a contract for the construction of the new electric light plant to be erected by the city.

2. The instructor displayed extreme interest in the instruction charts showing the distribution of electric current.

3. The defective electric lights detracted from the beauty of the exterior of the center building of the group.

4. The entering class misinterpreted the instructions regarding the examination in the History of Agriculture.

5. Mr. McNamara declined to carry out the transaction.

6. The disagreeable postal clerk antagonized the postmaster to such an extent that the latter suspended him.

7. Mr. McNeil was overcome with the magnitude of the undertaking.

8. At the same time do not overlook the supreme importance of the final paragraph in this circular.

9. This shortsighted policy, under the circumstances, can only result in financial shipwreck.

10. Grandmother made a superb shortcake.

11. I cannot understand how you can enter into an agreement with this contractor at this time.

12. Do you know whether or not your credit department will write us concerning the extra discount that is under consideration?

13. The factory will ship your order at once. Please let us know if the goods fail to arrive in first-class condition.

14. I do not understand how the work will be done any better under this new system than under the old system.

15. It is, in my opinion, the duty of the accounting department to enter at once the names of all doubtful accounts on a special ledger kept for this purpose.

SPEED STUDY XI

160. Analogical Word-Endings. The grouping of shorthand forms by analogy is a valuable aid to the memory and should be used wherever possible in developing skill in the execution of common word-beginnings, common word-endings, and particularly brief-form derivatives. The analogical drills given below supplement those of Chapter XI of the Manual.

Drill

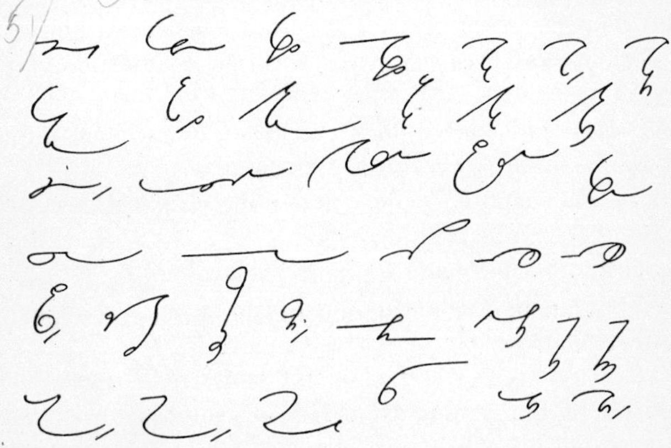

Key: inscription, prescribe, patiently, impatiently, composes, composed, composure, proposal, supposedly, disposal, opposite, deposit, disputes, secured, lecture, temperature, expenditure, pasture, annual, manual, continually, inquiry, inquiries, expired, extensively, agencies, assured, measurement, treasures, injures-injuries, injurious, reflected, inflicted, conflicts, attainment, results, consulted.

161. Additional Word-Endings.

Uate Drill

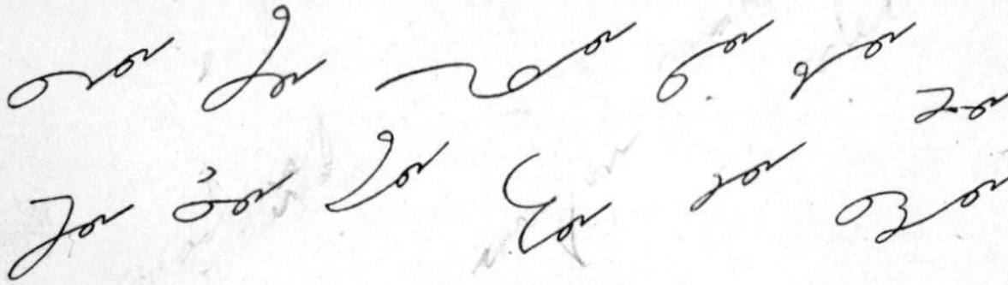

Key: actuate, evacuate, graduate, attenuate, extenuate, insinuate, infatuate, superannuate, eventuate, perpetuate, situate, accentuate.

Uation Drill

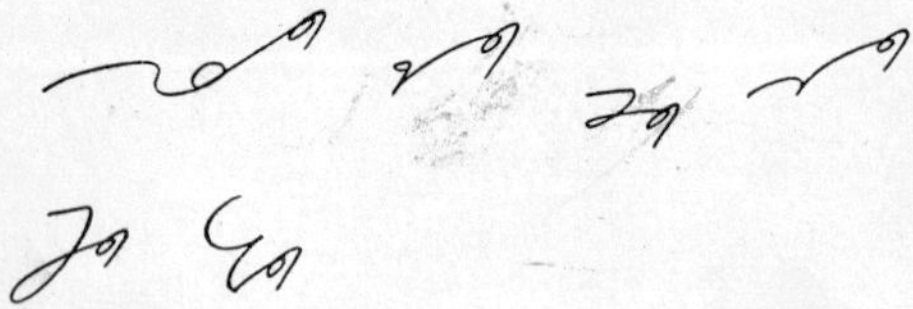

Key: graduation, extenuation, insinuation, continuation, infatuation, perpetuation.

Tial Drill

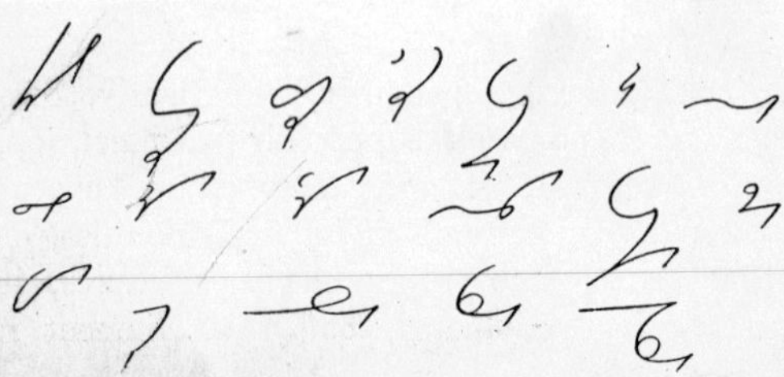

Key: judicial, beneficial, artificial, superficial, provincial, social, crucial, initial, substantial, circumstantial, credential, providential, essential, potential, influential, martial, partial, impartial.

Gence Drill

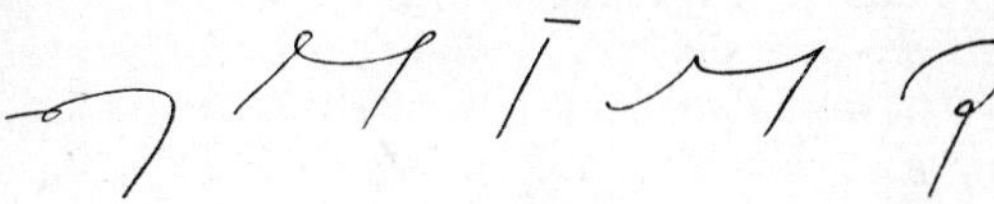

Key: negligence, diligence, intelligence, indulgence, divergence.

162. A Compendium of Directional Signs. The following outlines will be found useful in many types of dictation. The student will note that the forms for *east* and *west* have been slightly modified to secure facile joinings when used in these combinations.

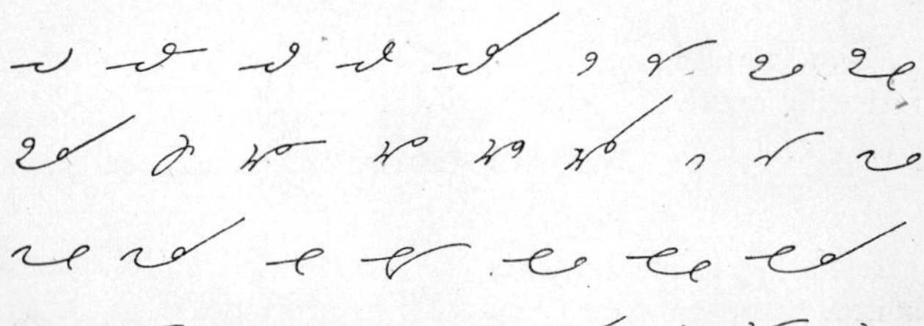

Key: (1) north, northern, northerly, northerly side, northerly direction, east, eastern, easterly, easterly side; (2) easterly direction, south, southern, southerly, southerly side, southerly direction, west, western, westerly; (3) westerly side, westerly direction, northeast, northeastern, northeasterly, northeasterly side, northeasterly direction; (4) northwest, northwestern, northwesterly, northwesterly side, northwesterly direction, southeast, southeastern, southeasterly; (5) southeasterly side, southeasterly direction, southwest southwestern, southwesterly, southwesterly side, southwesterly direction; (6) northbound, northbound track, southbound, southbound track, eastbound, eastbound track, westbound, westbound track, northeast corner, northeast quarter; (7) southeast corner, southeast quarter, northwest corner, northwest quarter, southwest corner, southwest quarter.

163. Special Phrase Drill.

Assistant (prefix),
Agent (suffix):

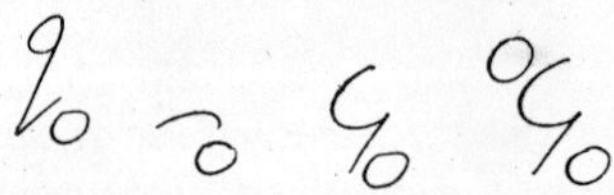

Key: advertising agent, claim agent, purchasing agent, assistant purchasing agent.

Auditor:

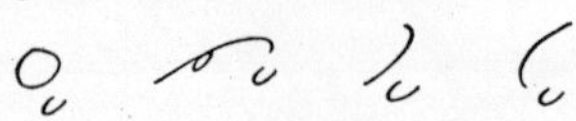

Key: assistant auditor, ticket auditor, freight auditor, passenger auditor.

Baggage:

Key: baggage master, baggage agent, baggage department, baggage check.

Chief:

Key: chief clerk, chief draftsman, chief engineer, chief counsel.

Division: 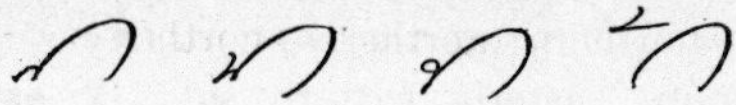

Key: western division, southern division, eastern division, central division.

Engineer:

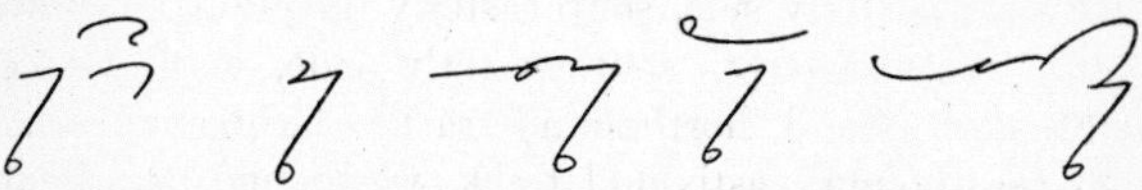

Key: engineer of construction, civil engineer, mechanical engineer, electrical engineer, locomotive engineer.

Freight: 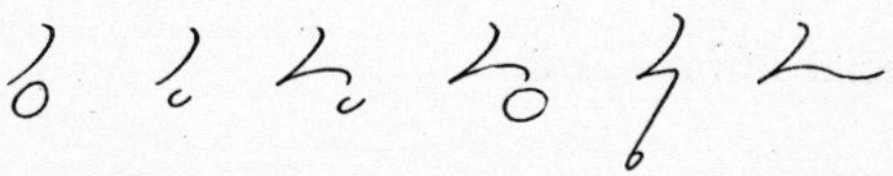

Key: freight agent, freight auditor, freight claim auditor, freight claim agent, freight engineer, freight car.

General: 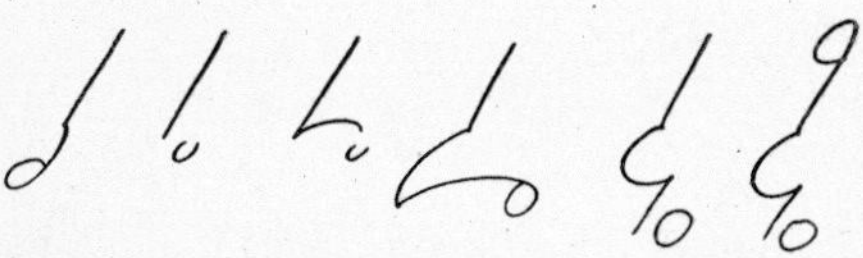

Key: general freight agent, general auditor, general claim auditor, general baggage agent, general purchasing agent, assistant general purchasing agent.

Manager: 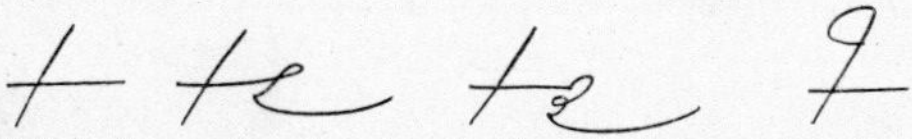

Key: general manager, general manager eastern lines, general manager western lines, assistant general manager.

Mechanical:

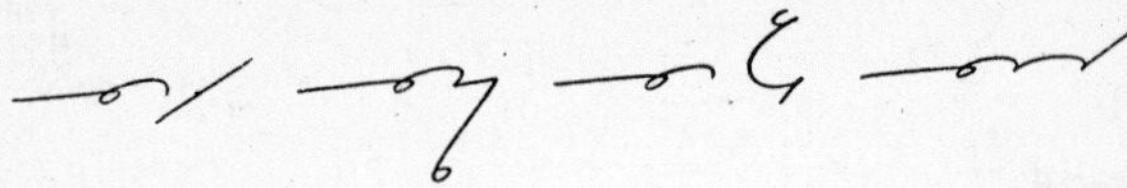

Key: mechanical department, mechanical engineer, mechanical operation, mechanical condition.

Passenger: 

Key: general passenger agent, assistant general passenger agent, passenger department, passenger coach, passenger car.

Superintendent:

Key: superintendent of telegraph, superintendent of the eastern division, superintendent of transportation, superintendent of shops, superintendent of motive power, mechanical superintendent.

Ticket: 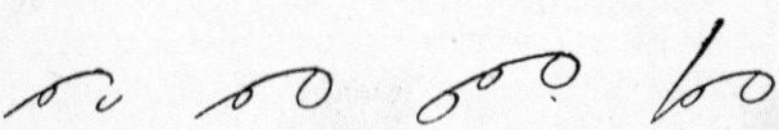

Key: ticket auditor, ticket agent, assistant ticket agent, general ticket agent.

Traffic: 

Key: traffic manager, passenger traffic manager, assistant passenger traffic manager.

164. READING AND DICTATION PRACTICE

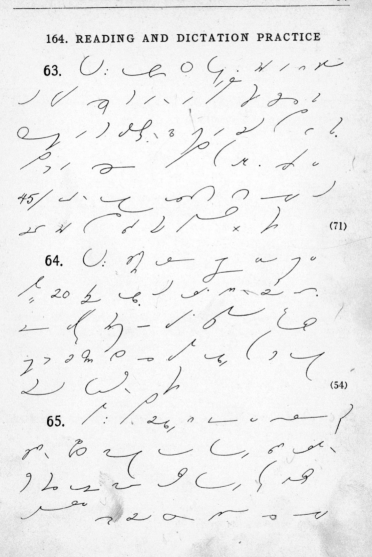

63.

(71)

64.

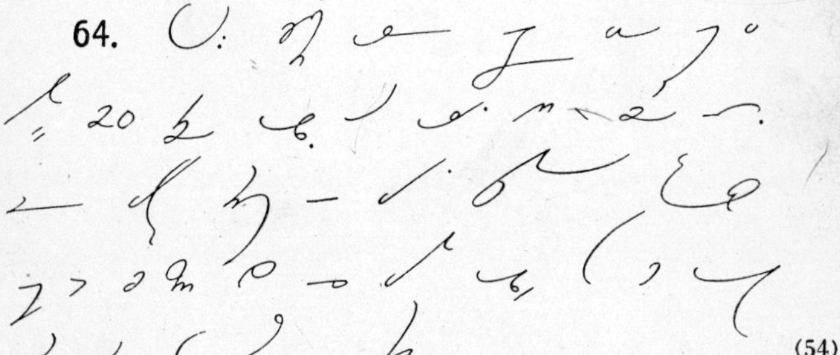

(54)

65.

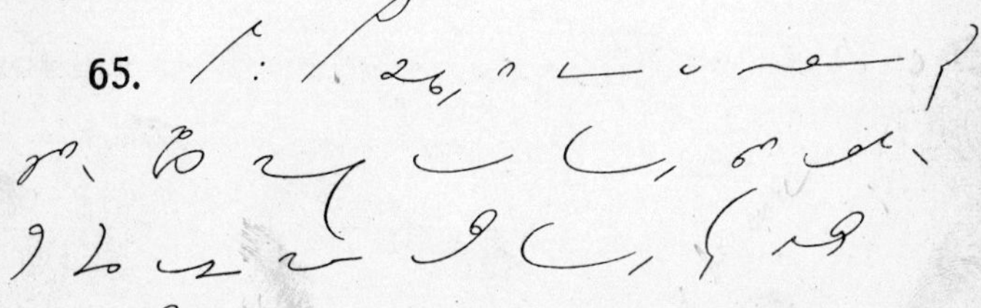

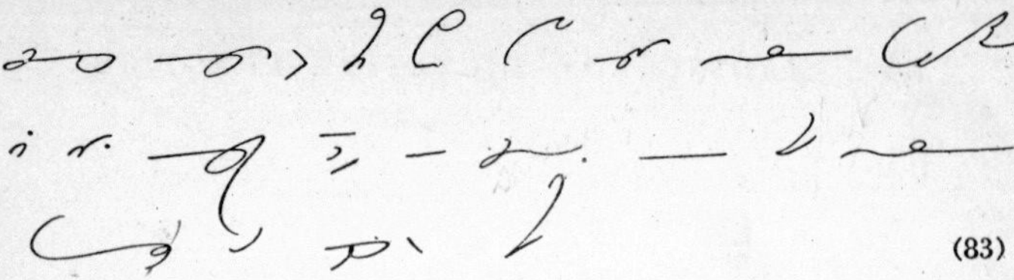

(83)

66.

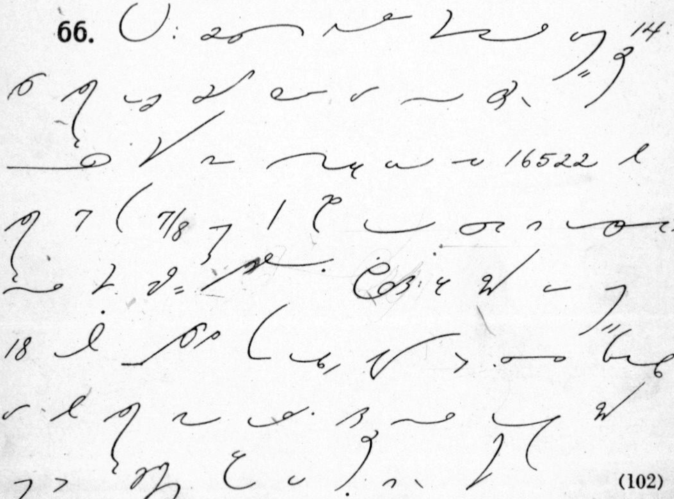

(102)

67.

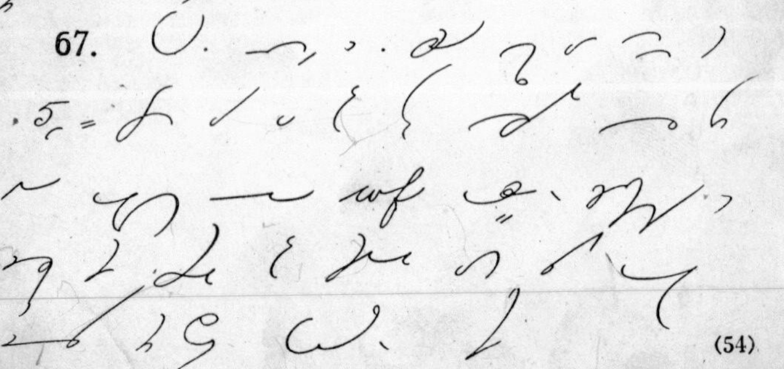

(54)

68.

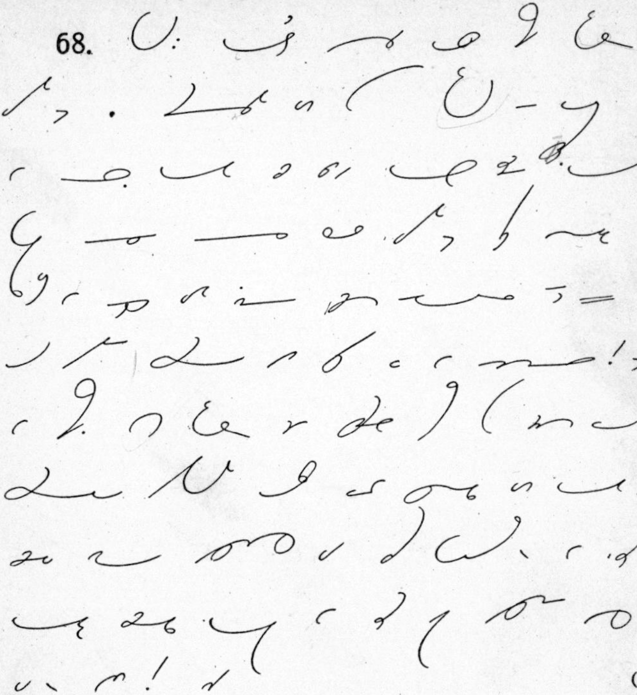

(99)

69.

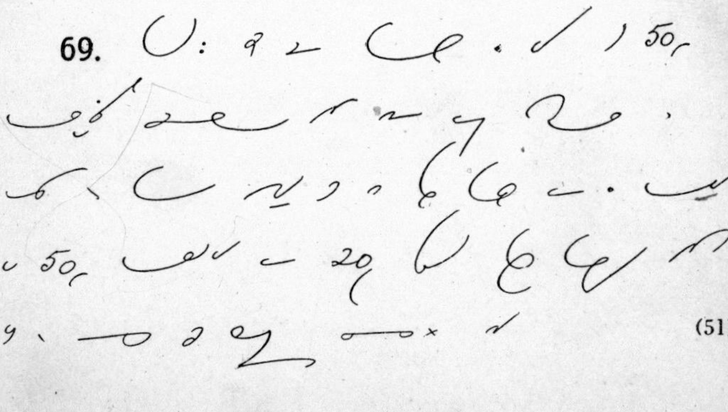

(51)

70.

(57)

71.

(75)

72.

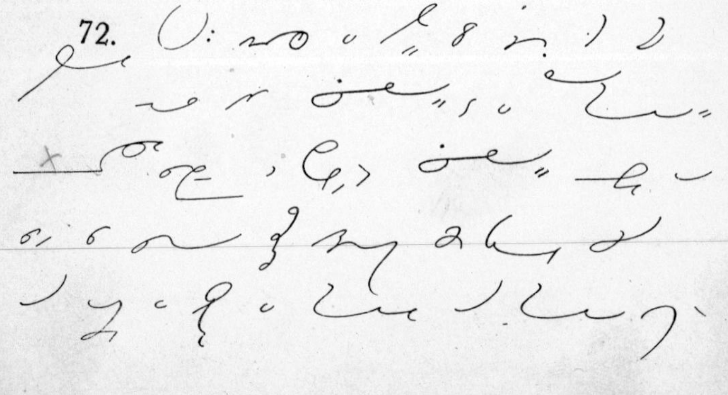

(100)

73.

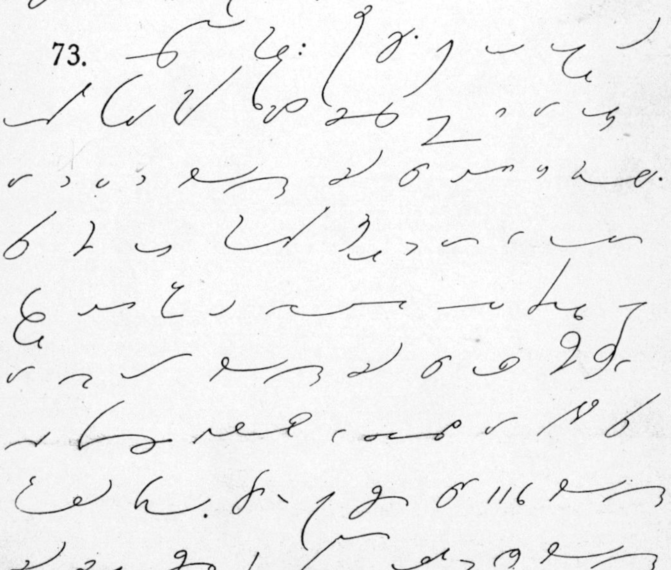

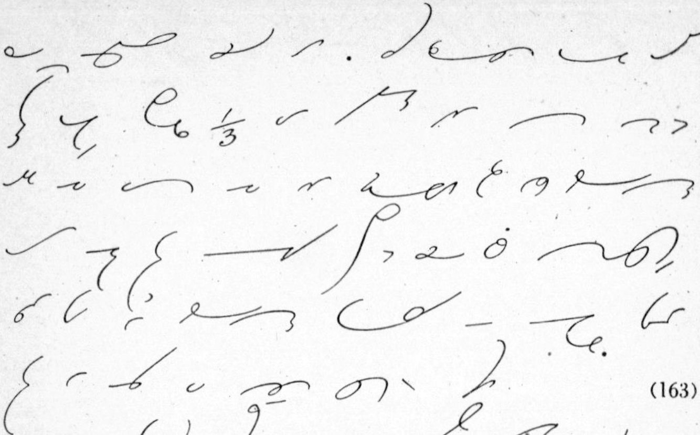

(163)

74.

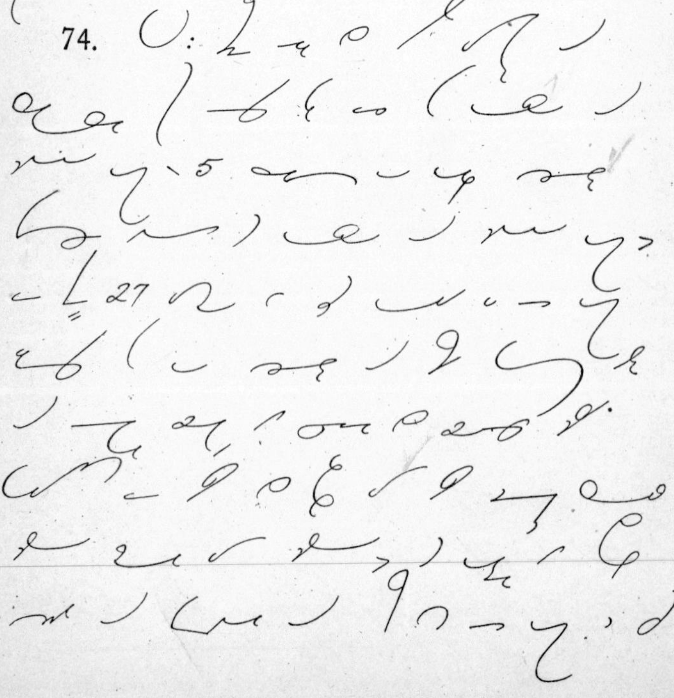

(260)

75.

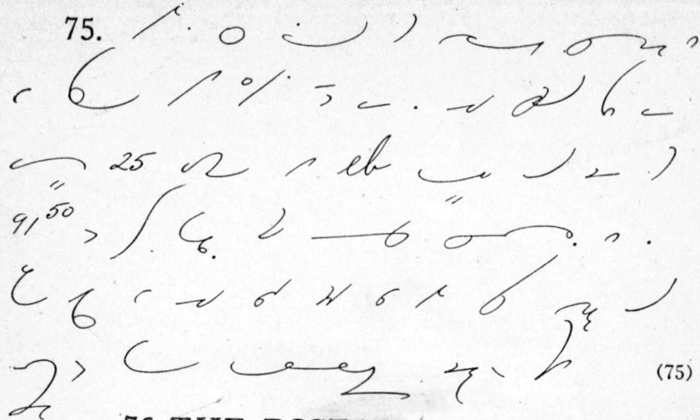

(75)

76. THE POSTAL SERVICE

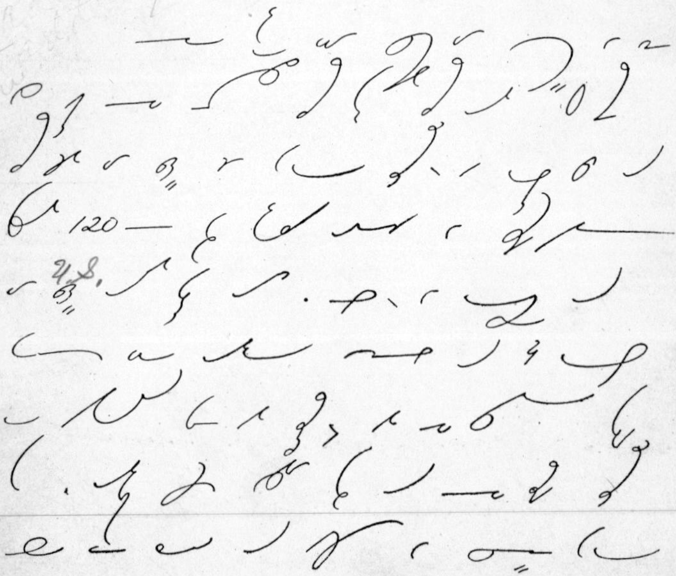

70
75,
94

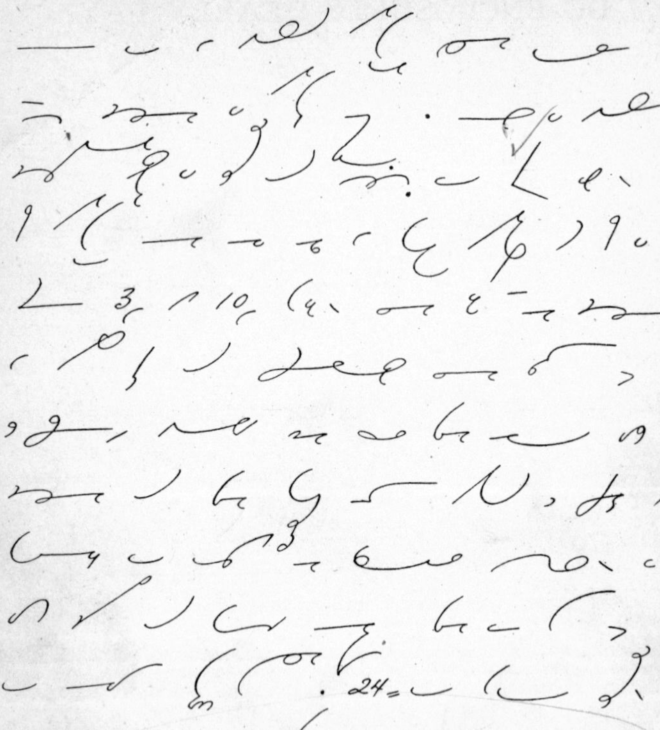

Congressional Record (446)

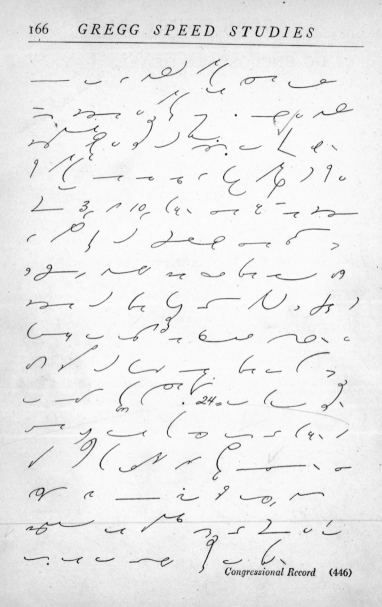

77. DO ENCLOSURES REALLY PAY?

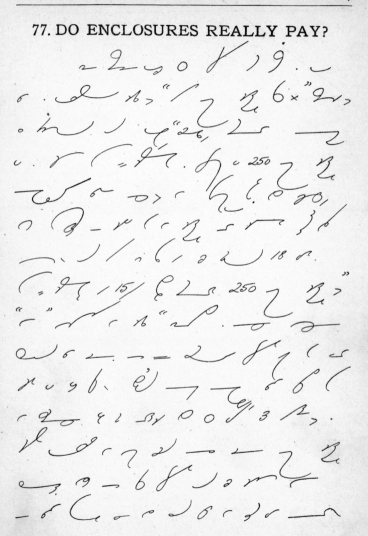

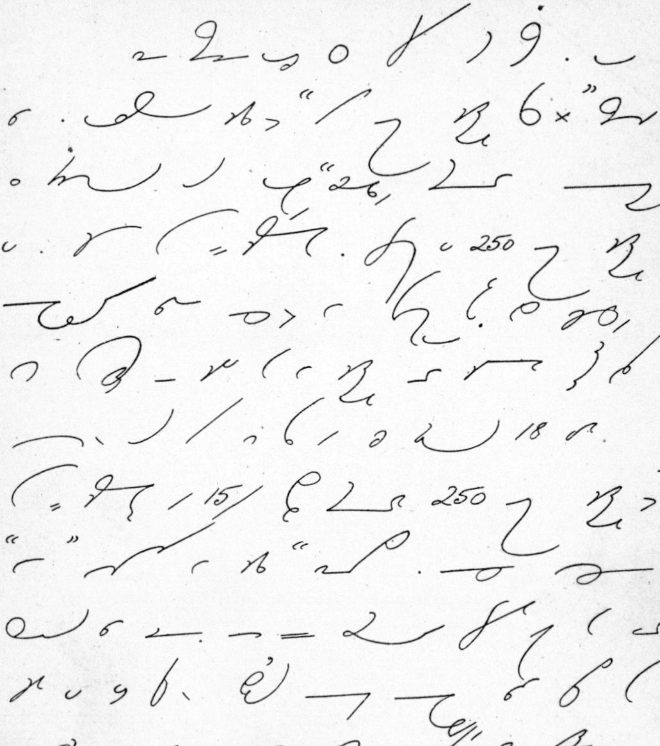

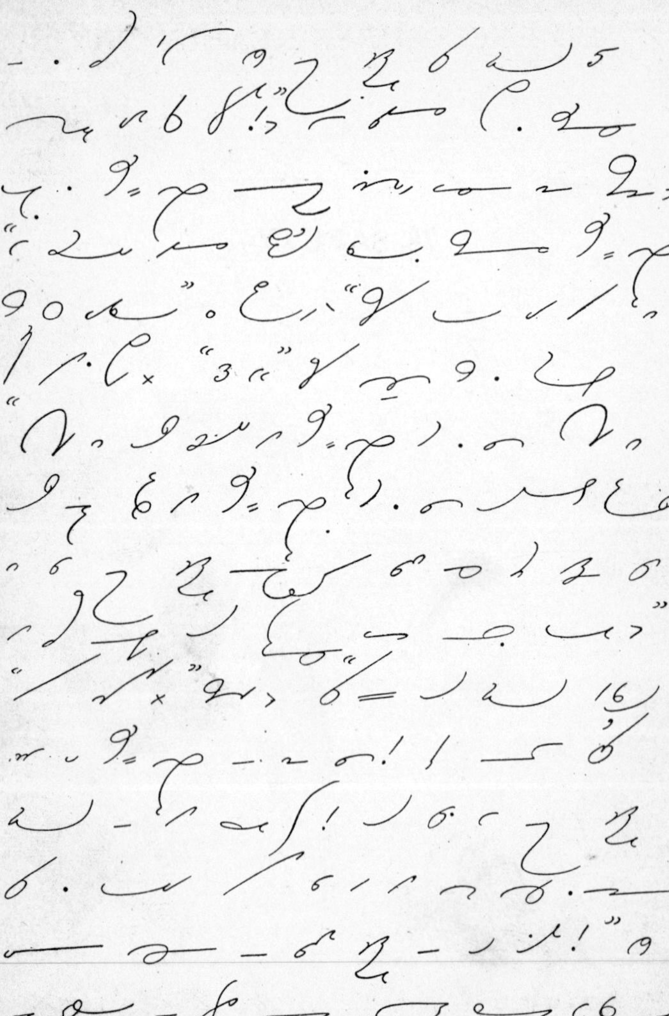

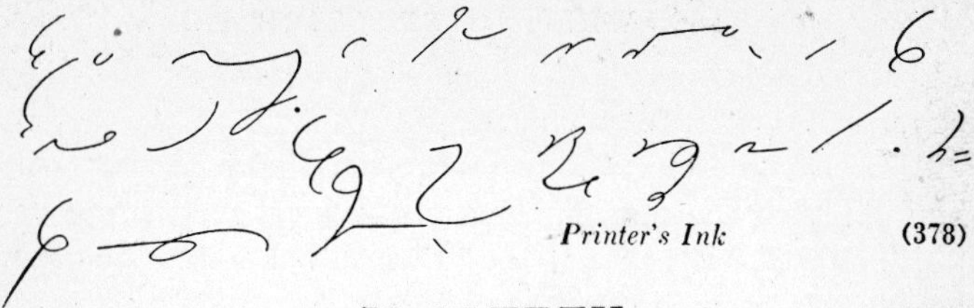

Printer's Ink (378)

78. SAFETY

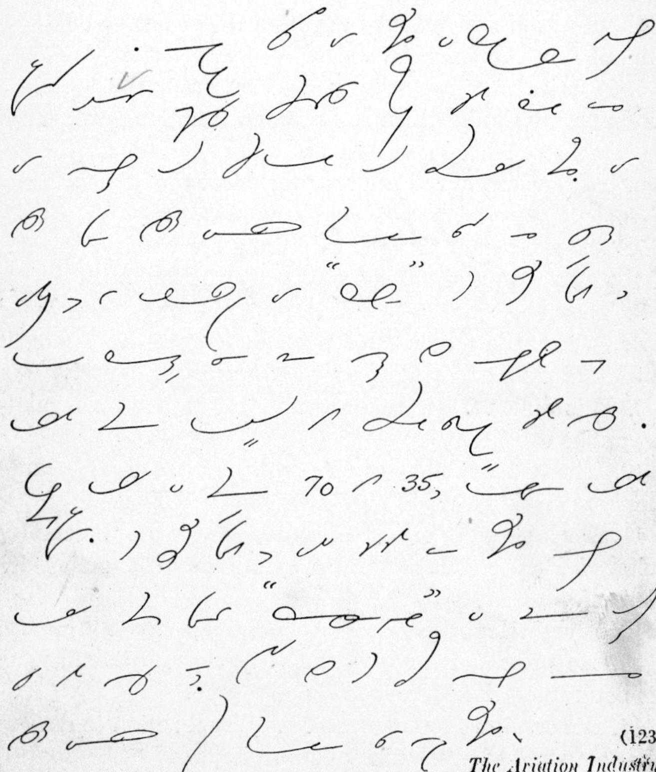

(123)

The Aviation Industry

165. WRITING PRACTICE

1. His description of the efficient tax measures used by the ancients required much explanation.

2. The two foremen were in continual dispute over who should inspect the consignments of electrical goods.

3. The collection agency that I consulted assured me that the high-pressure, intensive methods they employ always secure results.

4. As a trial assignment the prospective sales correspondent was asked to compose a set of five sales letters.

5. It is usually expensive to depart from the standard shipping procedure, which has resulted from long experience and extensive efficiency methods.

6. The senior elected a heavy technical course, consisting of zoology, physical geography, and physiology.

7. The radiogram and the cablegram are two illustrations of the application of applied electricity to modern life.

8. The article was a justification of the new typographic style, which the majority of printers felt was a drastic, if not a fantastic, departure from good taste.

9. It is difficult to formulate a practical plan for regulating public utilities.

10. The marketability of this stock is attractive, because there are stockholders in every state in the Union.

11. Enclosed are application blanks for an indemnity policy for your company and an endowment policy for yourself.

12. A chattel mortgage is a mortgage on personal property.

13. He presented a statement of assets and liabilities to his bank to establish credit.

14. His creditors took the necessary legal action to declare him in a state of involuntary bankruptcy.

SPEED STUDY XII

166. Geographical Prefixes and Suffixes Drill. (Supplementing Paragraph 241 of the Manual.)

—boro (borough): 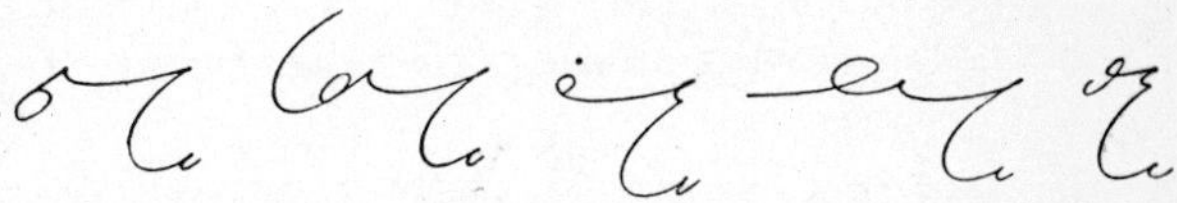

Key: Attleboro, Brattleboro, Hillsboro, Marlborough, Owensboro.

-burg: 

Key: Galesburg, Lynchburg, Ogdensburg, Plattsburg.

-bury: 

Key: Amesbury, Danbury, Fairbury, Salisbury, Waterbury.

-chester: 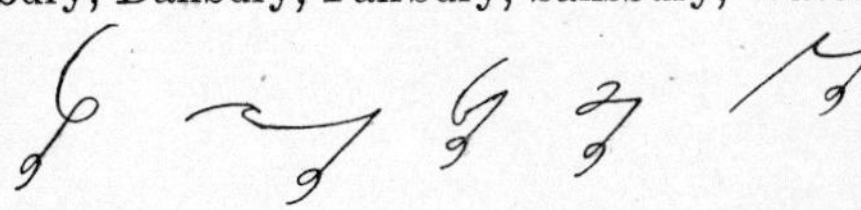

Key: Baychester, Colchester, Portchester, Winchester, Dorchester.

-field: 

Key: Clearfield, Fairfield, Mansfield, Wakefield, Winfield.

-ford: 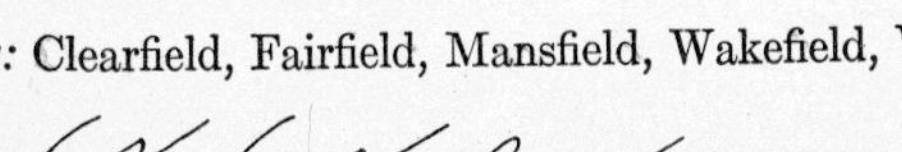

Key: Bedford, Bradford, Stamford, Weatherford.

Fort (-fort) 

Key: Ft. Collins, Ft. Dodge, Frankfort, Ft. Madison.

Grand: 

Key: Grand Haven, Grand Island, Grand Junction, Grandview.

-ington:

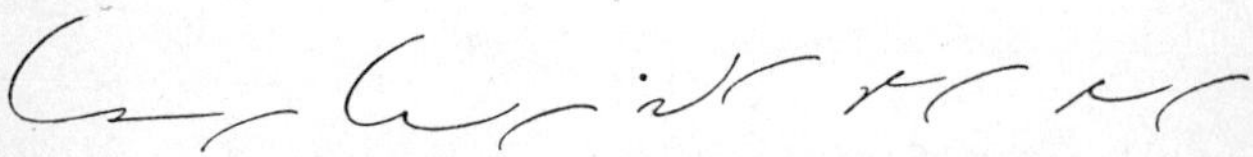

Key: Bloomington, Burlington, Huntington, Stonington, Torrington.

New: 

Key: New Albany, New Bern, New Britain, New London.

-port: 

Key: Glassport, Lockport, Logansport, Williamsport.

Saint (St.): 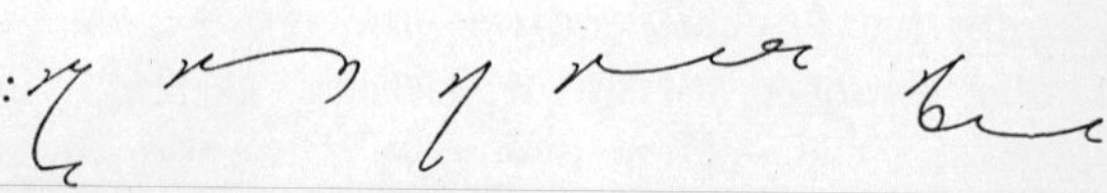

Key: St. Albans, St. Augustine, St. Joseph, St. Lawrence, St. Charles.

San: 

Key: San Angelo, San Bernardino, San Juan, San Rafael.

Santa: 

Key: Santa Barbara, Santa Cruz, Santa Fé, Santa Rosa.

–son: 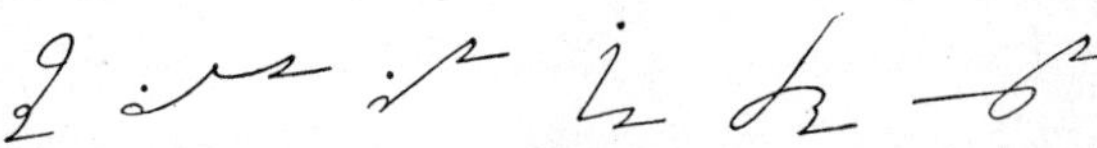

Key: Atchison, Henderson, Hudson, Hutchinson, Jackson, Madison.

–ton: 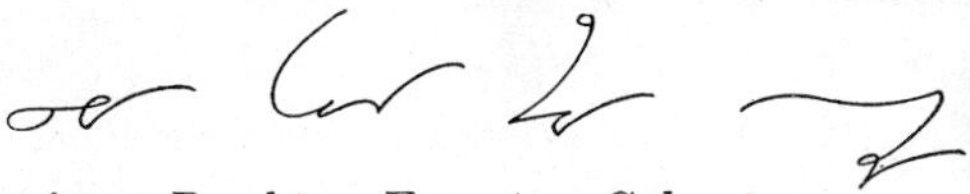

Key: Anniston, Brockton, Evanston, Galveston.

–town: 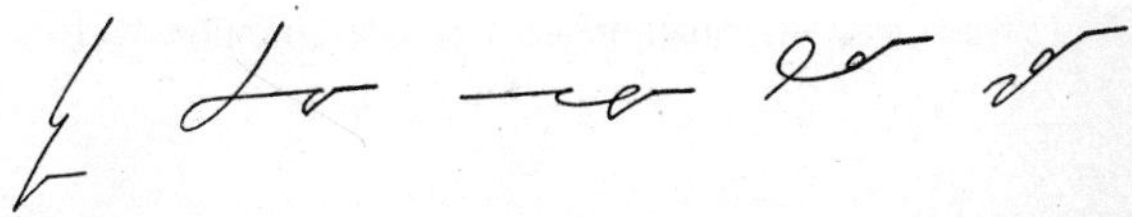

Key: Georgetown, Jamestown, Morristown, Tarrytown, Watertown.

–worth: 

Key: Ellsworth, Kenilworth, Leavenworth, Longworth.

167. Geographical Names. Shorthand outlines for a large number of foreign countries and cities have been conveniently arranged for quick reference in the following seven groups. The student should not attempt to memorize all these outlines at one time, but should learn them as he finds a need for them.

Group 1

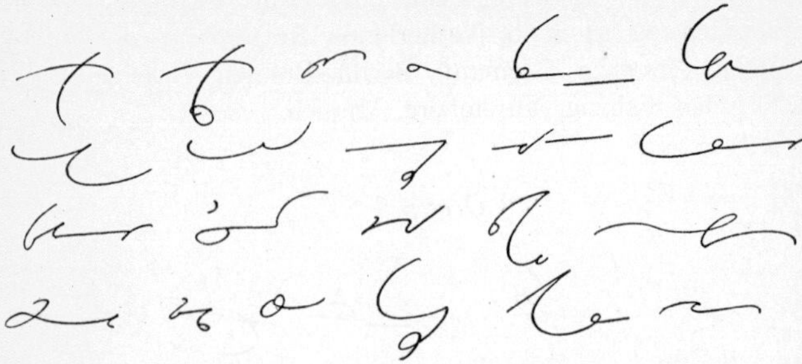

Key: Great Britain, Great Britain and Ireland, United Kingdom, England, Birmingham, Bristol, Liverpool, London, Manchester, Nottingham, Plymouth, Portsmouth, Southampton, Scotland, Edinburgh, Glasgow, Wales, Swansea, Ireland, Belfast, Dublin, Cork.

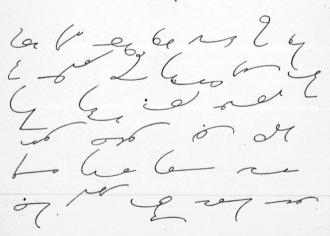

Group 2

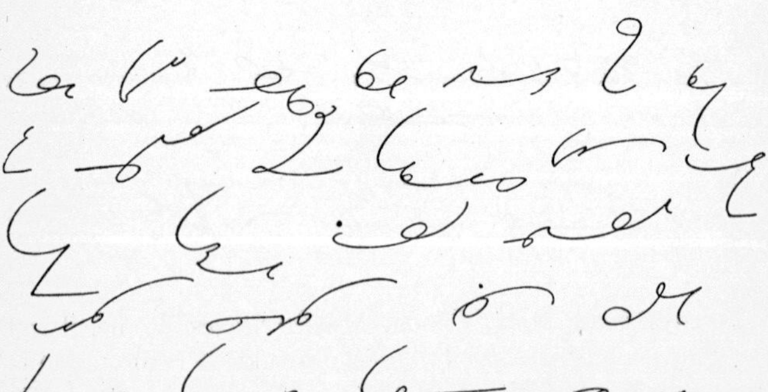

Key: France, Bordeaux, Marseilles, Paris, Toulouse, Havre, Cherbourg, Spain, Madrid, Seville, Barcelona, Portugal, Lisbon, Belgium, Brussels, Holland, Netherlands, Rotterdam, Amsterdam, The Hague, Antwerp, Germany, Berlin, Bremen, Cologne, Hamburg, Dresden, Leipzig, Nuremberg, Munich.

Group 3

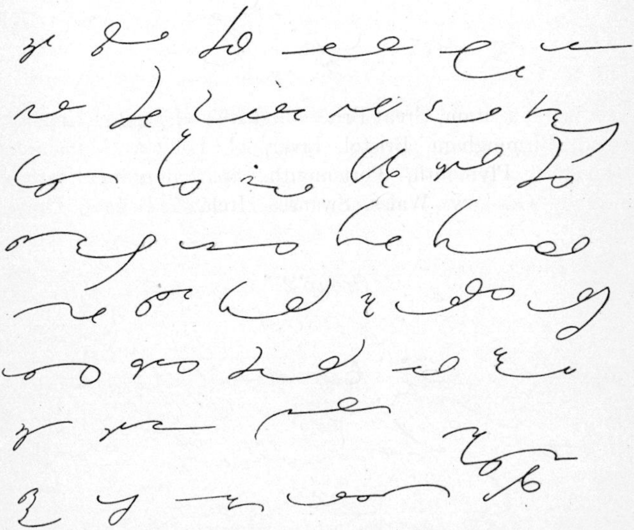

Key: Switzerland, Italy, Genoa, Milan, Naples, Rome, Turin, Venice, Florence, Trieste, Sicily, Czechoslovakia, Prague, Albania, Hungary, Budapest, Austria, Vienna, Yugoslavia, Rumania, Bucharest, Bulgaria, Greece, Athens, Poland, Warsaw, Lithuania, Latvia, Riga, Esthonia, Finland, Norway, Oslo, Sweden, Stockholm, Denmark, Copenhagen, Union of Socialistic Soviet Republics, Russia, Moscow, Leningrad, Odessa.

Group 4

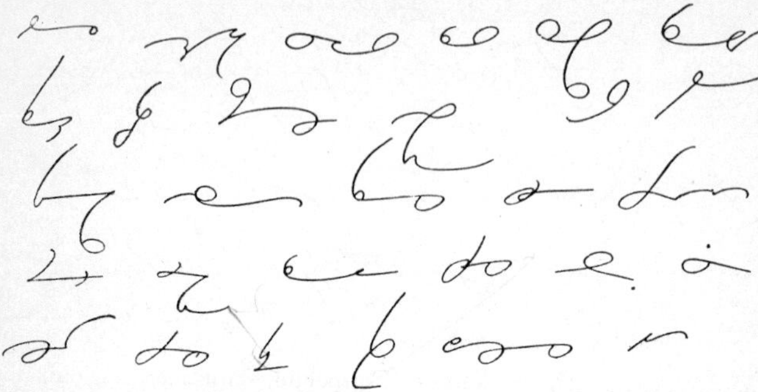

Key: Turkey, Constantinople, Angora, Syria, Arabia, Palestine, Jerusalem, Persia, Afghanistan, Kabul, India, Delhi, Bombay, Calcutta, Burma, Siam, Bangkok, Federated Malay States, Singapore, Ceylon, China, Nanking, Hankow, Canton, Shanghai, Chosen (Korea), Japan, Yokohama, Tokyo.

Group 5

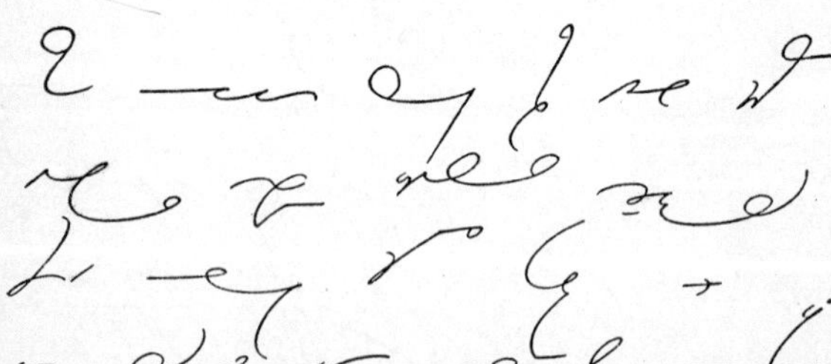

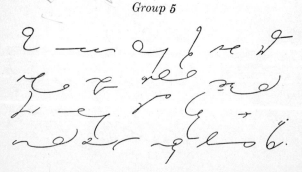

Key: Africa, Morocco, Algeria, Egypt, Tunis, Sudan, Tripoli, Cape Town, Australia, Queensland, Victoria, Melbourne, Sydney, Brisbane, New Zealand, Auckland, Wellington, Christchurch, Tasmania, Hobart.

Group 6

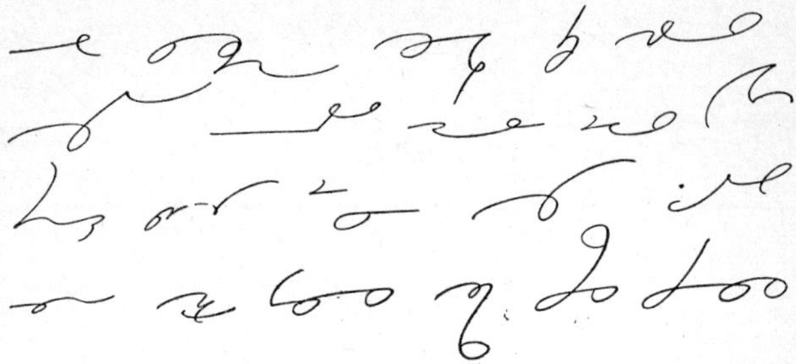

Key: Mexico, Aguascalientes, Campeche, Chihuahua, Coahuila, Guadalajara, Monterrey, Nuevo León, Sonora, Tampico, Vera Cruz, Yucatan, Central America, Guatemala, Honduras, Nicaragua, Costa Rica, Panama, Cuba, Havana, Jamaica.

Group 7

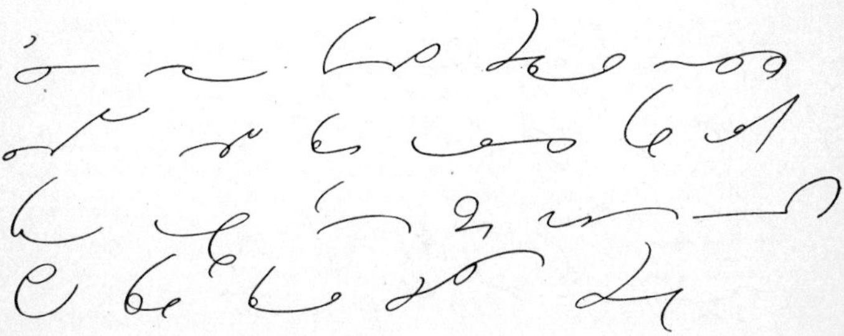

Key: South America, Colombia, Bogotá, Venezuela, Caracas, Ecuador, Quito, Peru, Lima, Brazil, Rio de Janeiro, Bolivia, La Paz, Paraguay, Asunción, Uruguay, Montevideo, Argentina, Buenos Aires, Chile, Santiago, Valparaiso.

168. Similar-Words Drill.

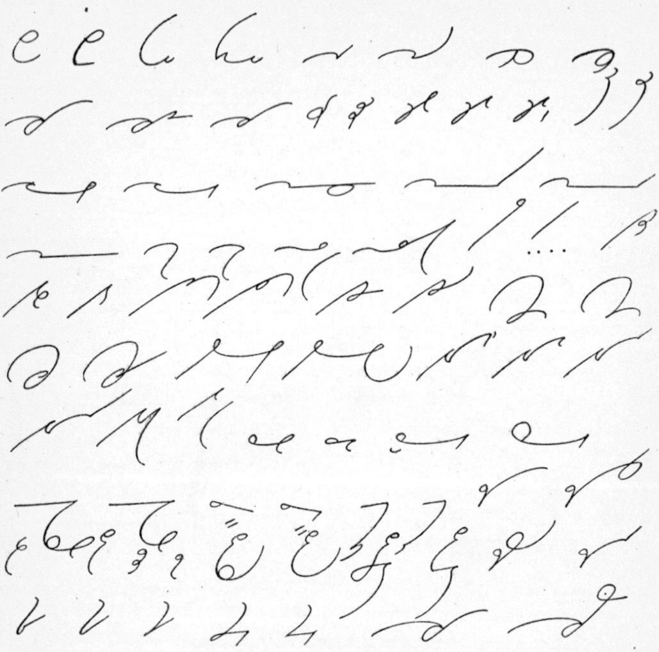

Key: appear, happen; borough, bureau; can't, count; cares, case; carton, cartoon, curtain; cessation, secession; cities, citizen, citizenship; civil, several; collision, collection; command, commend, comment, common; company-keep, complain-complete; creditable, credible; debtor, deter; decease, disease, desist; deduction, detection; descend, descent; defect, difficulty; defy, divide; diligence, diligent; destination, distance, distant, destined; disturb, distribute; earliest, earnest; illusion, allusion; embarrass, embrace; England, English; envious, invoice; esteem, estimate; except, expect; excess, exist; expand, expend; expansive, expensive; extant, extent; fault, fought, fort; finish, furnish; garden, guardian.

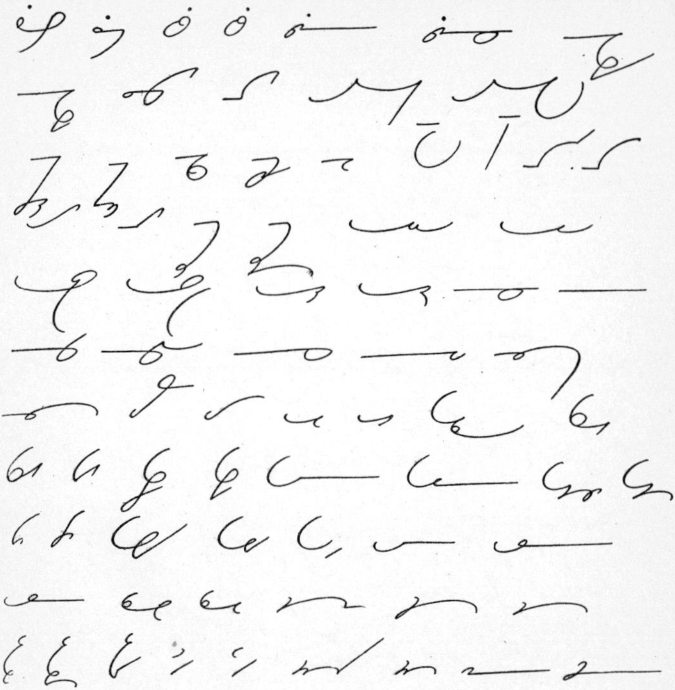

Key: hereafter, hereinafter; high, highly; human, humane; impassioned, impatient; inattention, intention; indulgence, indulgent; ingenious, ingenuous; inside, insight, instant; intelligent, intelligence; indent, intend; into, unto; invest, investigate; lawyer, lower; liable, likable; looks, luxury; man, men; matter, mature; memoranda, memorandum; negligence, neglect; ordain, ordinary; ours-hours, recent; parcel, partial; partition, petition; passionate, patient; permanent, prominent; persecute, prosecute; poor, pure; praised, pressed, presented; remark-room, remember-remain, remit; series, serious; signal, signature, significant; specify, specific; sport, support, circuit; succeed, success; woman, women.

169. Sentences on Similar Words.

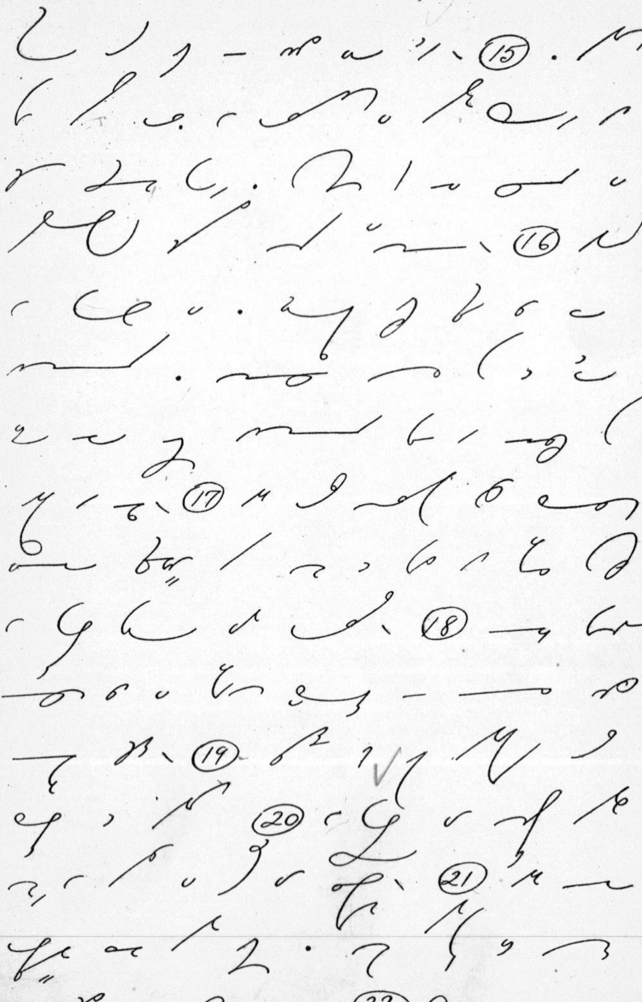
15
16
17
18
19
20
21
22

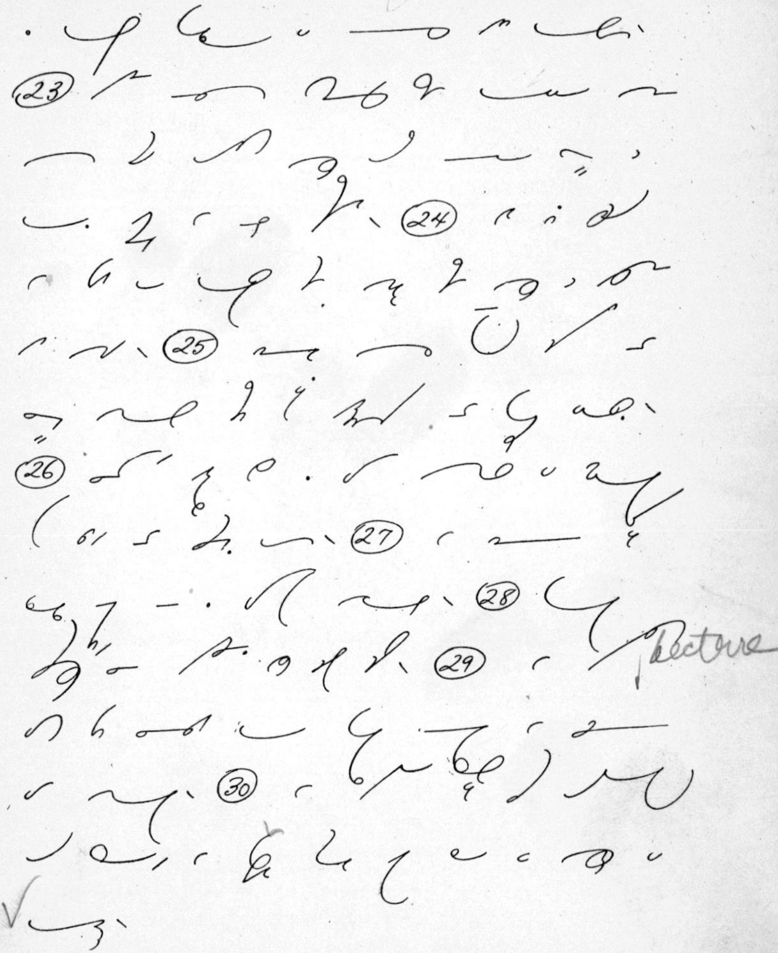
23
24
25
26
27
28
29
30

170. READING AND DICTATION PRACTICE

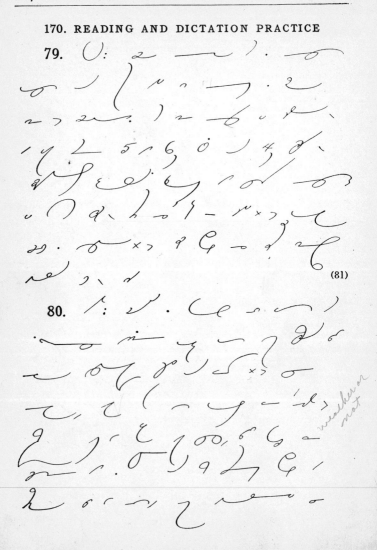

79.

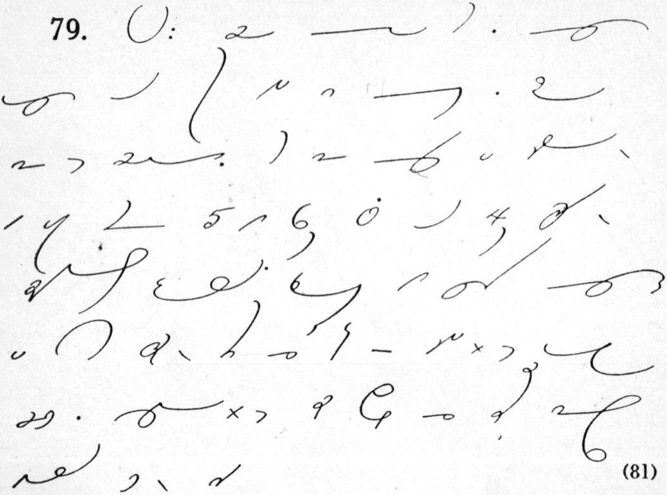

(81)

80.

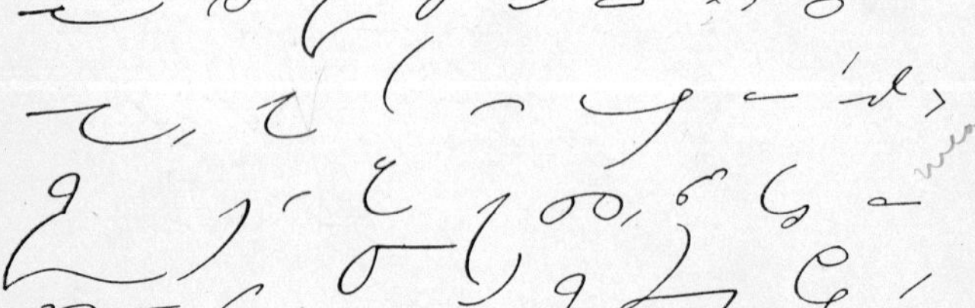

whether or not

(109)

81.

(134)

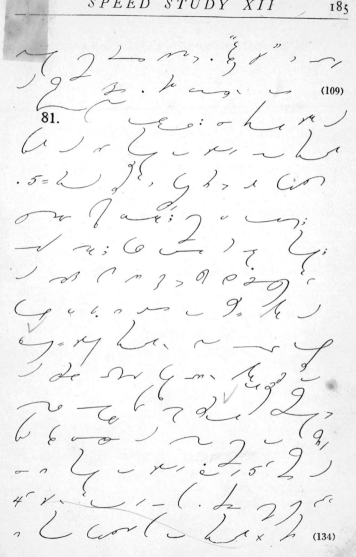

82.

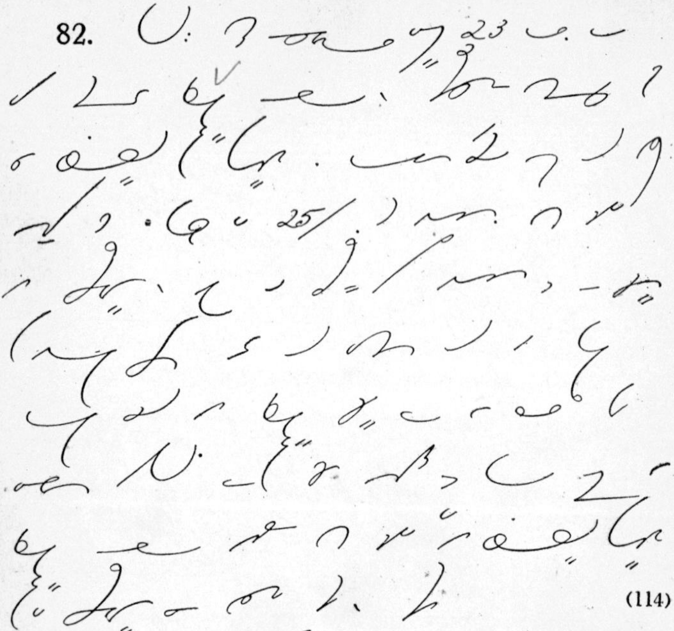

(114)

83.

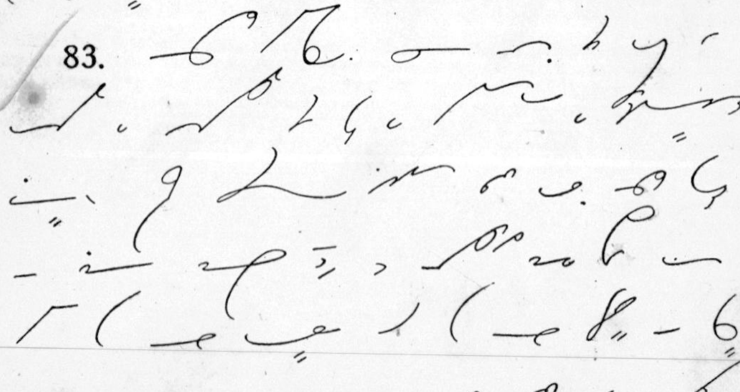

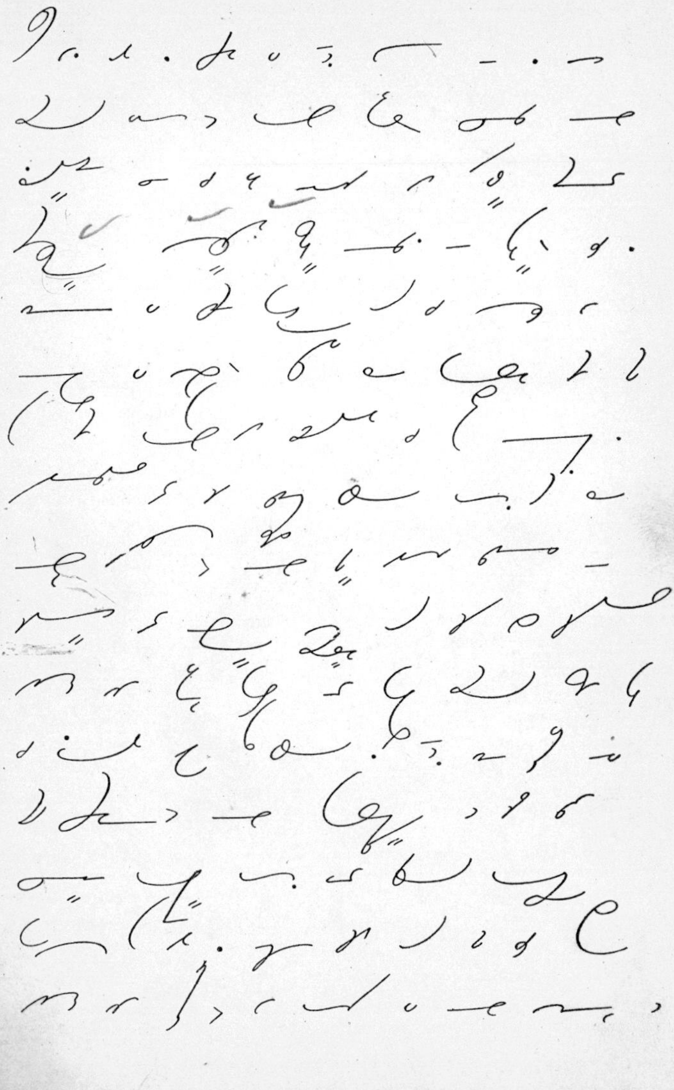

(282)

84.

(269)

85.

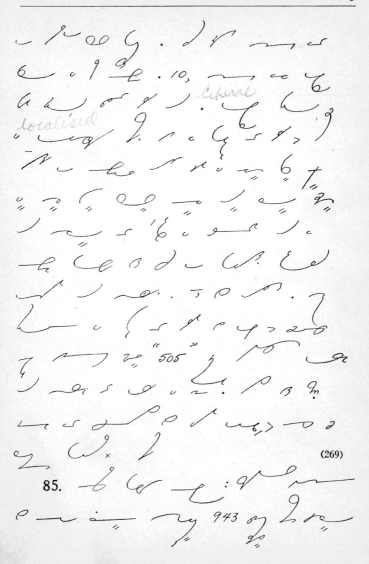

(69)

86.

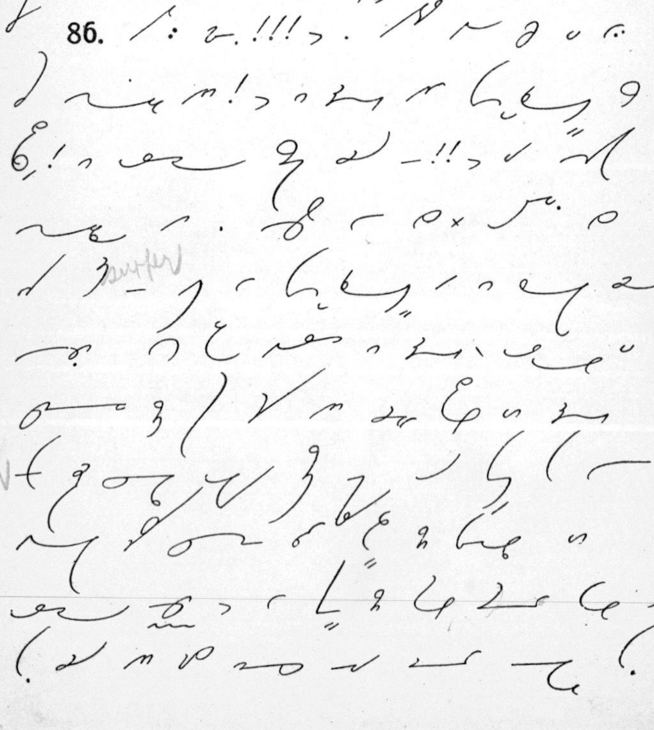

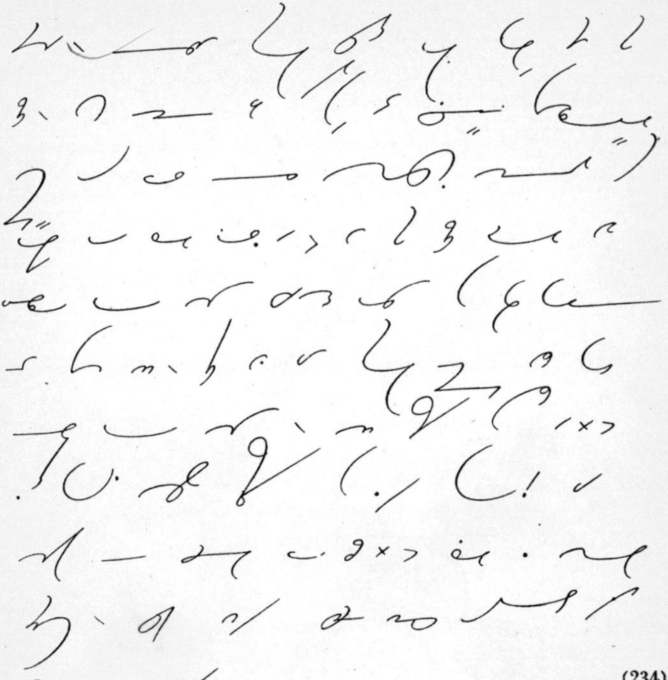

(234)

87.

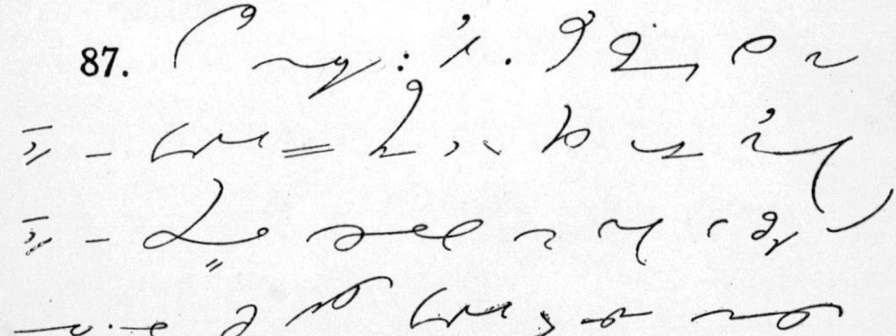

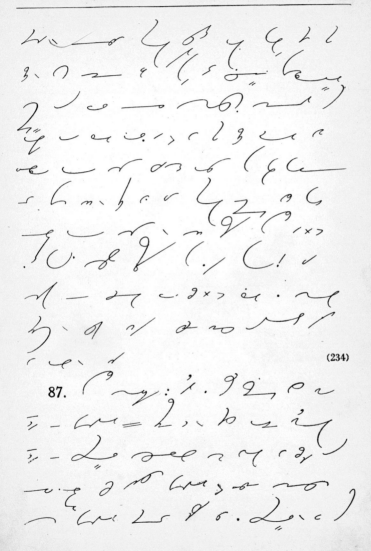

(165)

88. BOOK VALUE OF STOCK

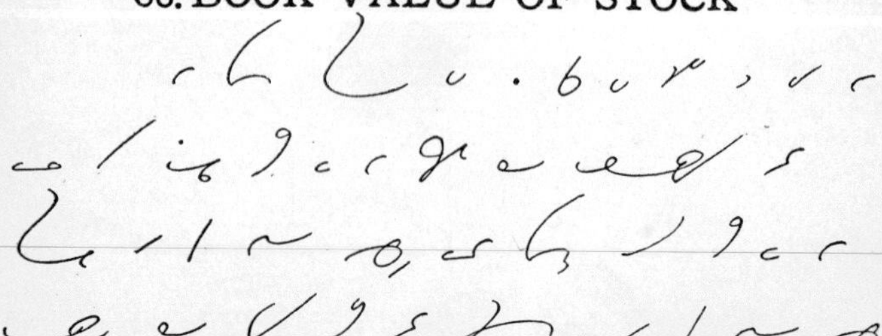

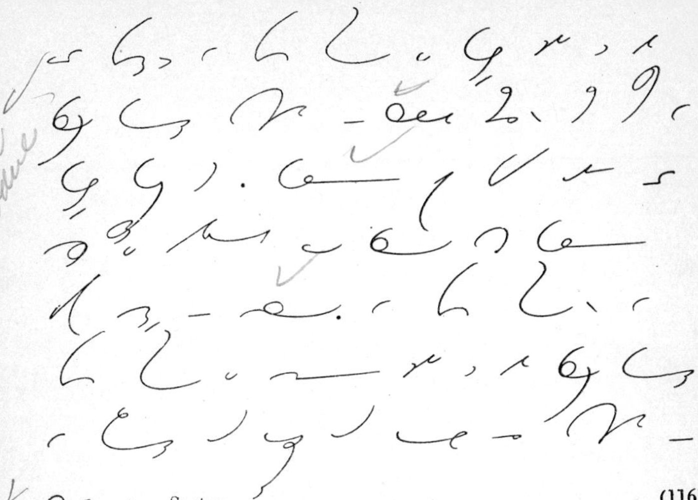

System (116)

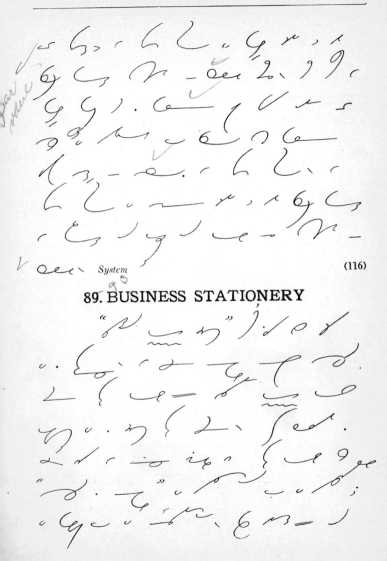

89. BUSINESS STATIONERY

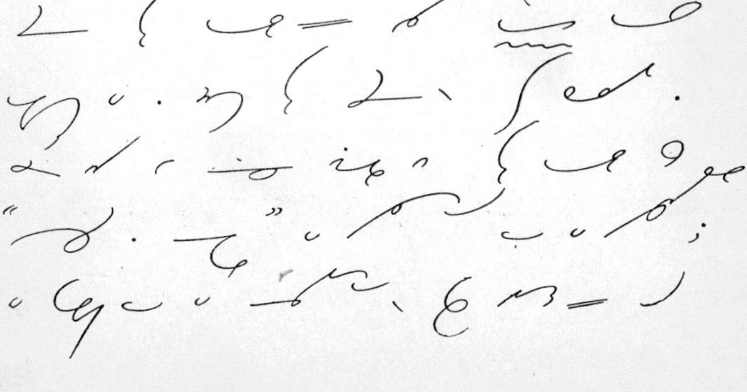

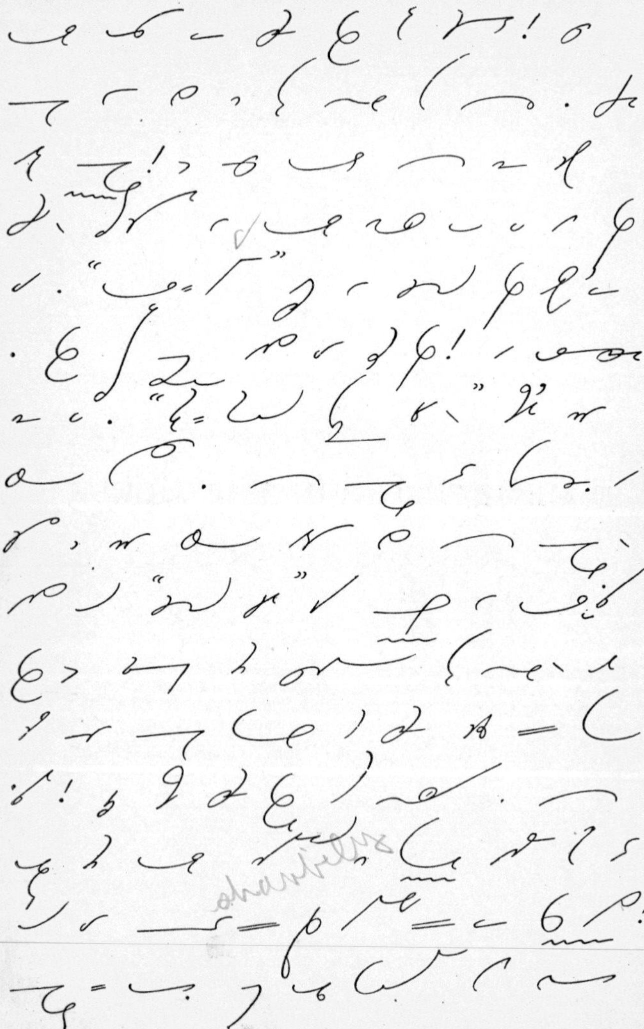

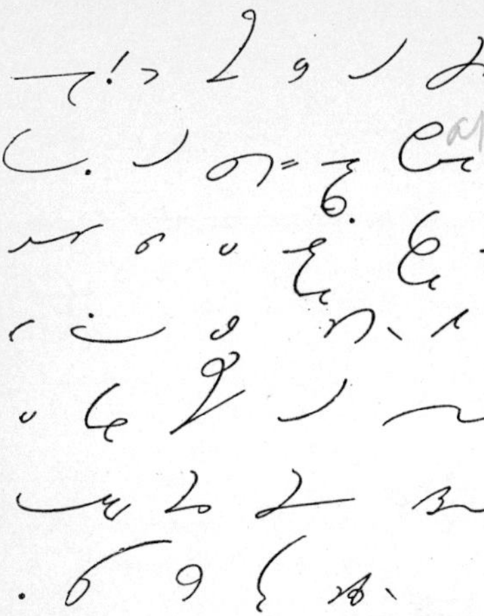

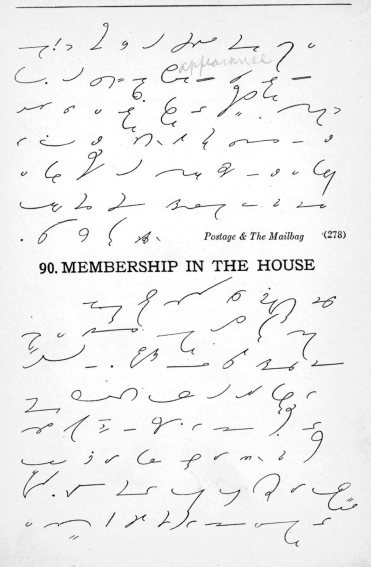

Postage & The Mailbag (278)

90. MEMBERSHIP IN THE HOUSE

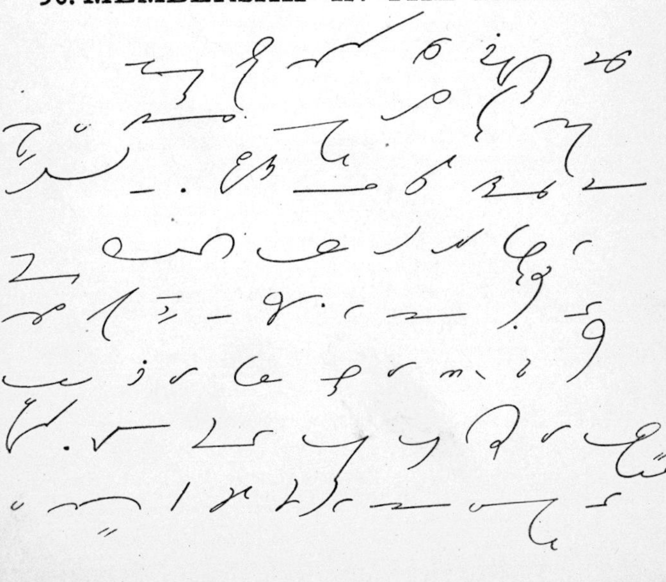

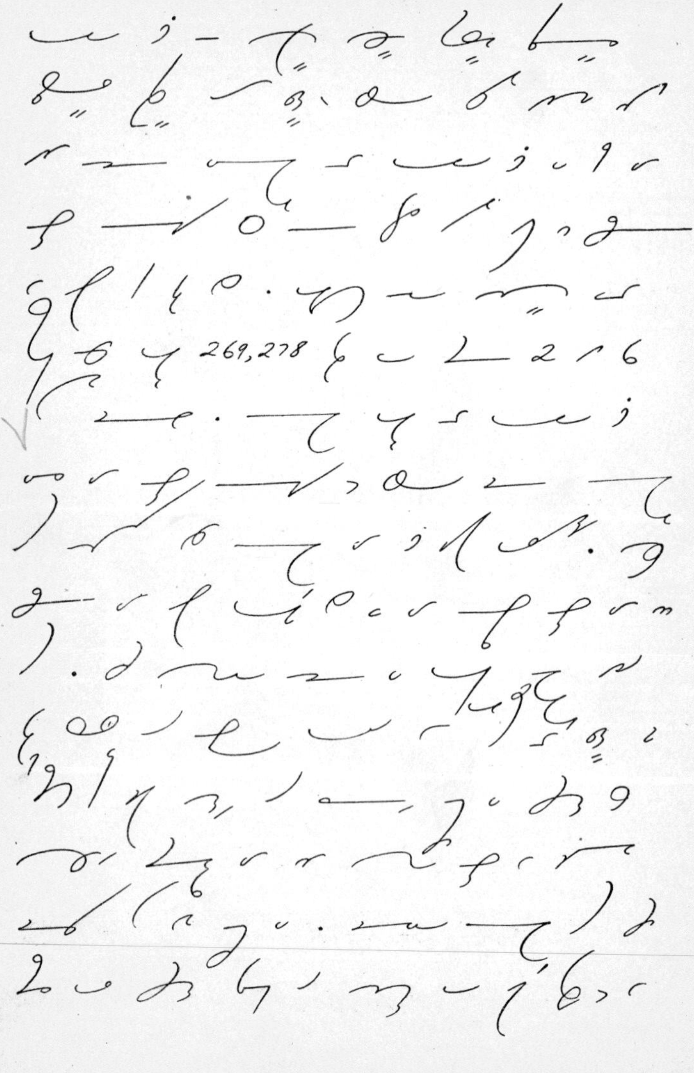

269,278
2
1
6

Congressional Record (450)

171. WRITING PRACTICE

1. The total amount of coal mined in Pennsylvania up to the present time reaches the staggering figure of nearly ten billion tons.

2. In the United States, zinc is obtained chiefly from Oklahoma, Kansas, New Jersey, and Montana; silver from Utah, Montana, Nevada, and Idaho; gold from California, Colorado, South Dakota, and Alaska.

3. In Massachusetts, customs officials are located in the cities of Boston, Fall River, Gloucester, New Bedford, Plymouth, Provincetown, Salem, Springfield, and Worcester.

4. Notice that "Pittsburgh," Pennsylvania, is spelled with a final *h*.

5. It is necessary to indicate the state clearly in addressing envelopes, as cities of the same name often appear in more than one state.

6. Yale University is located at New Haven, Connecticut; Harvard at Cambridge, Massachusetts; Dartmouth at Hanover, New Hampshire.

7. In 1790, the center of population of this country was located 23 miles east of Baltimore, Maryland; in 1810, 40 miles northwest of Washington, D. C.; in 1870, 48 miles east of Cincinnati, Ohio; in 1900, 6 miles southeast of Columbus, Indiana; and in 1920, 2 miles west of Whitehall, Indiana.

8. Prince Edward Island has the smallest and Northwest Territories the largest area of the Canadian provinces. In population, Yukon ranks lowest and Ontario highest. The densest average population per square mile is located in Quebec.

9. There was a substantial increase in the number of women in Congress and in many state legislatures.

91.

(46)

92.

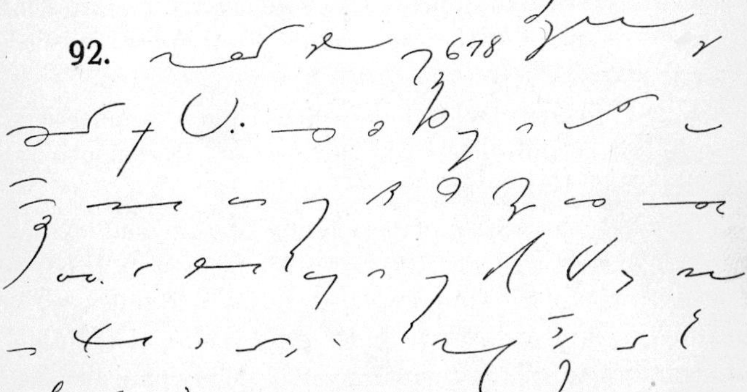

(62)

93.

(79)

94.

(260)

95.

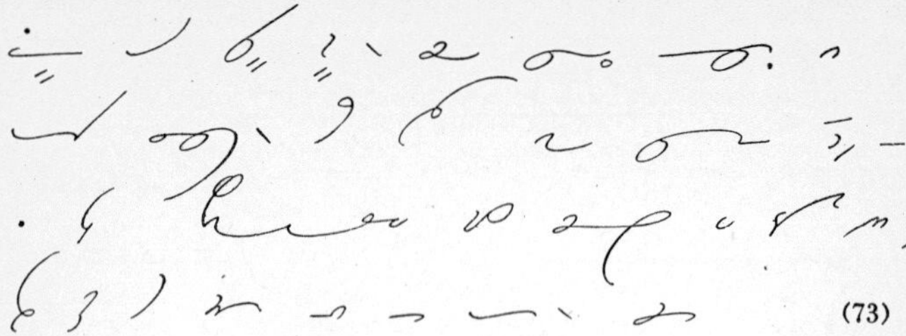

(73)

96.

(93)

97.

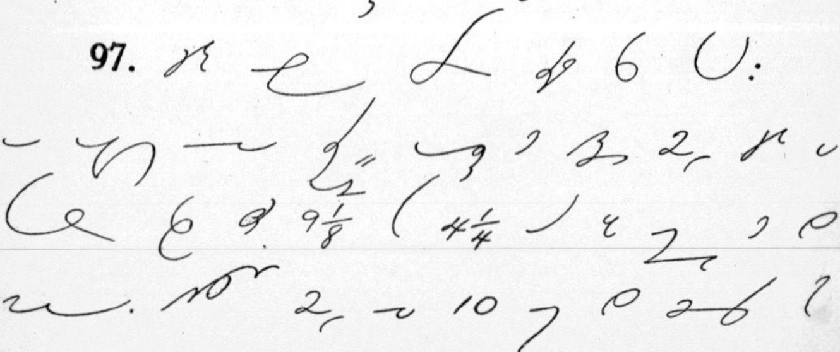

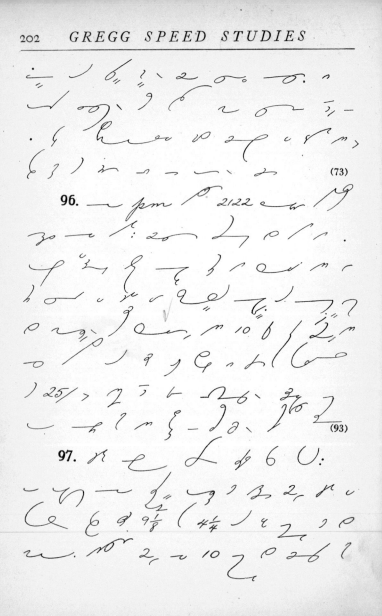

Dorothy Wagner

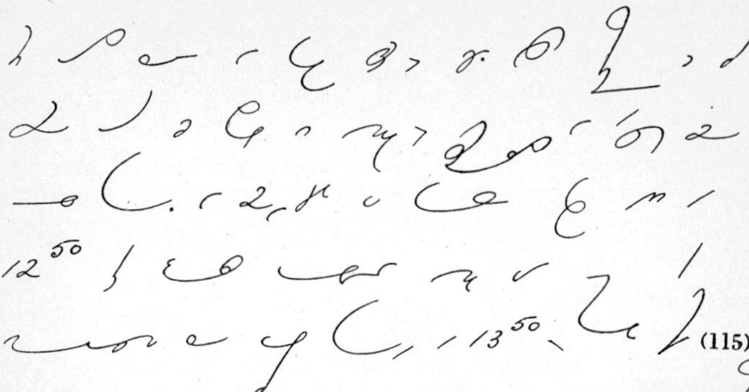

(115)

98.

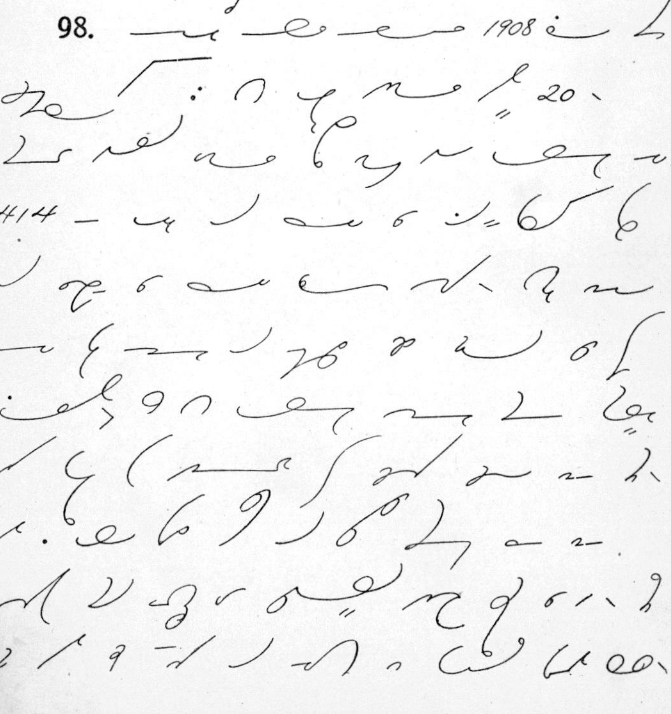

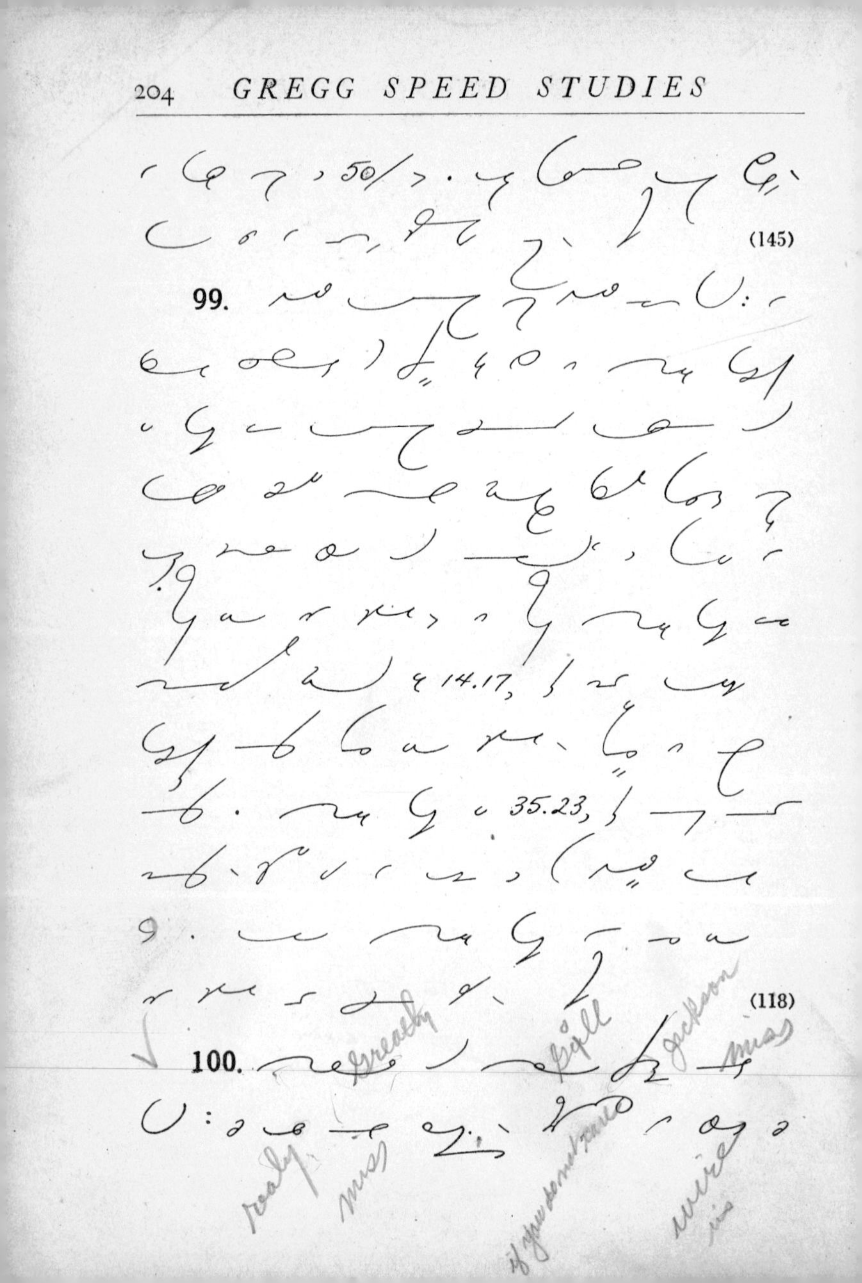

50/

(145)

99.

14.17,

35.23,

(118)

100.

greatly Bill Jackson miss

really miss if you do not want miss

(126)

101.

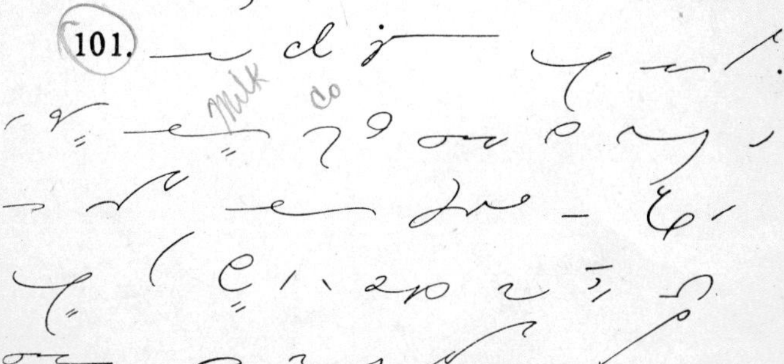

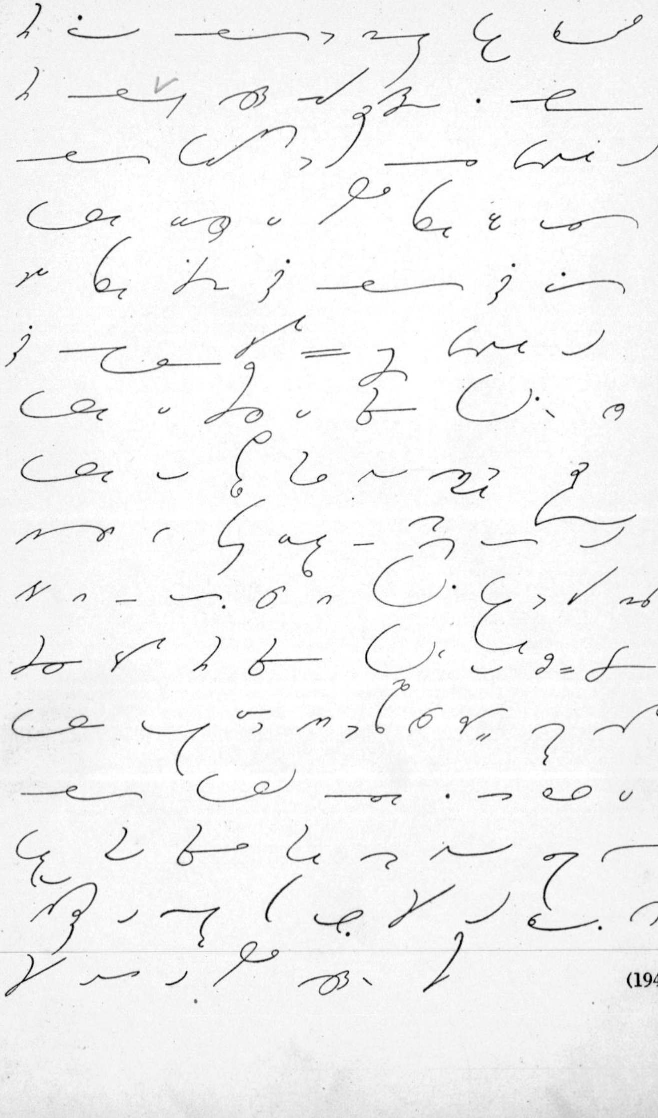

(194)

102. INITIATIVE

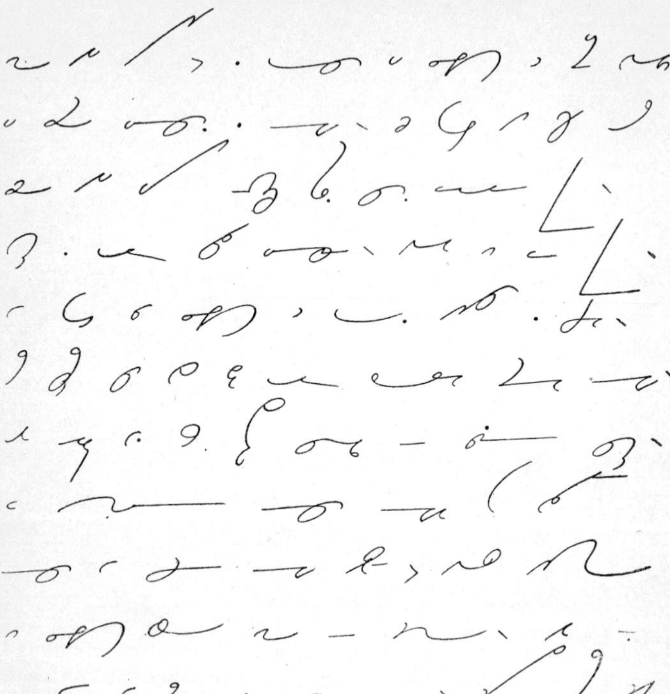

(300)

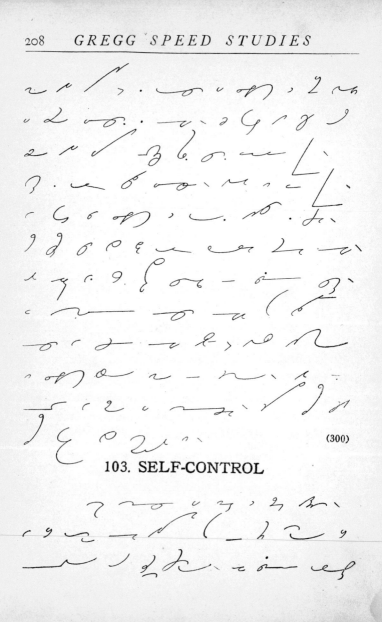

103. SELF-CONTROL

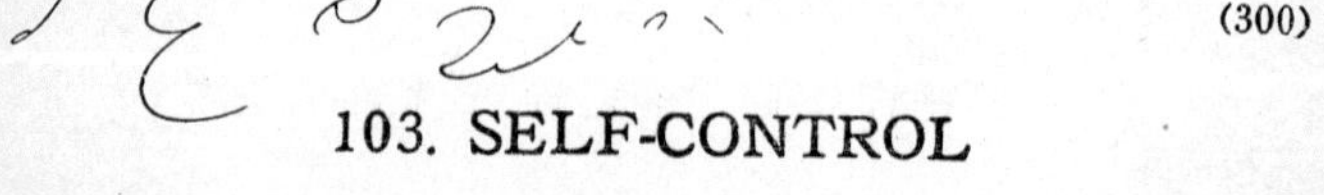

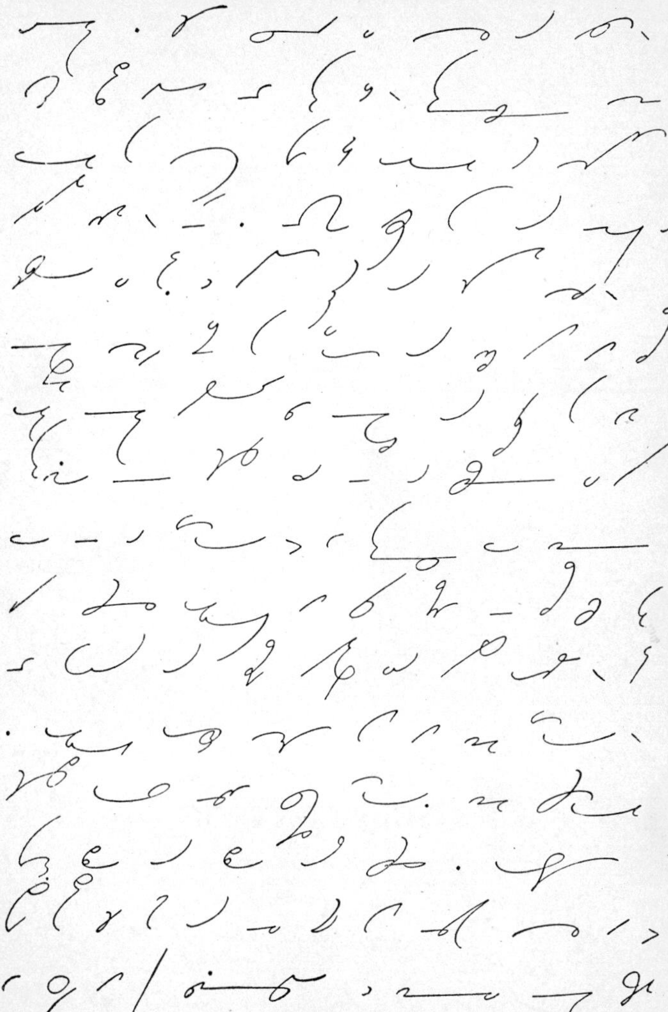

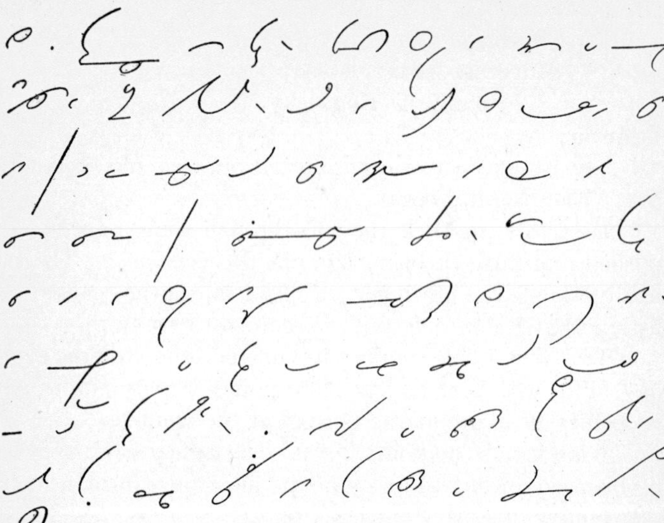

(350)

Office Manager
First National Company
815 State Street,
Frankfort, Kentucky

Dear Sir:

The bookkeeper reached into his pin tray and took out a pin. Then the fun began.

He tried[20] to stick the pin through some papers. He pushed and pushed, biting his lips as he pushed. The pin finally[40] landed in his finger. He said things that caused the little girl at the next desk to look up with[60] a start.

This very thing happens in lots and lots of offices every day. Pins with bent points, blunt points,[80] rusty points, and no points at all are at the bottom of the trouble.

What is to be done about[100] it? The logical solution of the problem, according to many of the most prominent firms in the country, is—use[120] our bank pins.

It takes only a slight pressure of the finger to push them through thick papers, because they[140] have long tapering points and short sharp stickers.

Moreover, being all brass, they won't rust, no matter how long they[160] lie in pin trays nor how long they are left in papers.

Two other features are worthy of special mention.[180] They have extra-large heads so they can't slip clear through the papers and so they may be easily and[200] quickly removed. They have a bright, lasting finish that is as smooth as velvet.

Yes, our bank pins will contribute[220] much to the smooth running of your office.

Here is a size card in case you have mislaid the one[240] we sent you.

Very cordially yours, (246—1.28)

Office Manager
Hanford & Mumford
Jefferson City, Missouri
Dear Sir:

Good pins are as essential to the proper functioning of an office as good pencils, good typewriters, or[20] good billing machines.

Our bank pins are good pins and cost surprisingly little.

Please put the enclosed samples of size[40] 4 to a rigid test. Fold a sheet of heavy paper several times and stick the pins through it. They[60] glide through easily, don't they?

Their long tapering points and short sharp stickers are responsible for their ability to perform[80] this feat.

They are made of the best brass wire. They won't rust. You know how provoking it is to[100] try to remove a rusty pin from a bunch of papers. You almost tear your finger nails off in the[120] process.

Our bank pins will not treat you in any such fashion. You may leave one of these bank pins[140] in a sheaf of papers indefinitely. It will come out as easily as it went in. You can use it[160] again, for that matter.

They are now used in the offices of many prominent firms. These firms are pleased with[180] the service they give, as is proved by the fact that they come back again and again for more.

You[200] will see from the attached list that, regardless of their many good qualities, our bank pins are reasonable in price.[220]

Send along an order. Here is a size card to help you make it up. Put the pins to a[240] thorough test in your office on your work. You will be much pleased with the result.

Sincerely yours, (258—1.30)

104.  (38)

105. 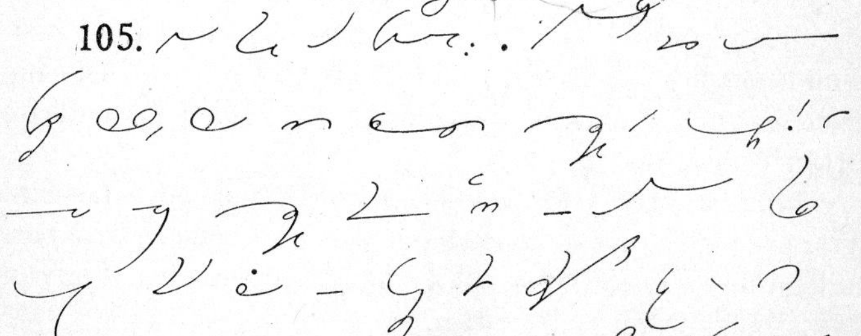 (76)

106. 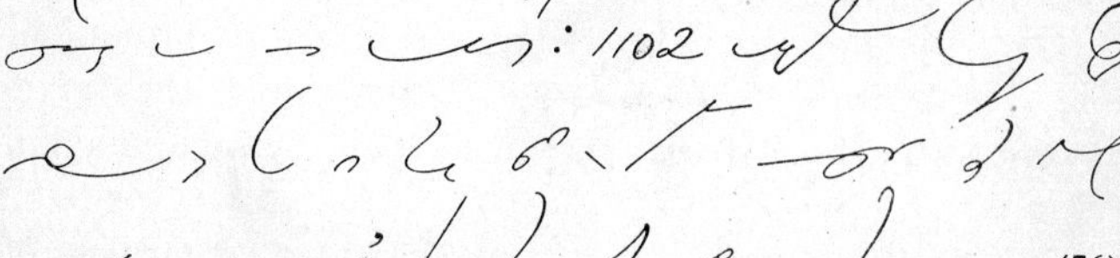

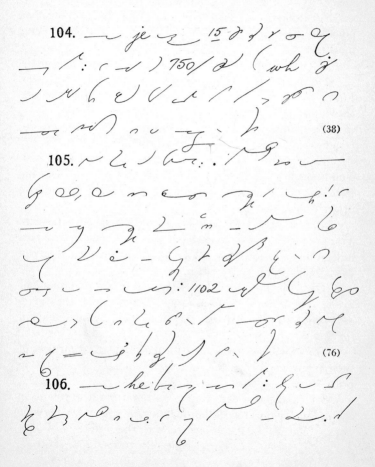

(183)

107.

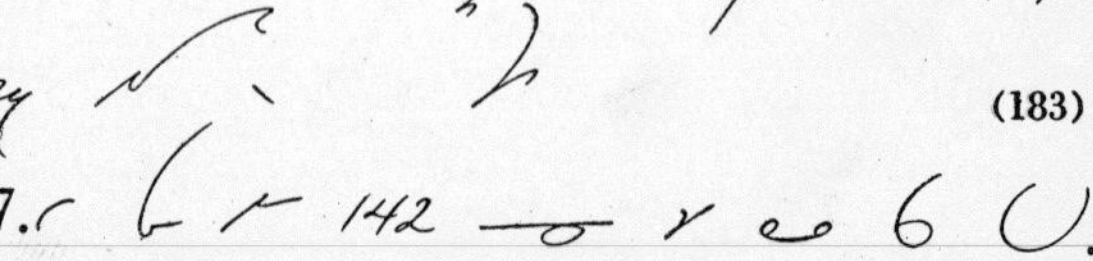

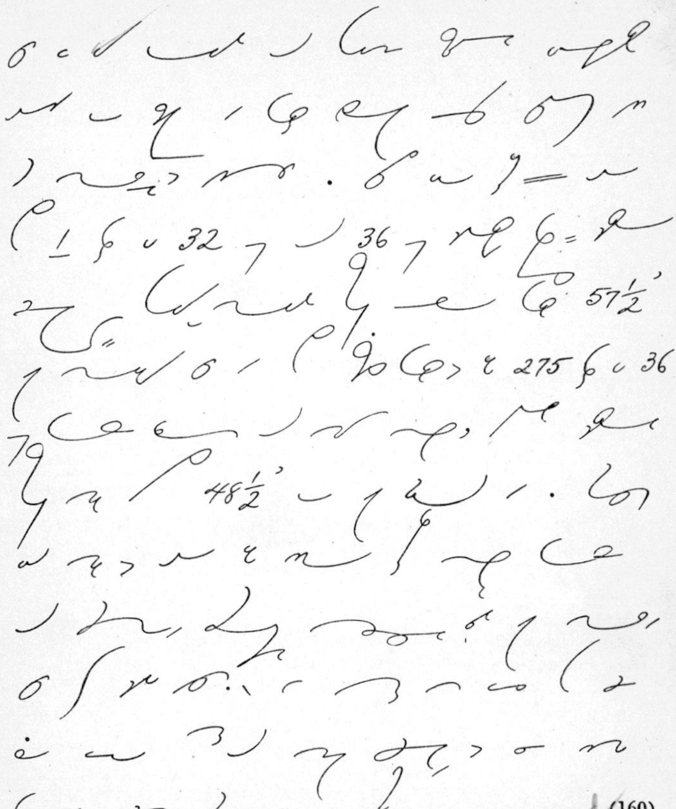

(160)

108.

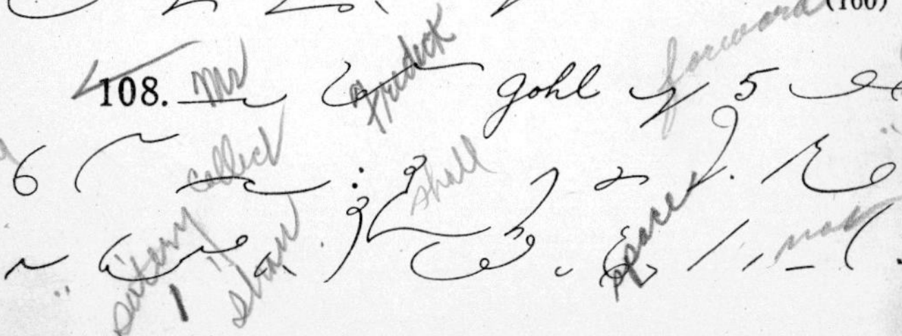

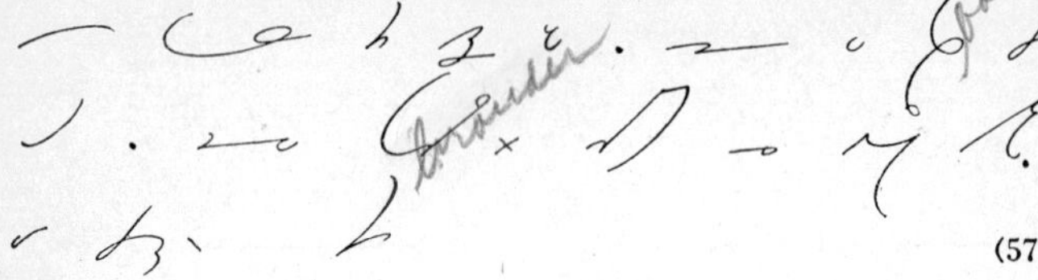

(57)

109

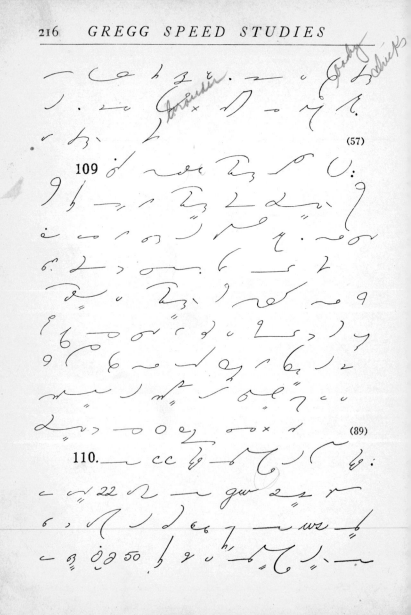

(89)

110.

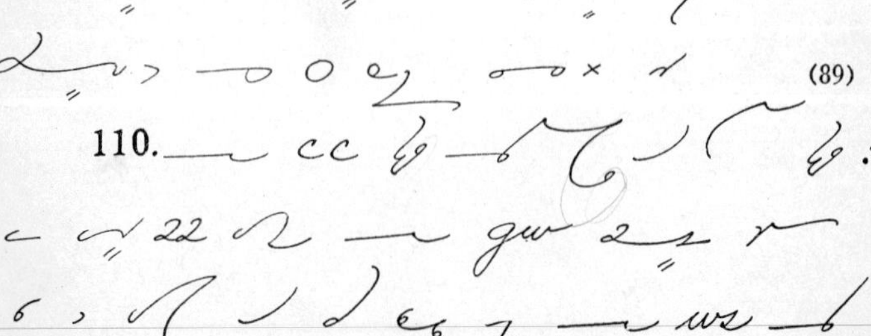

(154)

111.

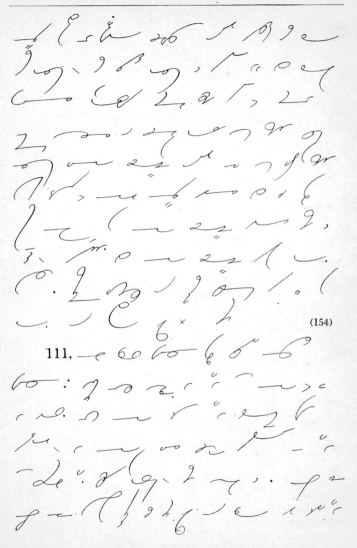

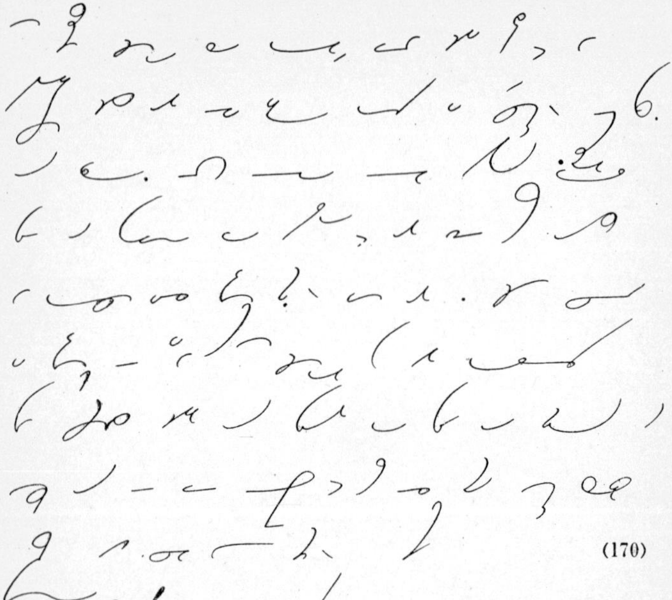

(170)

112.

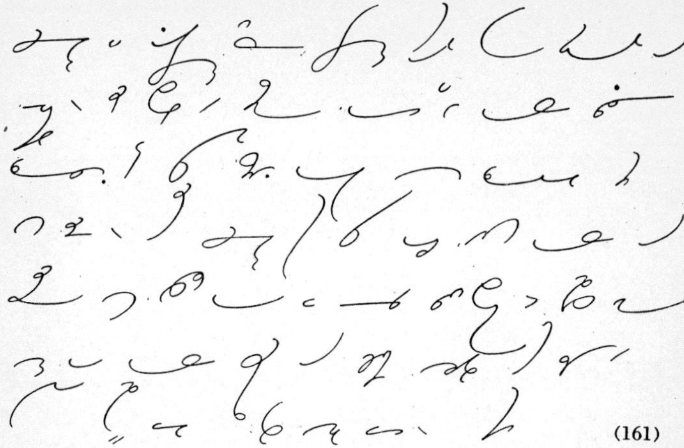

(161)

113.

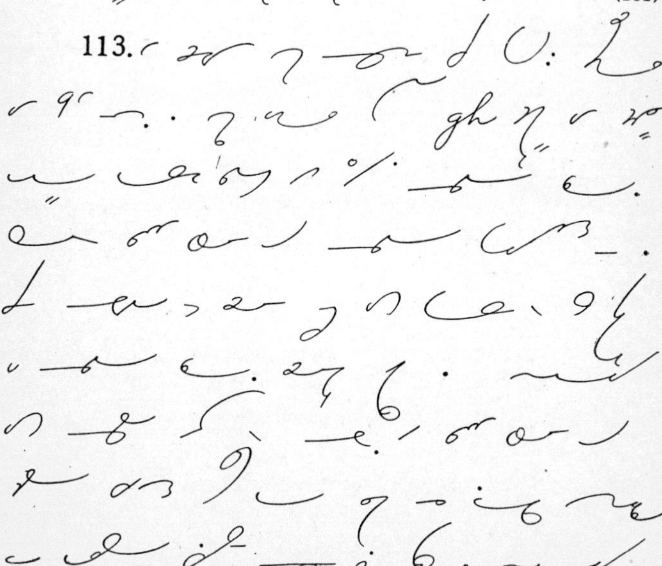

(134)

114.

(108)

115. FLAT-TOP DESK PHILOSOPHY

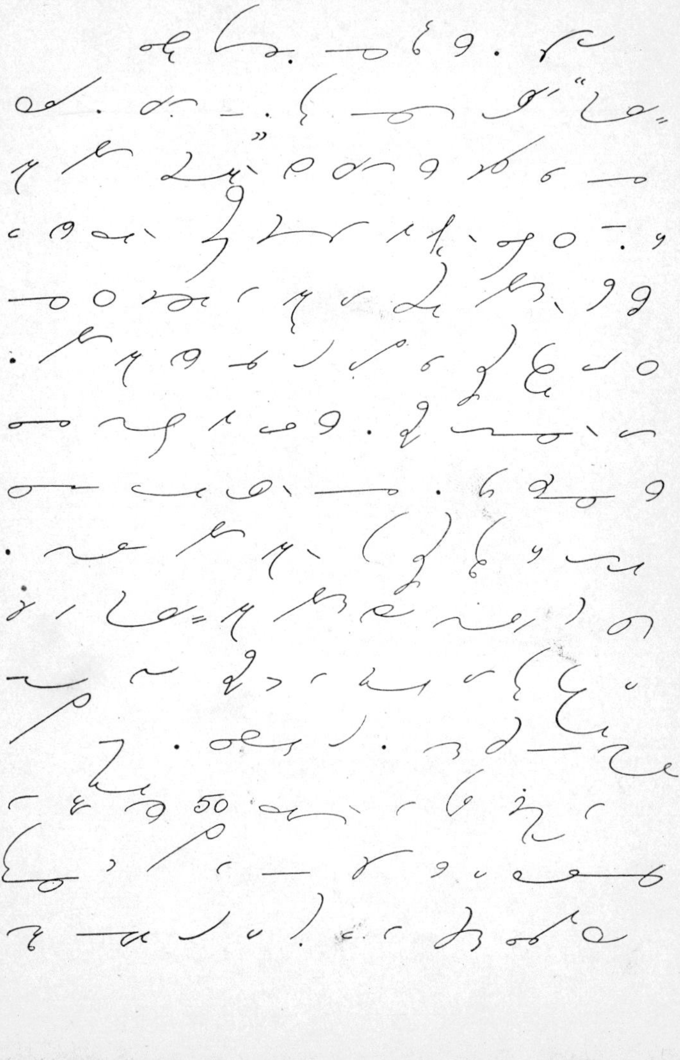

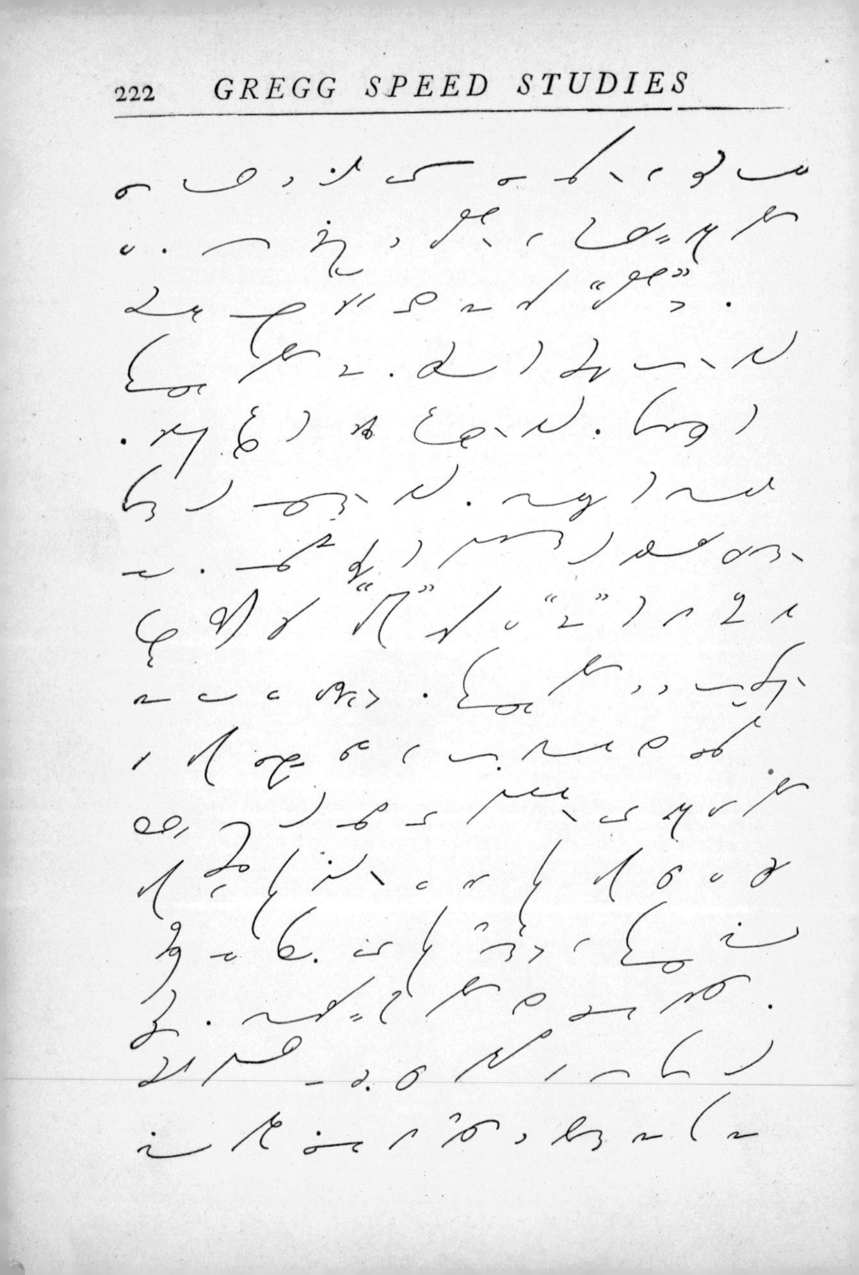

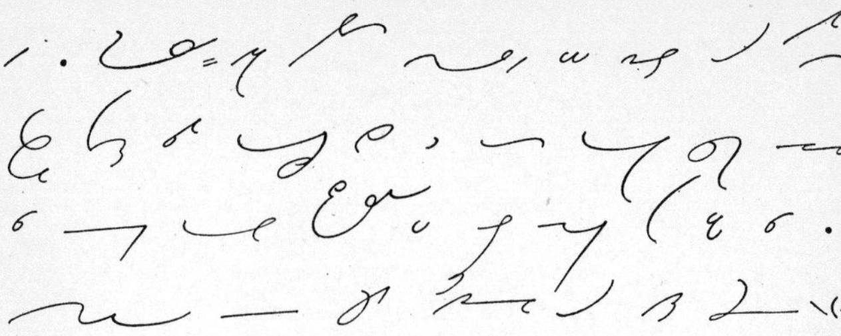

(400)

116. BUSINESS DRESS

(300)

Dear Friends:

We note with a great deal of pleasure your arrival in Greenville and we understand that you intend[20] to make this your future home.

We want to extend our congratulations to you and we feel sure you will[40] like our city. It is our sincere hope that you will find living here both pleasant and successful.

Our store[60] is located across the street from the Court House. We shall appreciate it if you will make yourself entirely at[80] home in our store. We shall particularly appreciate it if you will call on us at any time we can[100] be of possible service to you. Your neighborhood grocer, (109—1.39)

Dear Mrs. Brown:

Do you ever think about the men behind the scenes who are paid for reading the minds[20] of our patrons?

All day long they think about you. They study your tastes. They analyze your wishes. They plan[40] new services for you. Hour by hour they strive to anticipate your desires, to the end that long before you[60] feel a need the means will be at hand to meet it.

By our records of your purchases they know[80] what has pleased you. Through agents in foreign lands and experts in the world's market centers, through papers and letters[100] and the cable and the telegraph, they are ever on the watch for news that will help them find what[120] will please you.

Hence, all that is new and good lies before you on our counters. All the artistry of[140] every nation is at your instant service through your charge account.

We want you to use that account to the[160] fullest advantage. It is yours. This store itself is your store.

Very cordially yours, (174—1.29)

Dear Sir:

You have recently received some printed matter from us and you have been kind enough to allow one[20] of our men to tell you something about the merits of our system of heating.

If you had actually experienced[40] the advantages of our system of heating instead of being told about them, and if you had grown to know[60] the benefits that come from the even distribution of warmth and the constant supply of clean air given by our[80] heating system, we feel that you would have invested in it long ago. A quick heating response and a fuel[100] saving of 25 per cent are other features known to our thousands of users.

Although we have grown to[120] be the greatest organization in the industry, this company will never become so large that I am not personally interested[140] in every individual prospect. Therefore I am writing to ask that you tell me frankly where we have failed in[160] our endeavor to add your name to the long list of satisfied users in your own city.

Will you please[180] take the time and trouble to write me personally? I shall consider it a real favor if you will extend[200] this courtesy to me. I should like to know just what impression we have created and what information we have[220] failed to give you. I am asking this because if you knew the story as we know it, and as[240] more than a million satisfied users know it, you would install our system in your own home immediately.

I know[260] that you are busy and that I am asking something out of the ordinary, but I do not need to[280] tell you that I am deeply interested, and I shall be extremely grateful for an answer to this letter.

Cordially, (300—1.34)

SPEED STUDY XV

117.

(55)

118.

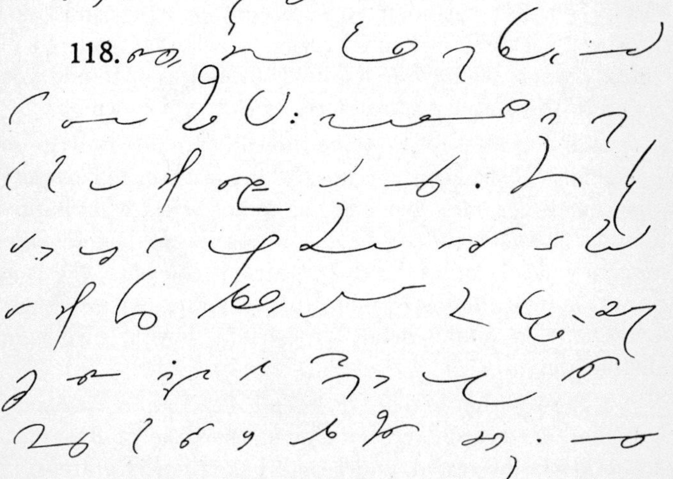

(76)

119.

(130)

120.

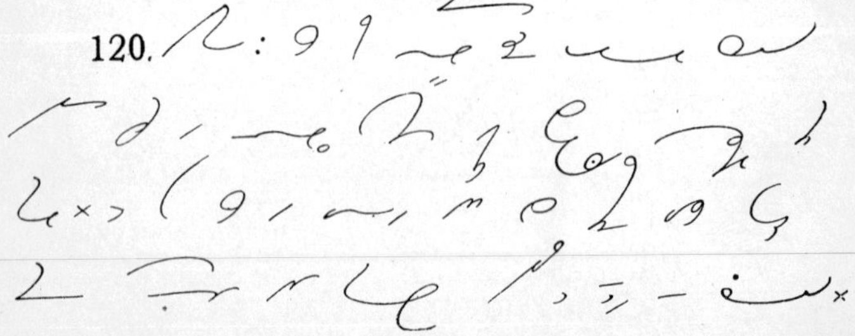

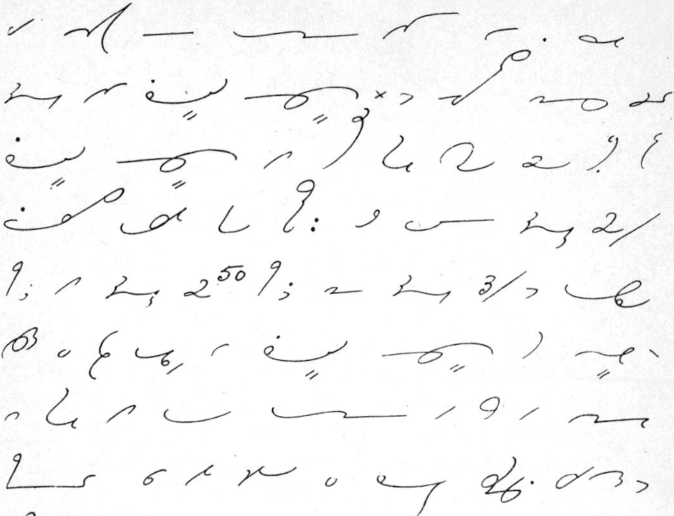

(177)

121.

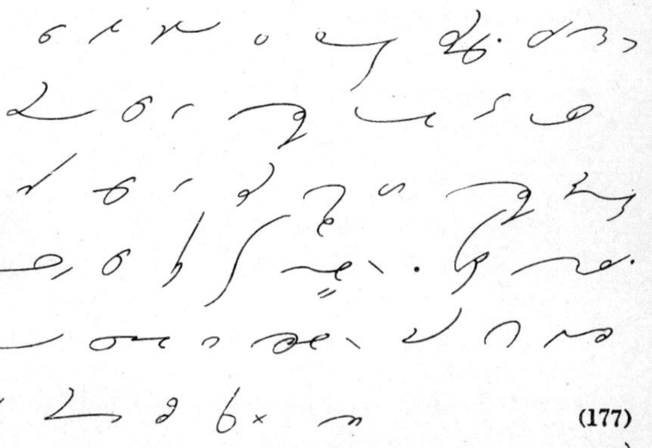

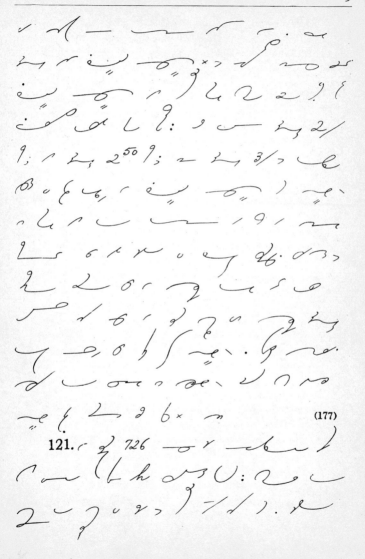

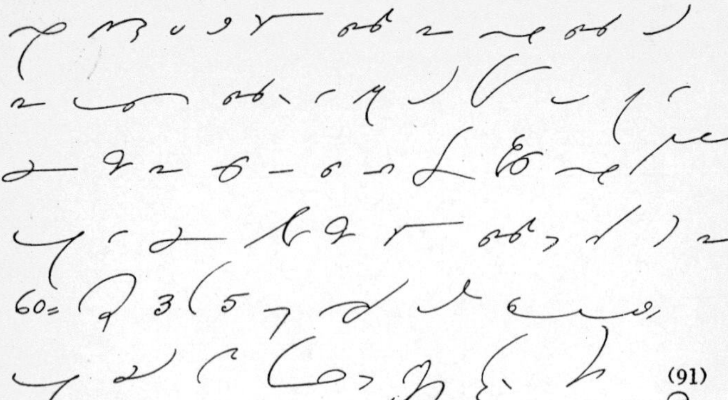

(91)

122.

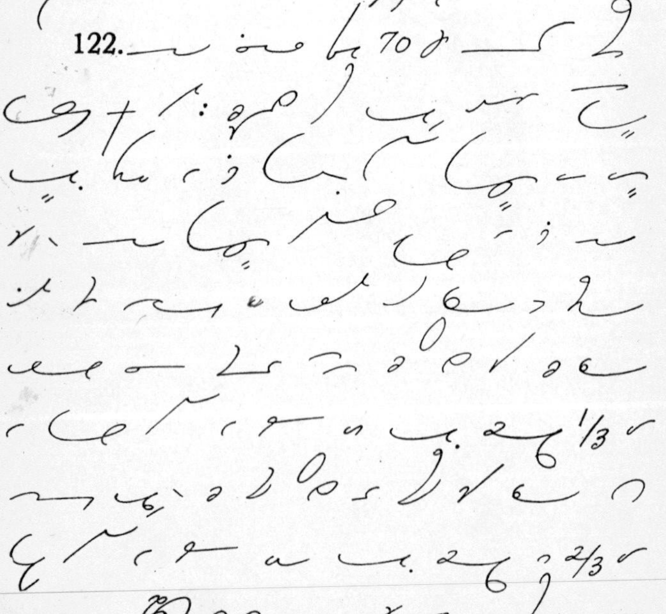

(109)

123.

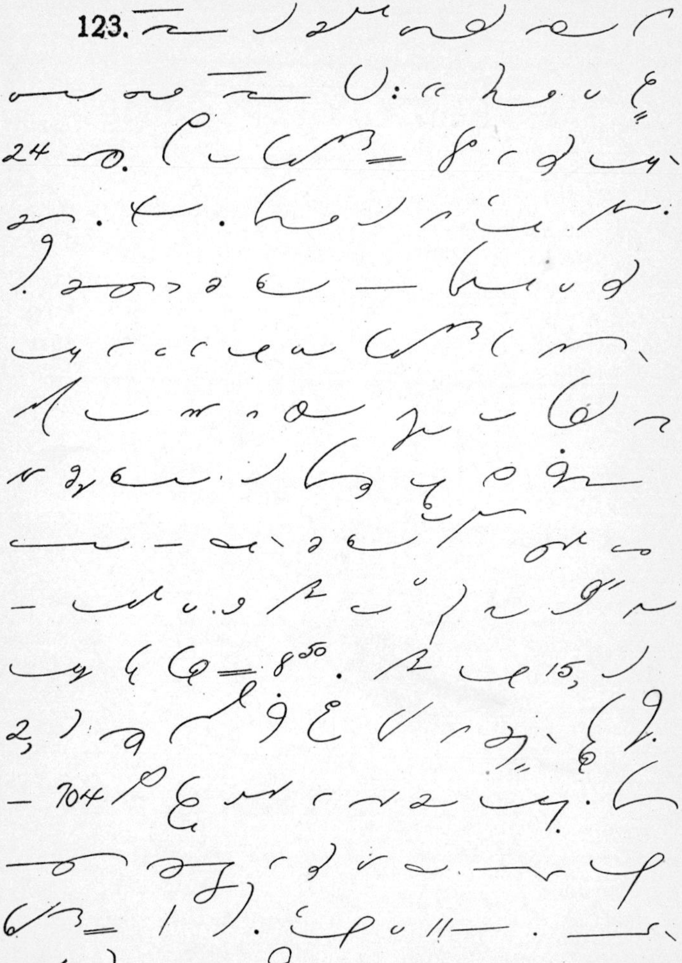

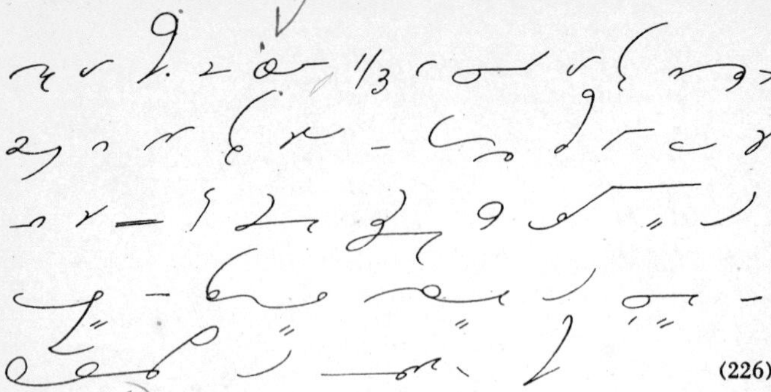

(226)

124.

(55)

125.

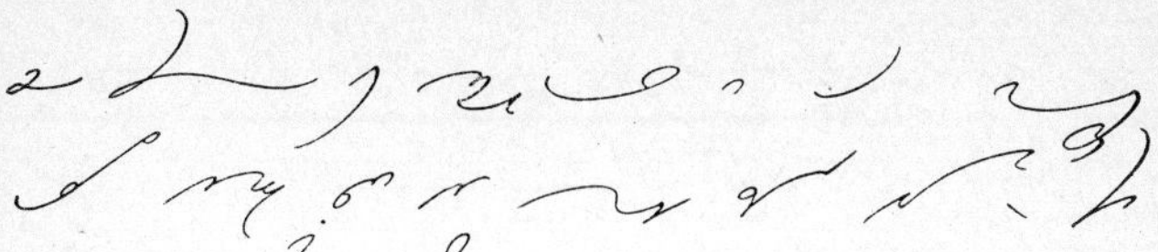

(100)

126.

(124)

127.

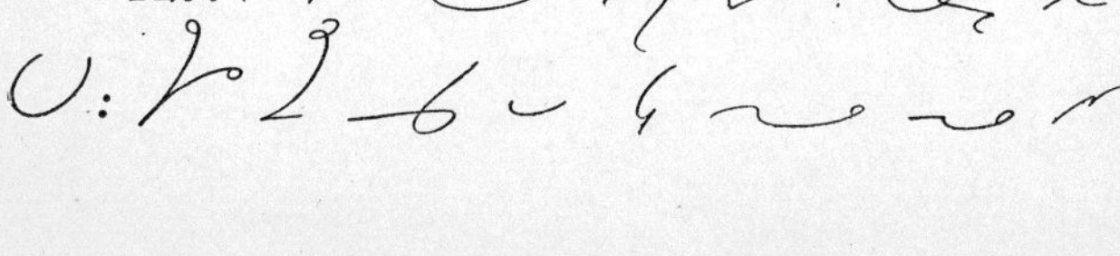

(162)

128. WHEN TO STOP STUDYING

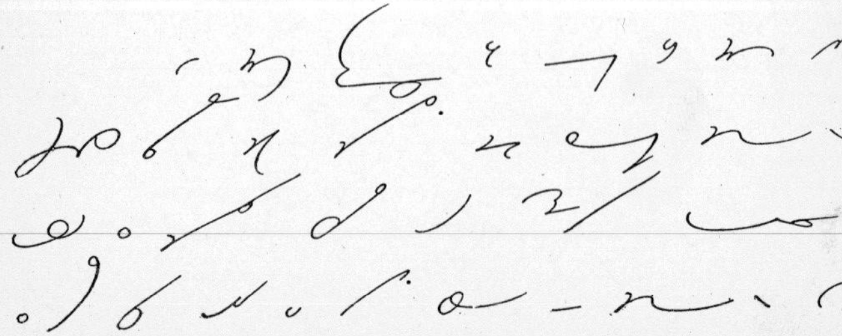

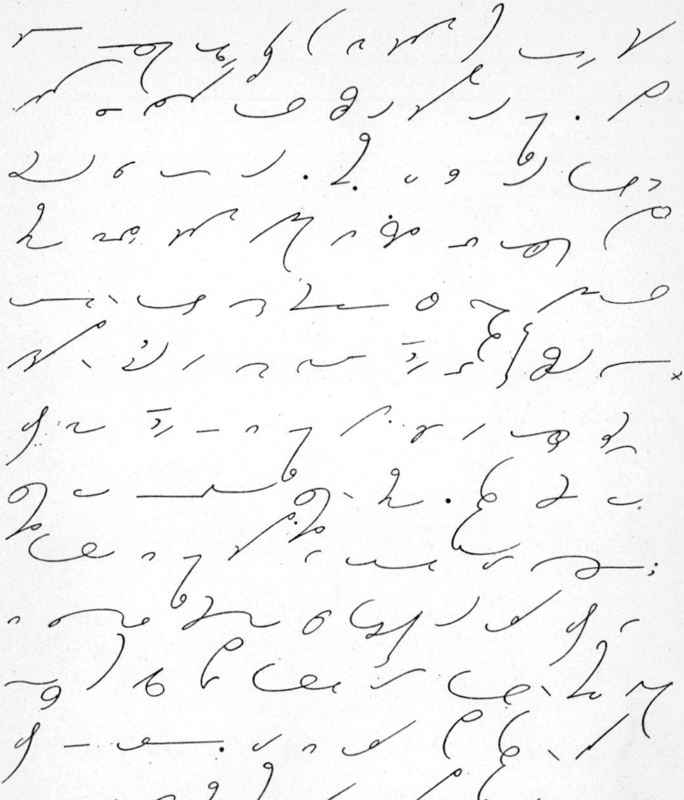

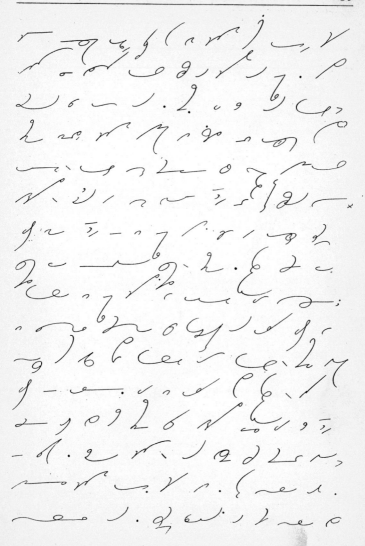

(600)

Mr. George Stebbins
Care of Carter and Sons
50 South Main Street
Ypsilanti, Michigan

Dear Sir:

Did you ever arrange to meet somebody downtown at exactly two o'clock and then hustle down there at[20] exactly the right time only to find your friend among the missing? If you have ever done that, standing first[40] on one foot and then on the other while you searched your brain to remember whether it really was two[60] o'clock and whether it really was that particular street corner on which you had agreed to meet—then you can[80] appreciate what we have just gone through.

Last year we sold you coal, yet this fall when the first cold[100] winds began whistling around the corners and the telephone began to ring all day long with people wanting more of [120] that fine coal we sell, we have had no order from you.

To tell you the truth we are all[140] rather worried here at the office. Everyone of us, from the person who took your order over the telephone to[160] the driver who delivered your coal, tried to give the kind of service you wanted to have.

And now it[180] is past the middle of January and another year has started, and we have not had any order from you.[200] We considered you one of the family and had hopes of meeting you every fall and winter. So here we[220] are waiting on the corner, so to speak, and we shall be overjoyed to see you or to hear from[240] you.

Very cordially yours, (244—1.34)

Mr. John Olsen
General Manager, Best Brothers
628 Huron Street
Hibbing, Minnesota

Dear Sir:

Sometimes it takes very little to upset a fellow!

Would you believe me if I should tell you[20] that just this morning a little metal tab, colored a bright but significant blue, took all the joy out of[40] life for me?

For that little bit of blue metal, directly above the information in regard to your account with[60] us, seemed to say, as plain as could be, "I wouldn't be on this card if it were not that[80] this customer of last year has not been on our order books this winter."

So here I am, writing to[100] see if I can find out why this particular color has had to go on your card file this season.[120]

Usually when our good friends come in to see us with an order for that shiny black coal of ours[140] that glows such a cheery red in the furnace on these chilly nights, every fellow in our organization does his[160] level best to treat them white by doing the job up brown.

Then we put a pink metal tab on[180] the record card. We do that to show that we are tickled pink to have our customers come back to[200] us.

Now I am just wondering whether we may still expect an order from your household that will assure you[220] of a good supply of the right kind of coal for a few months until the warm weather begins and[240] that will also change the blue metal tab to a pink one.

Very cordially yours, (255—1.28)

129.

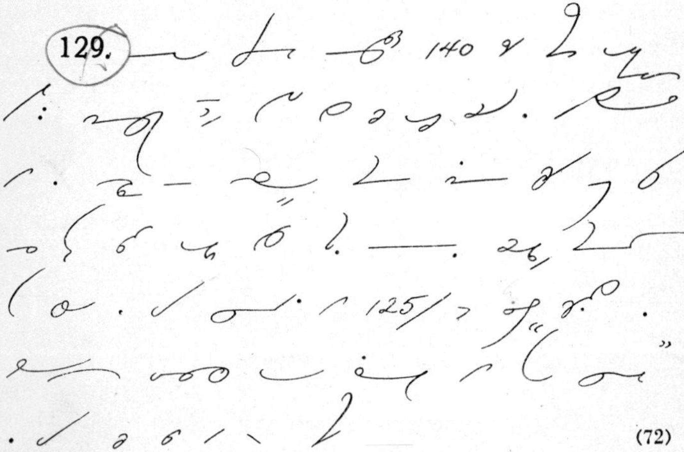

(72)

130.

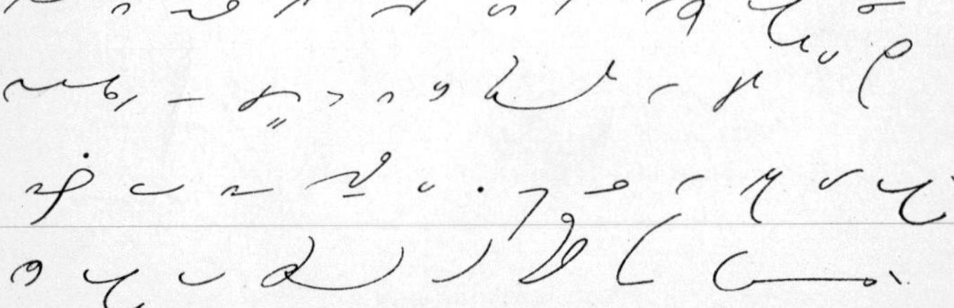

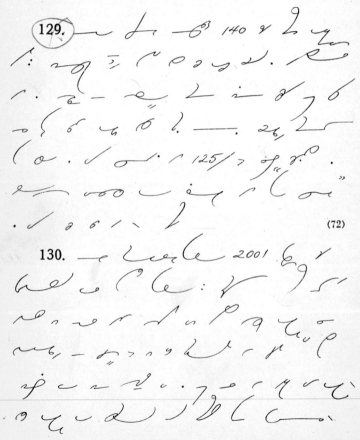

(109)

131.

(82)

132.

(179)

133.

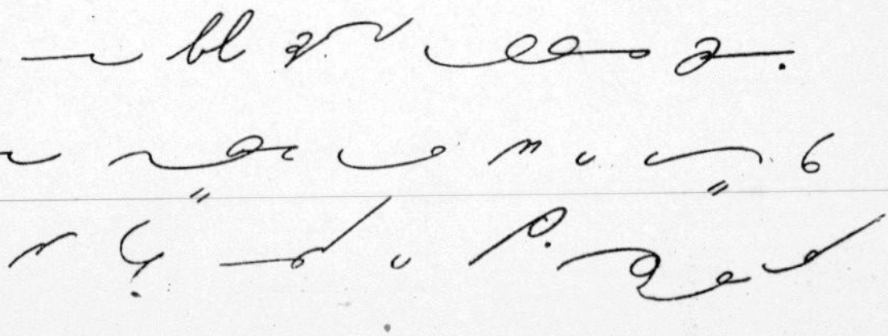

(128)

134

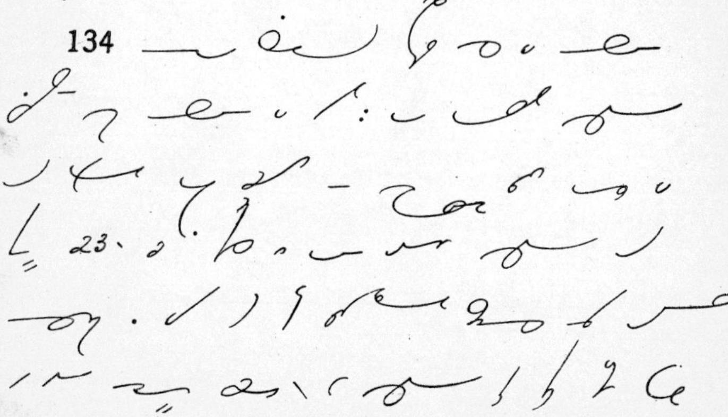

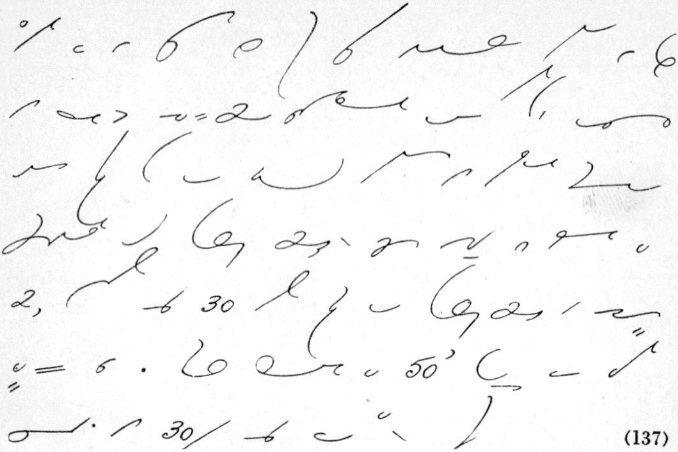

(137)

135.

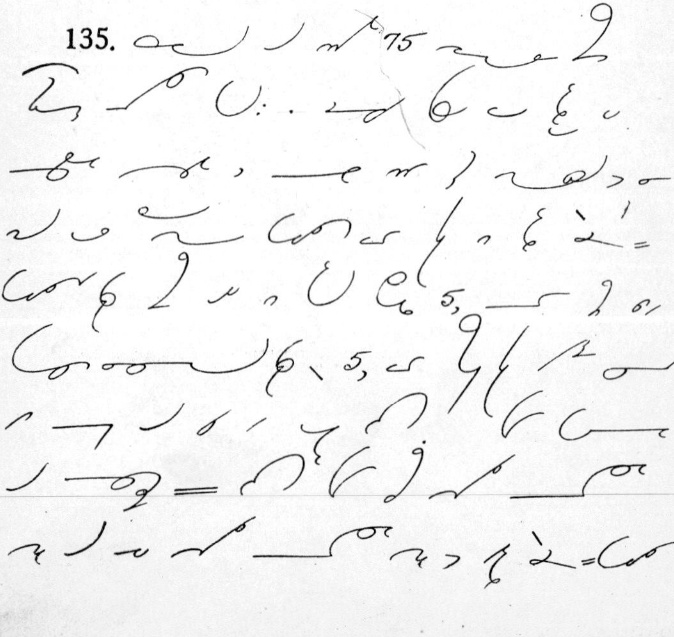

(186)

136.

(50)

137.

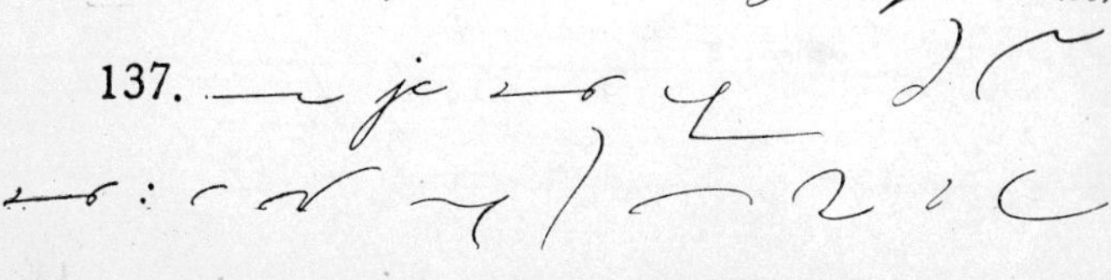

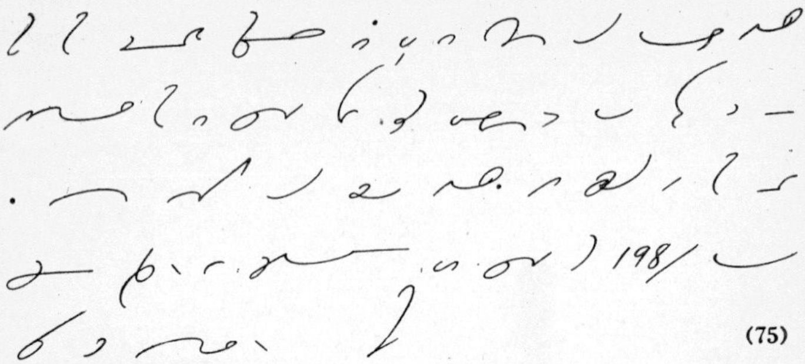

(75)

138.

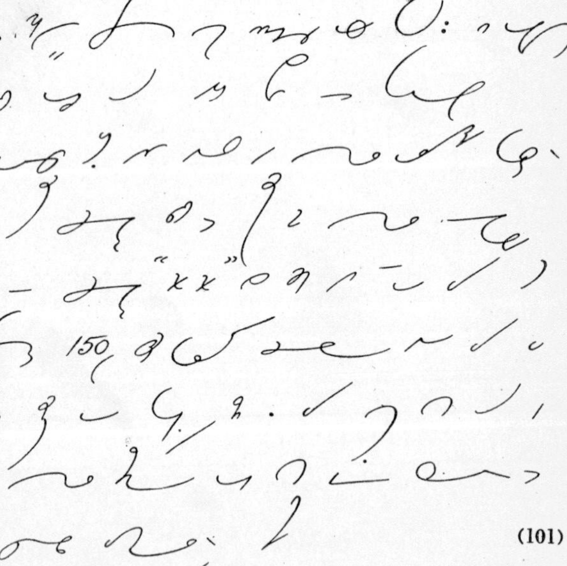

(101)

139.

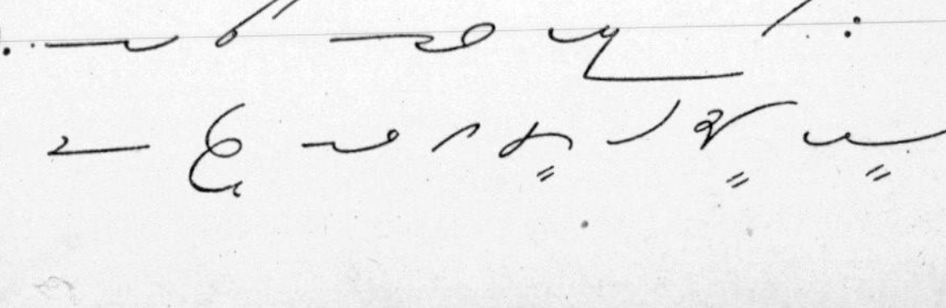

(214)

140. BUSINESS ENGLISH

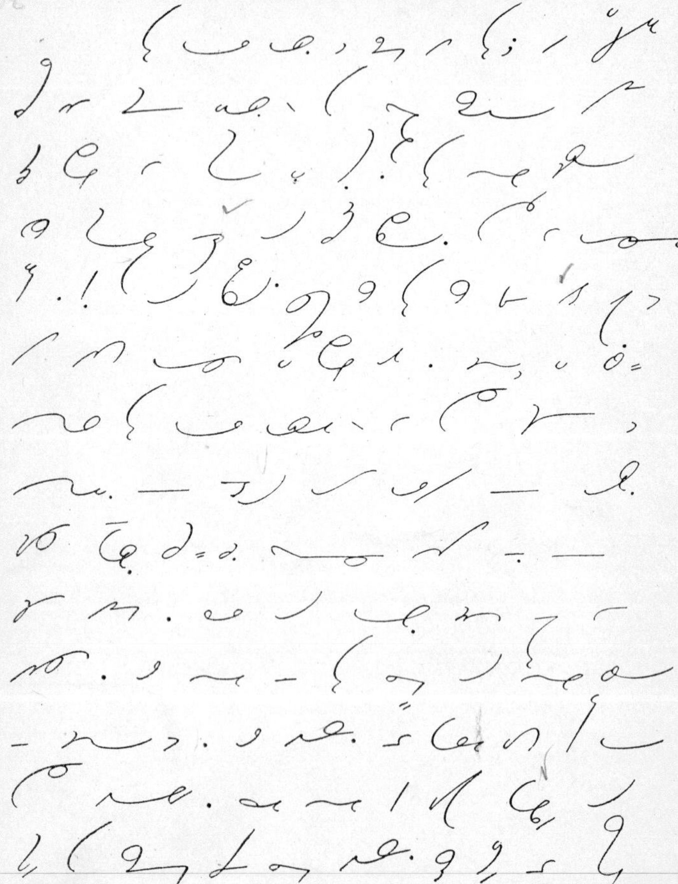

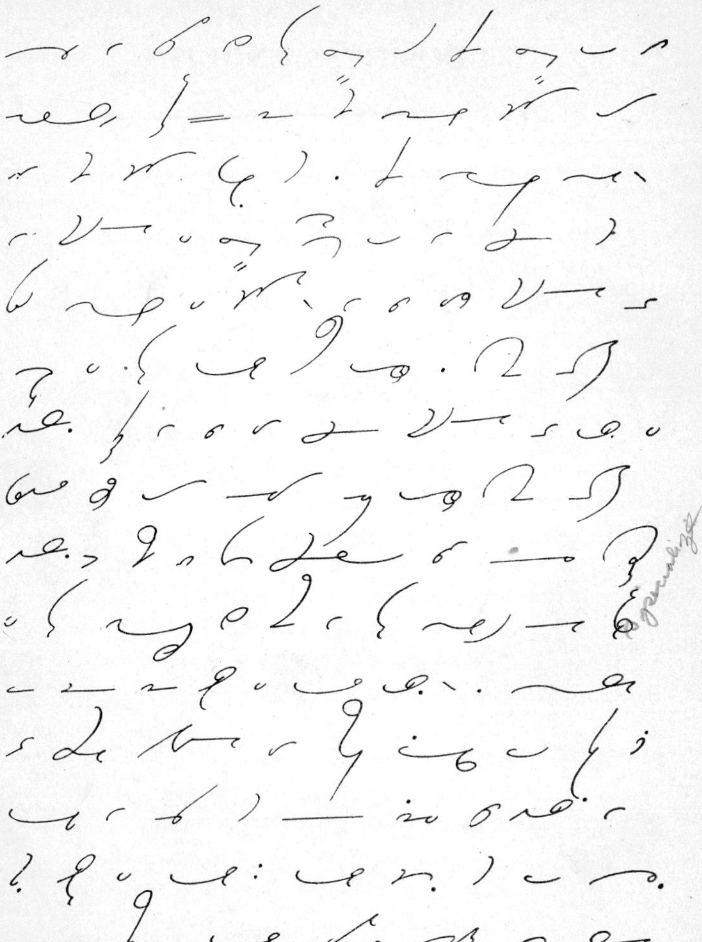

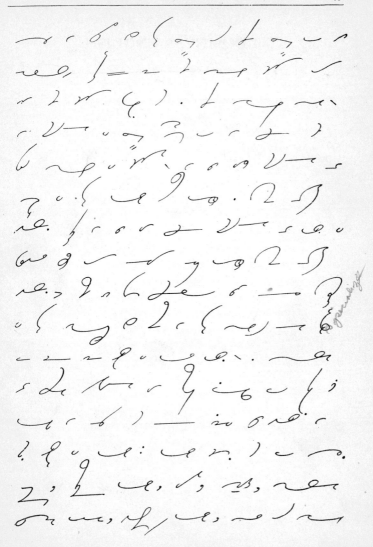

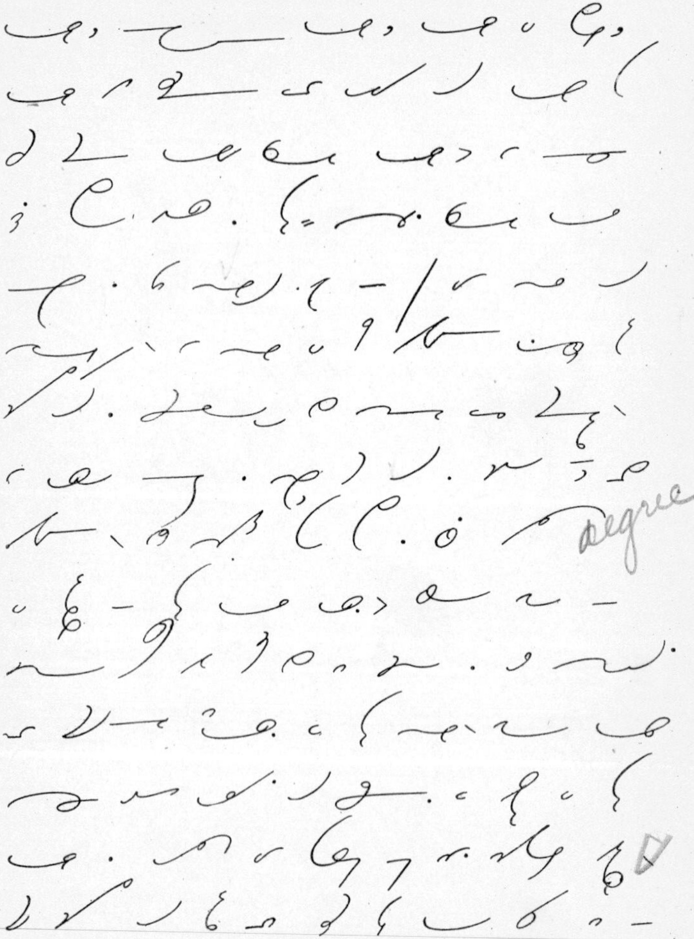
degree

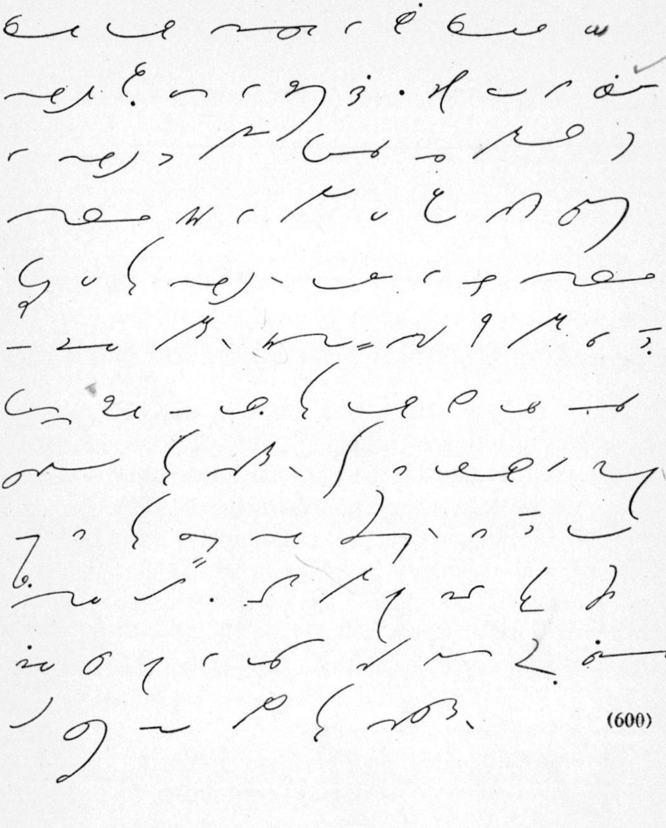

(600)

Dear Sir:

Now that the days are getting short a decided increase in the flashlight business may be noticed. We[20] have already felt this increase in the orders received from our distributors. They are getting in a complete stock to[40] take care of the demand from the dealers. We have also received many letters direct from the dealers telling us[60] that they have noticed this increase and that they are preparing orders for the distributors.

In most cases these dealers[80] have told us that the increase has been due in great part to the window displays, which they have made[100] to tie up with our fall advertising.

You want to get your share of this growing business and we want[120] to help you just as much as we can. We are sending you with this letter some window-display material,[140] together with a copy of the national advertising that will appear next week in several popular magazines.

Your best opportunity[160] to stimulate your sales of flashlights and flashlight batteries is to arrange a special window display featuring the same sales[180] arguments used in this advertising, which will appear in three of the great magazines of national circulation. Remember that one[200] of the best features of any window display is a good assortment of flashlights attractively arranged.

Has our salesman called[220] on you recently? If not, a post card addressed to this office will bring him to you within a few[240] days. He has many good ideas to increase your sales of flashlights and batteries. He can give you helpful suggestions[260] about the arrangement of your window display and about other forms of publicity that will increase your sales. We are[280] glad to cooperate with any of our **dealers** in this way or in any other way we can.

Yours truly, (300—1.47)

Gentlemen:

Did you ever stop to figure how much rent you pay each month for the space occupied by your[20] show windows? Did you ever stop to figure how much of a return you get out of the space used[40] by your store windows?

If you have never done this you may be surprised to find that your show windows[60] are not even paying for themselves, to say nothing of bringing you in the substantial profit that you have a[80] right to expect from them. If this is the case, the sooner you do something about it the better off[100] you will be.

Your show windows can be made to become your best money makers, even though you, like many[120] other dealers, have very little time to devote to arranging window displays.

Paints and varnishes are largely sold through suggestion.[140] That is why so many of our agents use the various window displays that we send them during the paint[160]-selling season.

Our window displays are made for one purpose—to sell paint. Each one has a message about paint[180] and each one gets that message over quickly and effectively.

With our great national advertising campaign working for you, and[200] with our window displays in your windows to tell people that you keep in stock the paints that they have[220] seen advertised, there is no reason why you cannot make a big success of your paint department.

The mere fact[240] that your store carries and sells the paints that are so well known and that have such a good reputation[260] should help you sell many other items.

Five thousand other progressive dealers all over the United States are doing a[280] large and profitable paint and varnish business by using our plan of stimulating paint sales.

Very cordially yours, (298—1.37)

SPEED STUDY XVII

141. 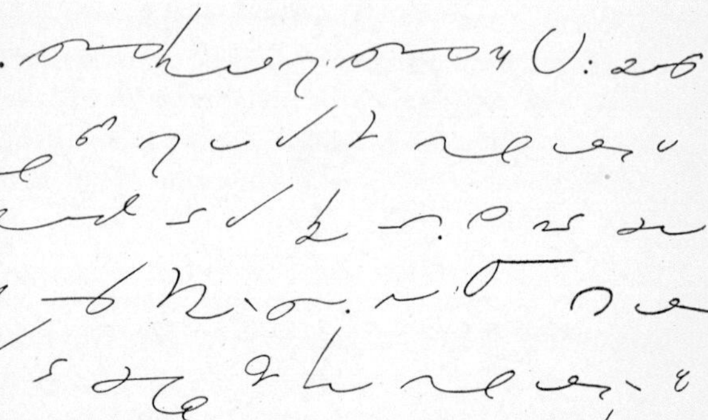

(147)

142. 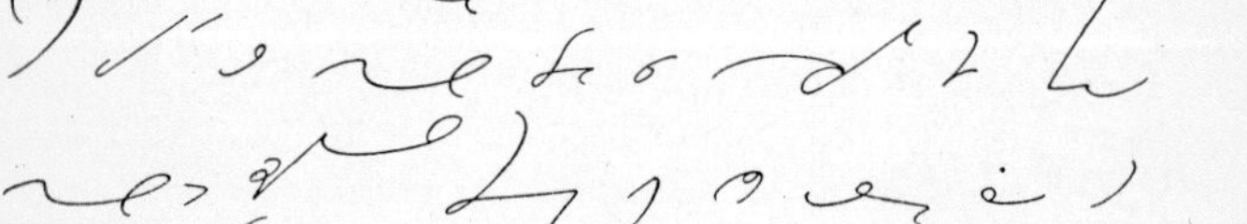

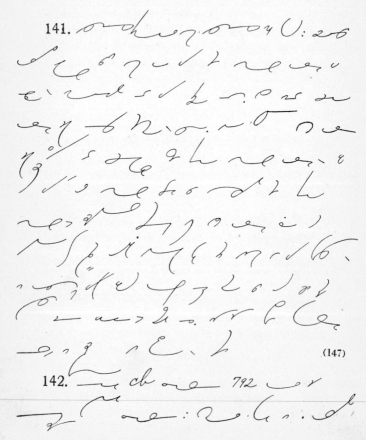

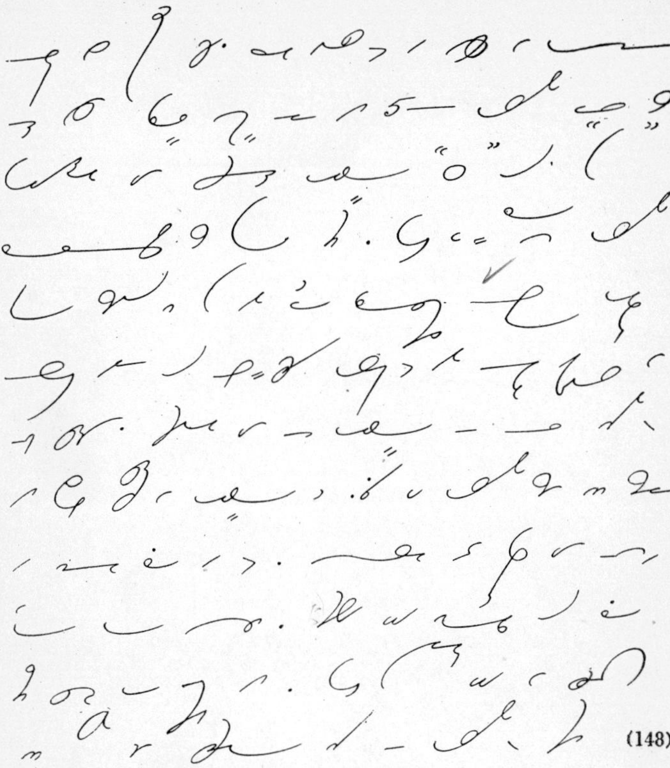

(148)

143.

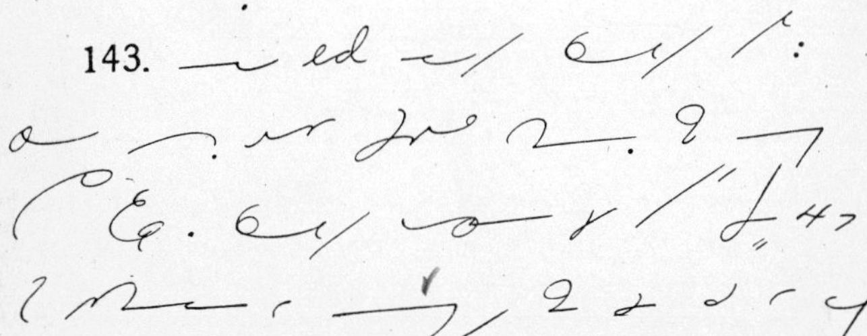

(161)

144.

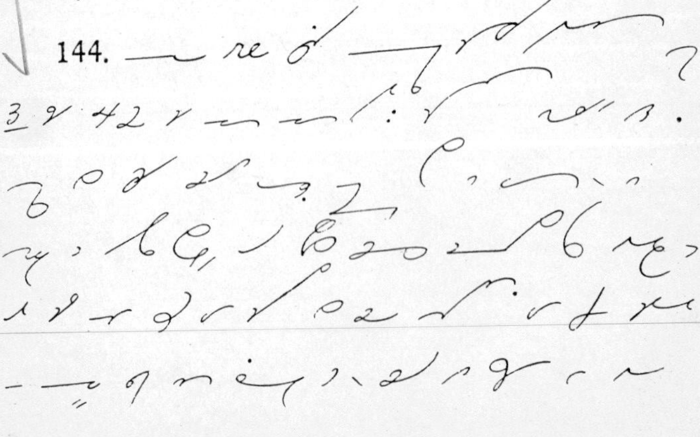

(255)

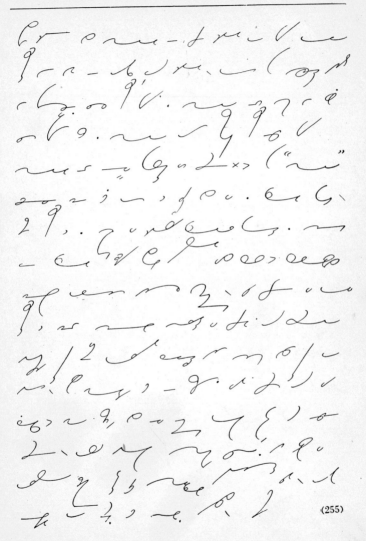

145.

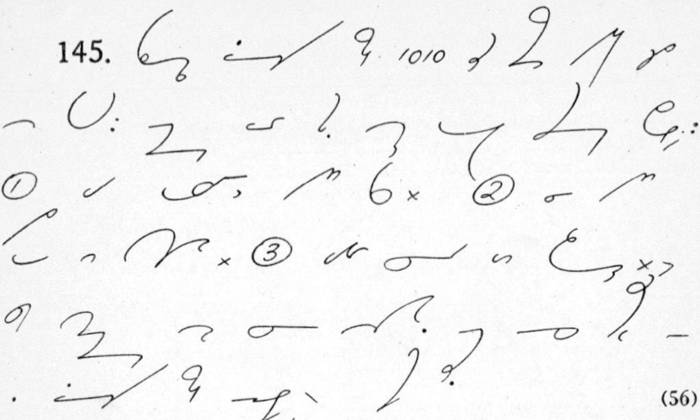

(56)

146.

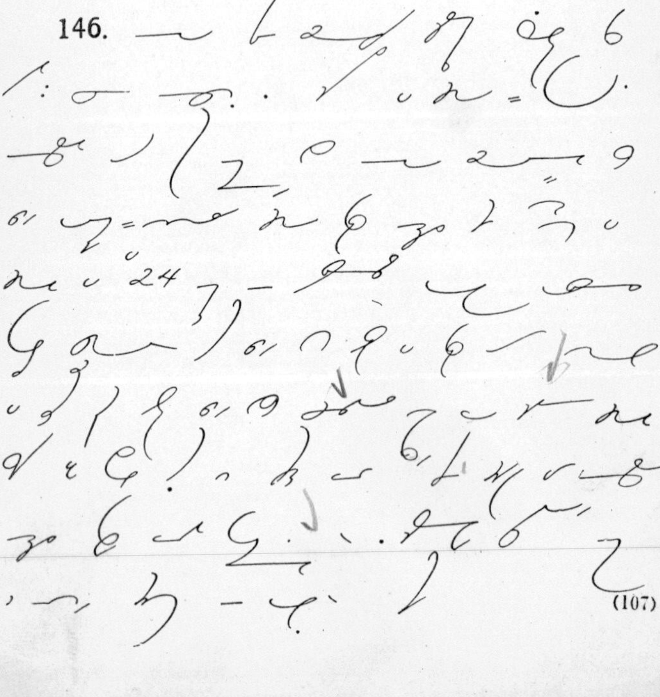

(107)

147.

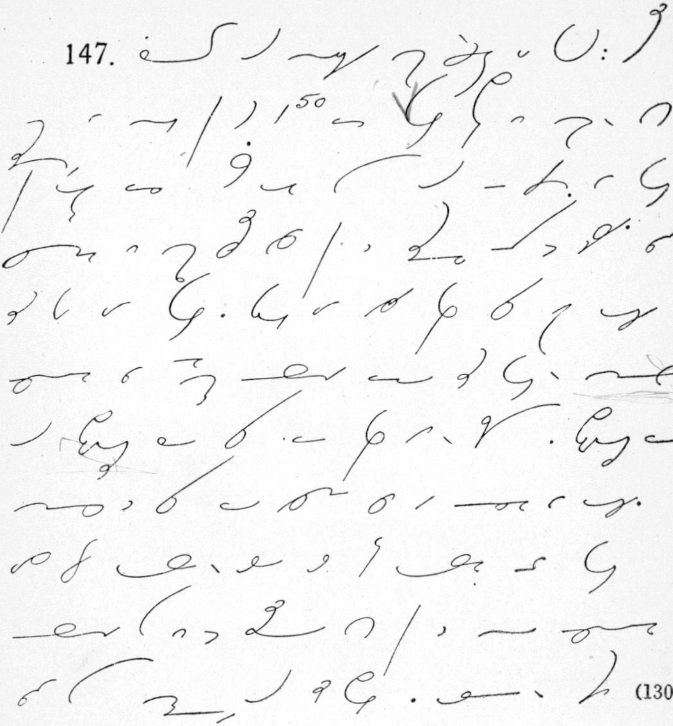

(130)

148.

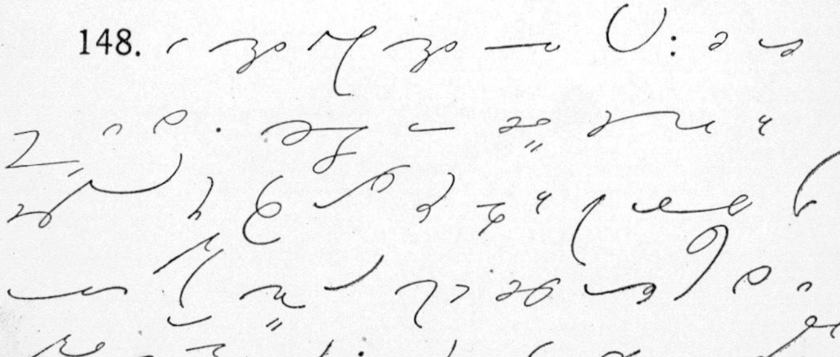

(131)

149.

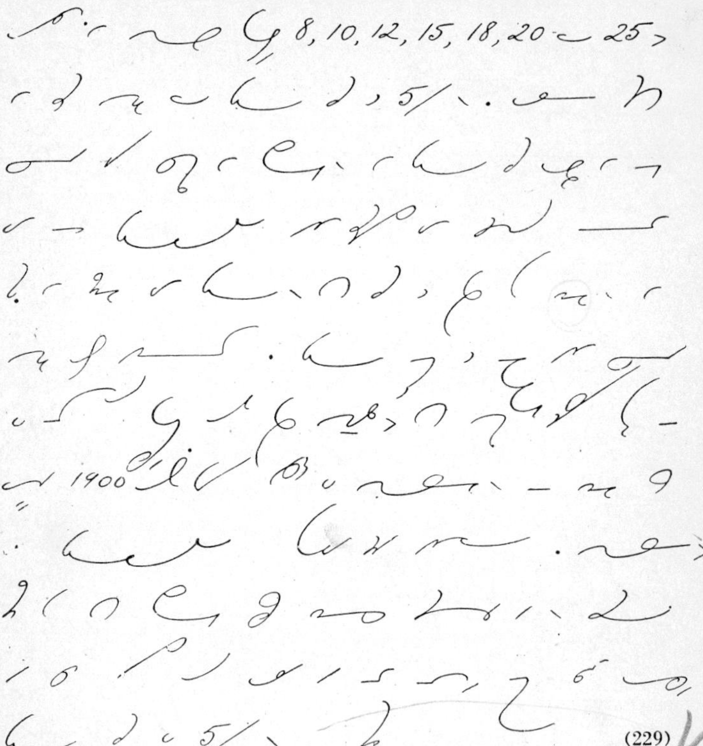

(229)

150. "IF I HAD ONLY KEPT ON!"

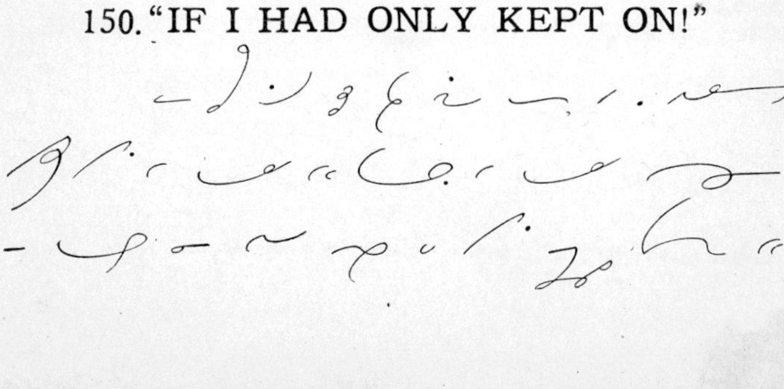

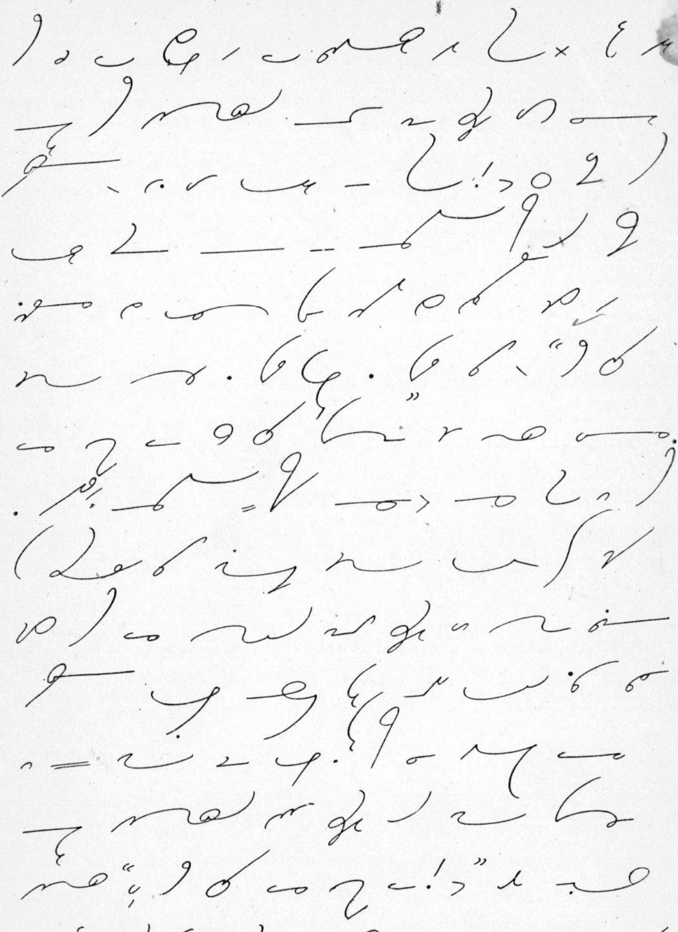

Orison Swett Marden (395)

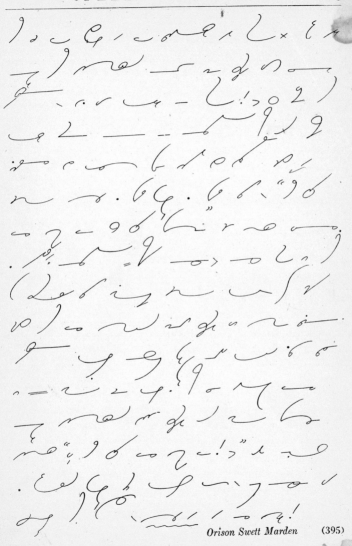

151. NINE LESSONS IN LIVING

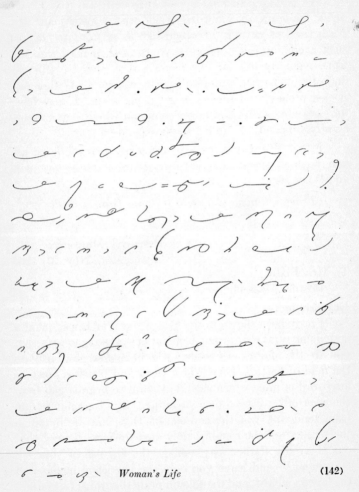

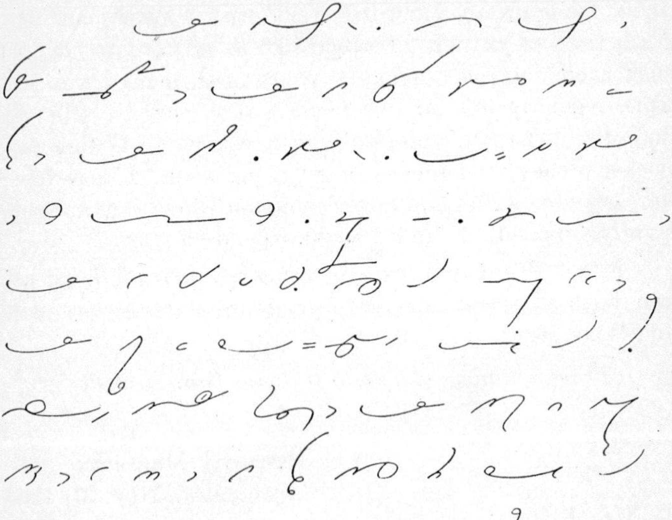

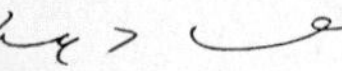 *Woman's Life* (142)

Dear Howells:

We had so charming a visit at your house that I have about made up my mind to[20] reside with you permanently. I am tired of writing. I would like to settle down in just such a comfortable[40] home as yours, with a man who can work regularly four or five hours a day, thereby relieving one of[60] all painful apprehension in respect to clothes and pocket money. I am easy to get along with. I have few[80] unreasonable wants and never complain when they are constantly supplied. I think I could depend on you.

P. S. I[100] should want to bring my two mothers, my two boys—I seem to have everything in twos—my wife and[120] her sister. (122—1.35)

(*Thomas Bailey Aldrich to William Dean Howells.*)

Executive Mansion
Washington, Nov. 21, 1864

To Mrs. Bixby,
Boston, Massachusetts

Dear Madam:

I have been shown in the files of the War Department a statement of the Adjutant General of[20] Massachusetts that you are the mother of five sons who have died gloriously on the field of battle. I feel[40] how weak and fruitless must be any word of mine which should attempt to beguile you from the grief of[60] a loss so overwhelming. But I cannot refrain from tendering you the consolation that may be found in the thanks[80] of the republic they died to save. I pray that our Heavenly Father may assuage the anguish of your bereavement,[100] and leave you only the cherished memory of the loved and lost, and the solemn pride that must be yours[120] to have laid so costly a sacrifice upon the altar of freedom.

Yours very sincerely and respectfully,

A. Lincoln, (140—1.38)

Acheson & Fowler
Hoboken, New Jersey
Gentlemen:

Would it be to your advantage for your dyer to know the one *best* temperature for each process—how[20] to eliminate spoilage, save steam and water, and produce uniformly dyed products?

Would you care to have your dye-house[40] foreman know the *facts* about temperature—that vital factor in modern dyeing procedure?

Without cost of a red cent—"Temperature[60] Control in the Dye House" will tell you the whole story. This booklet will be sent *free* to those interested[80] in better dyeing. From cover to cover it is chock-full of information, pictures, diagrams, all about such subjects as[100] Chemicking,* Boiling-out, Mordanting, Washing, Dyeing, Drying, etc. It contains the correct temperature for each process and much valuable information[120] for the betterment of the product. Each subject is covered in a practical, concise, non-technical manner—written by the[140] industry's best authority on the subject.

These booklets cost us real money—to eliminate waste, we are sending them only[160] when requested. Secure a copy, read it, and pass it on to the dye-house foreman and the dyers. Their [180] reading will mean dollars to you. The enclosed postal card is for your convenience.

Yours very truly (197—1.58)

*"Chemicking" means bleaching with a dilute solution of chloride of lime; "mordanting," fixing the color in dyeing.

SPEED STUDY XVIII

152.

(117)

153. sd

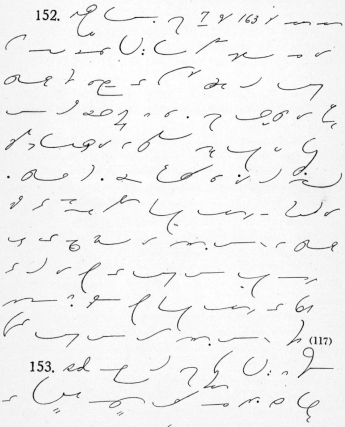

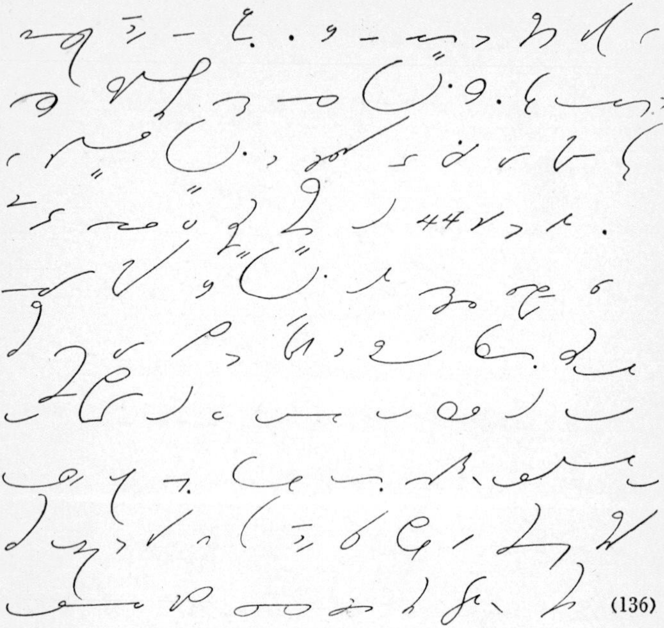

(136)

154.

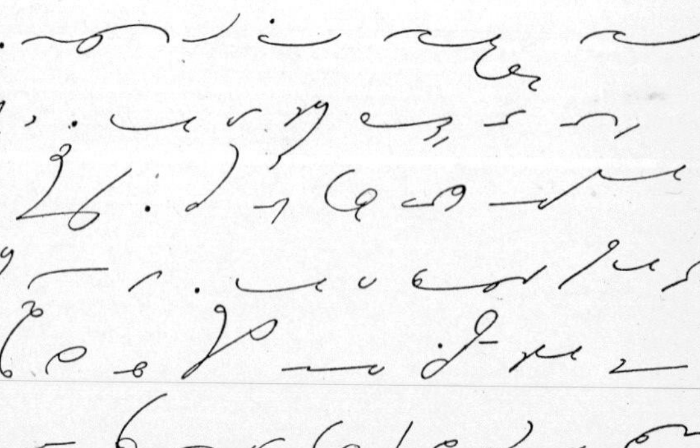

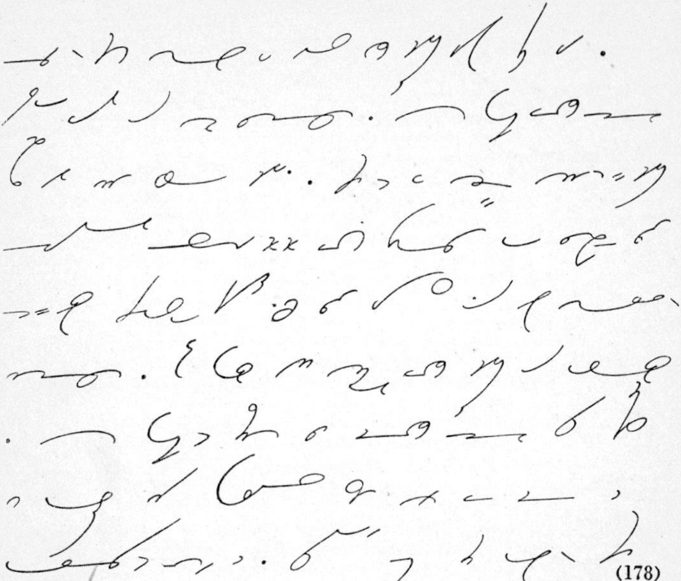

(178)

155.

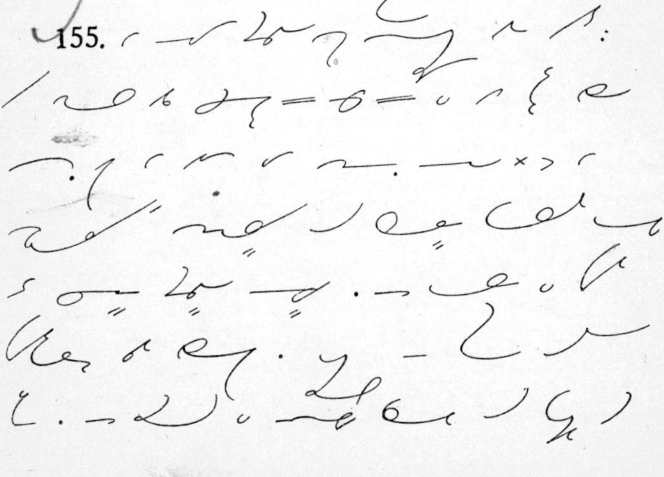

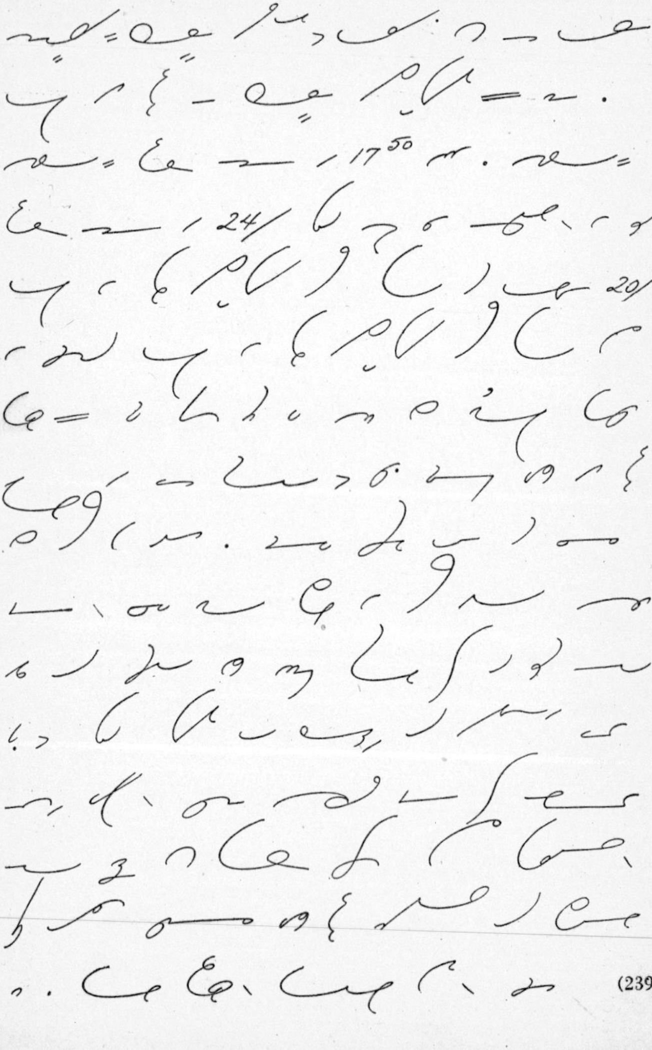

(239)

156.

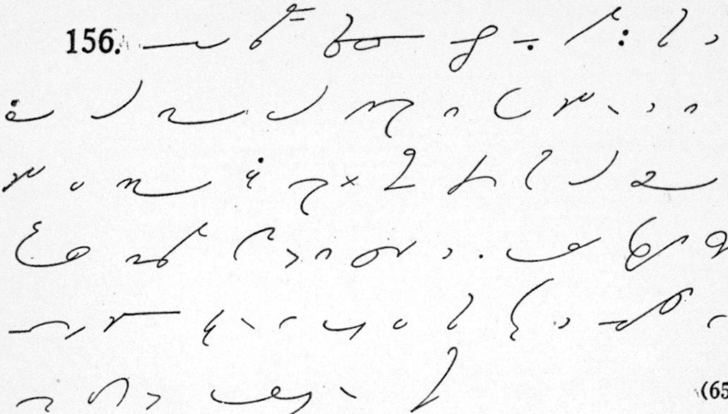

(65)

157.

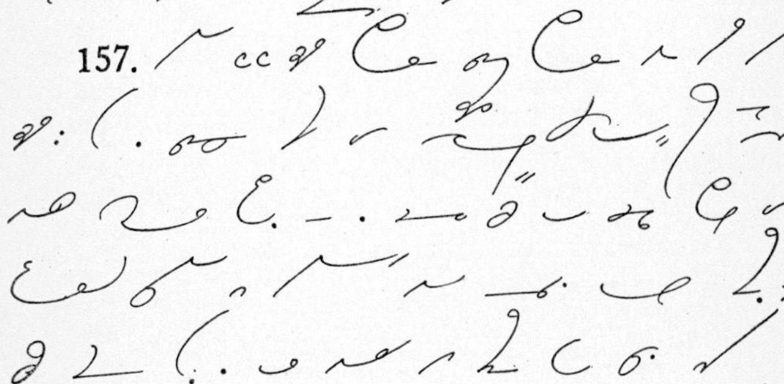

(90)

158.

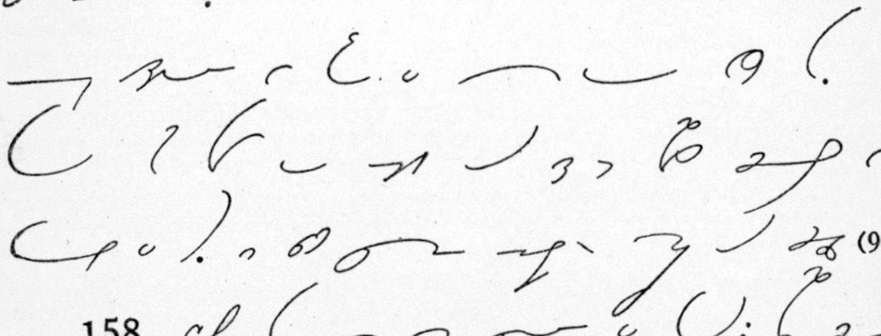

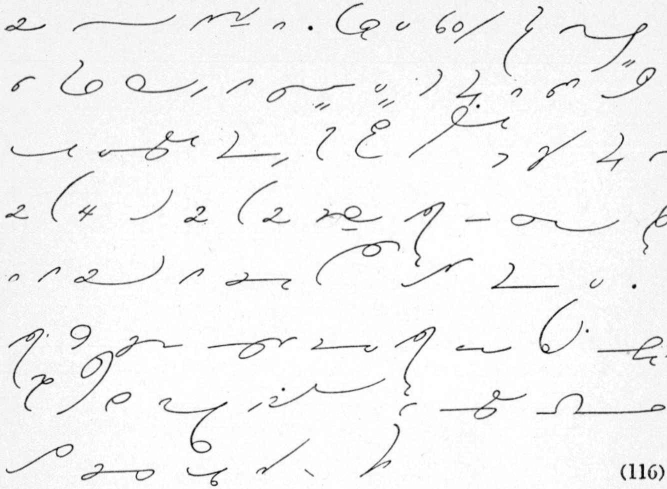

(116)

159.

(172)

160.

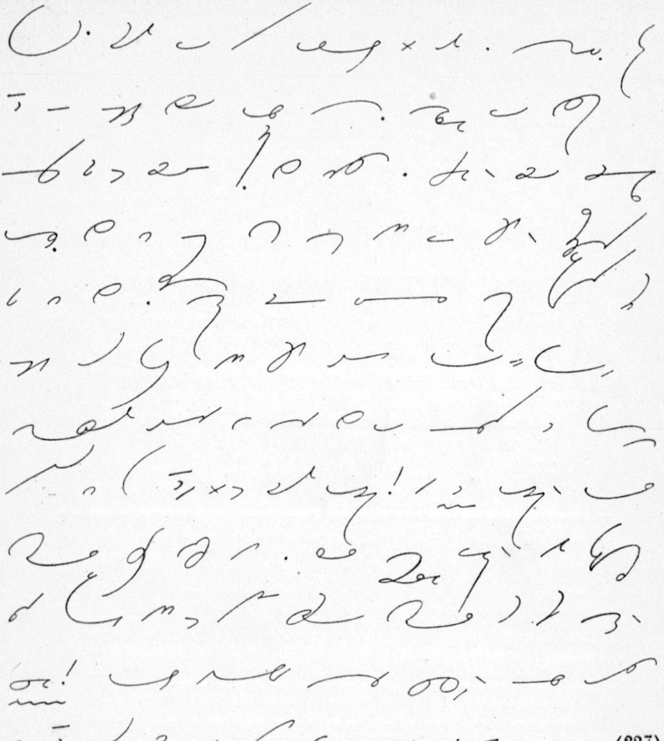

(227)

161.

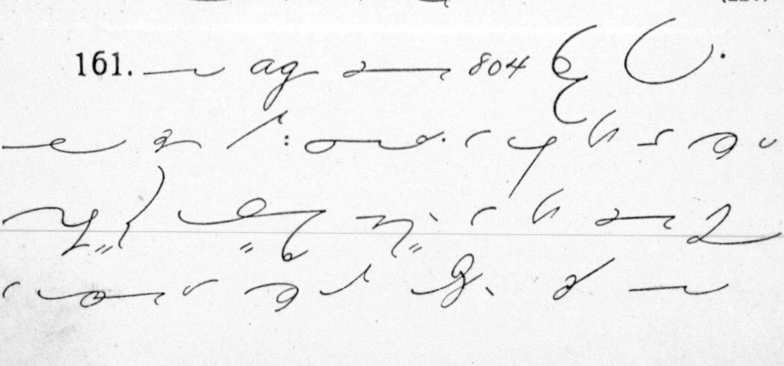

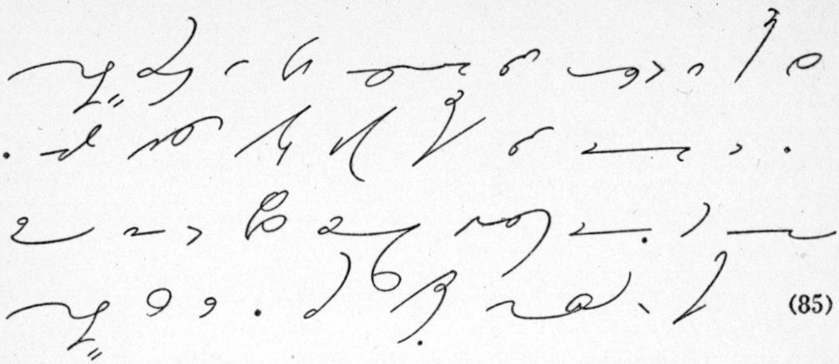

(85)

162. SIX RULES FOR SUCCESS

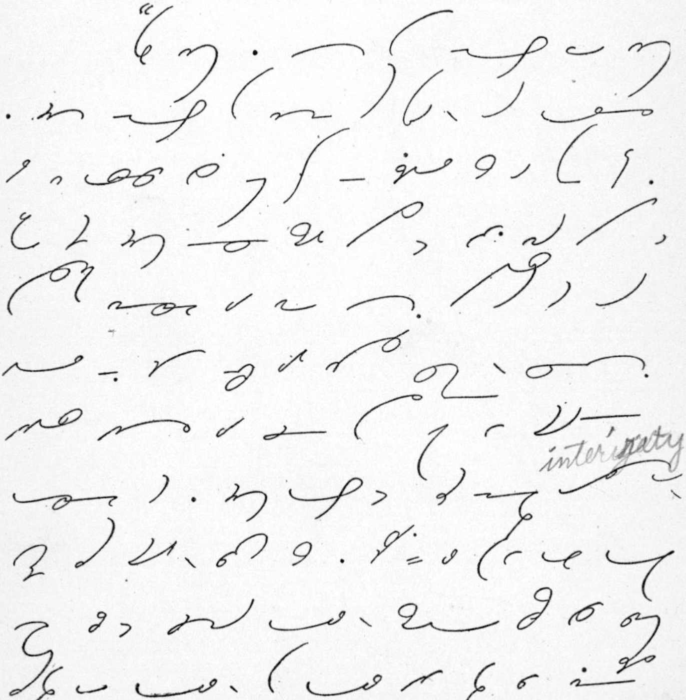

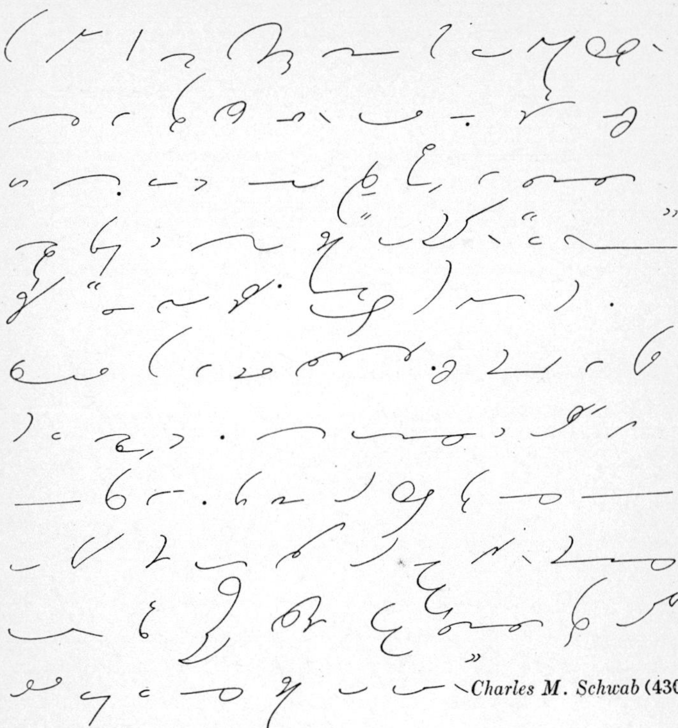

Charles M. Schwab (430)

163. PLAYING THE GAME

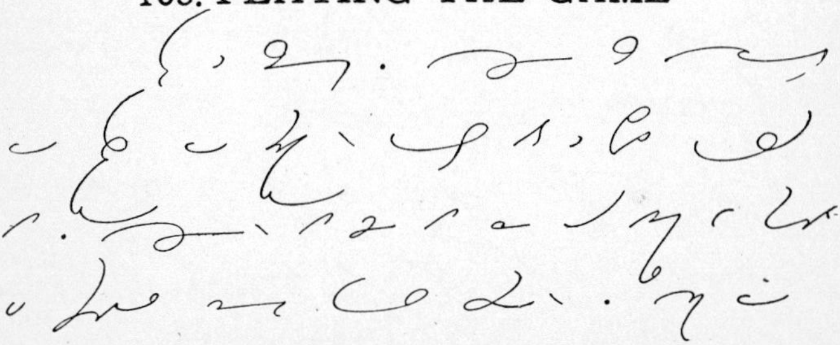

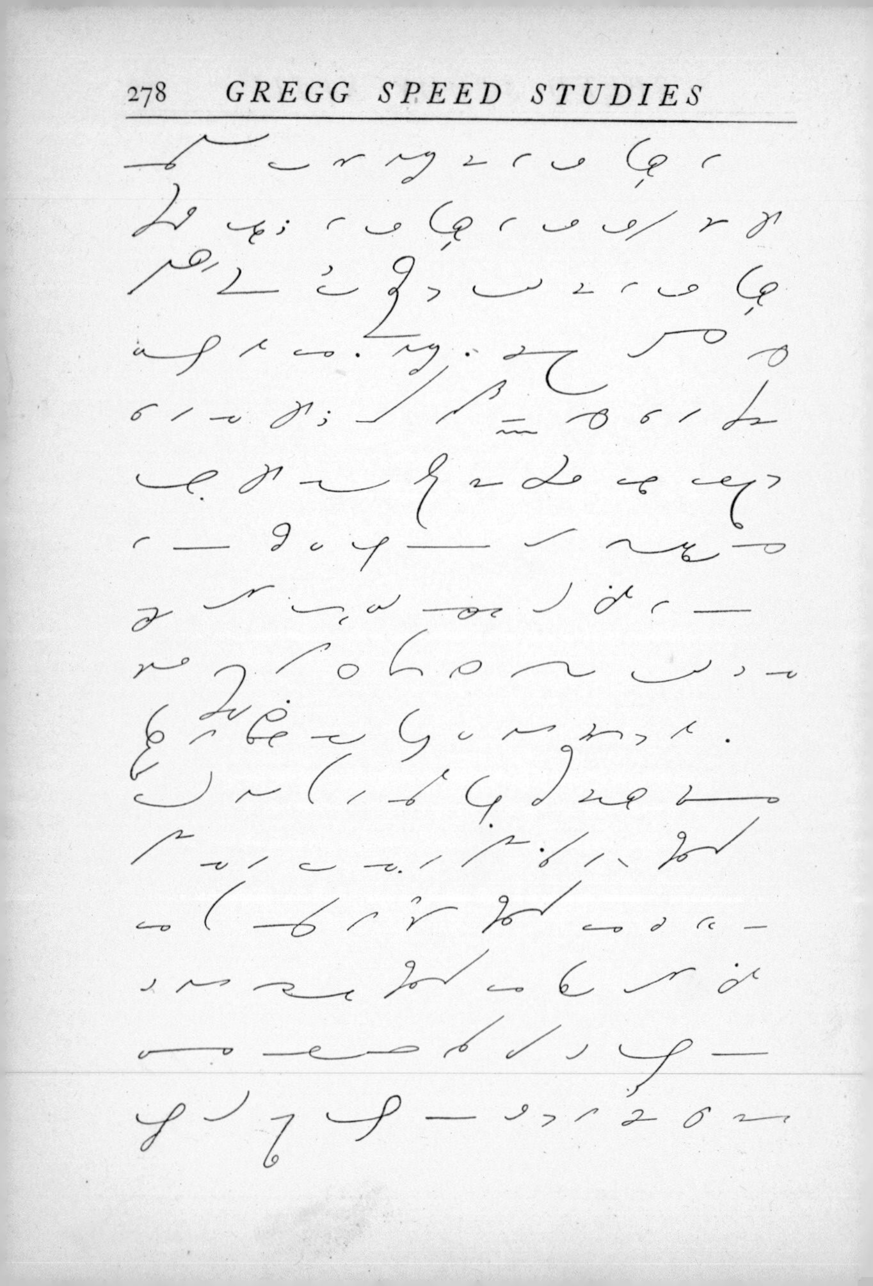

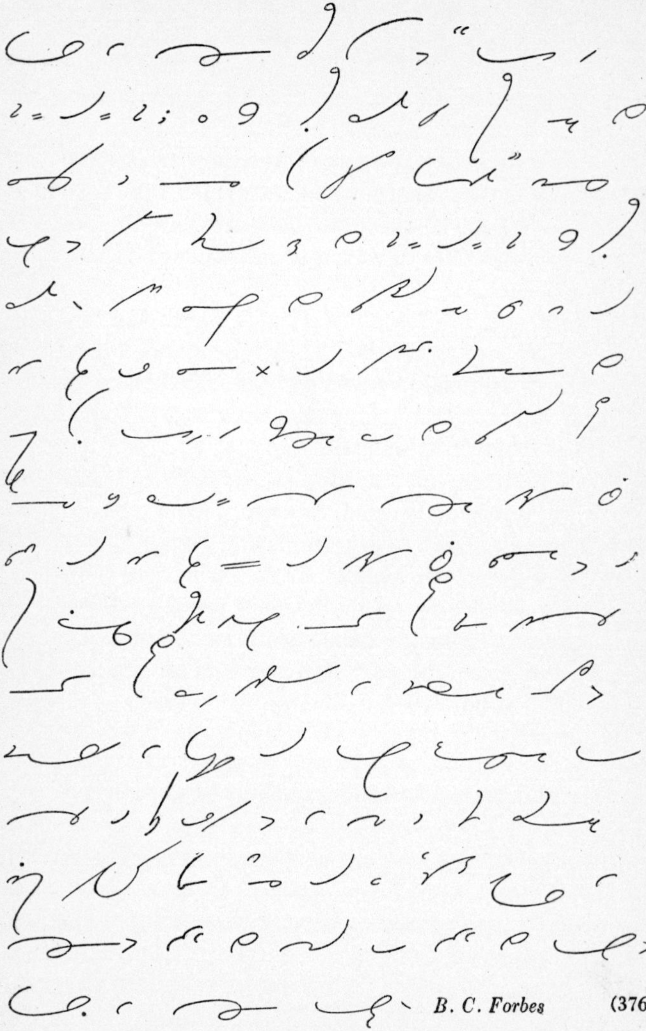

B. C. Forbes (376)

Dear Sir:

Will you let us provide you with a watchman to protect your home against the thieves who are[20] so active nowadays?

This watchman of ours will guard your home for a salary of approximately ten cents a day.[40] If a thief breaks into your home and steals your valuables the watchman will make good your loss. Not only[60] that, but he will repair the doors or windows that the thief damaged in his attempt to enter the house.[80]

Without any additional salary this watchman will be a personal bodyguard to you and to any member of your immediate[100] family over eighteen years of age. He will make good any loss in the case of a holdup occurring within[120] the limits of the United States or Canada.

This watchman will also protect you from any claims for damages because[140] of personal injuries. A servant may become careless and meet with an injury or a delivery boy may be hurt[160] while in your house. In that case, this watchman will take care of any claims that may be made against[180] you, and if necessary he will fight a lawsuit in your name but at his expense. If he should[200] lose the suit he will pay any damages that are awarded to the injured person.

If the glass in doors[220] or windows in your home is broken as a result of almost any accident, this watchman will repair the damage[240] without cost or trouble to you.

He will also repair without cost to you any damage to your home or[260] its contents caused by water leaking through the roof or windows, by the bursting or leaking of water pipes, or[280] by the explosion of any heating or cooking equipment.

If you have to leave your home as a result of[300] damage done by fire, lightning, or a windstorm, the watchman will pay you a sum equal to the rental[320] value of your home for the length of time required to make repairs.

This sum will pay any expense to[340] which you are put by having to go to a hotel. In addition to this he will make, without cost[360] to you, whatever repairs are required in your home.

If you want further information about what this invaluable watchman can[380] do for you at so small a cost, a telephone call will bring me to see you.

Yours truly, (399—1.37)

Gentlemen:

Try your knife or a file on the enclosed piece of copper wire and you'll see how hard a[20] wearing surface chromium plating gives. Chromium is the hardest known metal—ranking next to the diamond in hardness. You can[40] write your name on glass with this piece of chromium-plated copper wire!

Chromium as used in our patented plating[60] process is one of the greatest contributions to economy and longer wear in manufacturing history. Manufacturers everywhere are using this[80] process for increasing the wearing quality of piston pins, bearings, shafting, gears, machine parts, dies, and an infinite variety of[100] parts where greater wearing quality is a sales asset or manufacturing economy.

And this is all in addition to its[120] silvery non-tarnishing beauty and extreme resistance to rust and acids.

We are equipped to handle your requirements on a[140] production basis and invite an opportunity to chromium-plate a sample for you to make your own tests. The enclosed[160] post card will bring you further information without obligation.

Yours very truly, (172—1.66)

To our Stockholders:

It is gratifying to inform our stockholders that during the first half of the present fiscal year[20] our earnings exceeded our dividend requirements for the entire twelve months. Our earnings were over $10,000,000 after charges[40] and taxes, which are more than 25 per cent greater than the first six months of our previous best[60] year.

At the present rate our dividends require $3 per share. In these first six months we have earned[80] $3.37 a share.

This record was made possible by a steady increase in our production, shipments,[100] and sales. It now seems certain that March will be our greatest month yet, in which we shall have shipped[120] more than 4,500 cars. Nearly 1,000 of them will be Eights, for we have practically doubled[140] our production of Eights.

We did this by introducing early in March nine new Eight models at new and lower[160] prices. These are standard in design and therefore lower in cost, yet they preserve strictly the fine traditions of our[180] Eight quality, beauty, comfort, and performance.

Now we are able to offer the buying public its choice of 53[200] models, and at prices ranging from $8,725 to $2,250,[220] exclusive of freight and government tax.

Very truly yours, (229—1.45)

Mr. George P. Floyd
Dear Sir:

I have just received your letter with check on Flagg & Savage for twenty-five dollars. You must[20] think I am a high-priced man. You are too liberal with your money. Fifteen dollars is enough for the[40] job. I send you a receipt for fifteen dollars, and return to you a ten-dollar bill.

Abraham Lincoln, (59—1.32)

SPEED STUDY XIX

164.

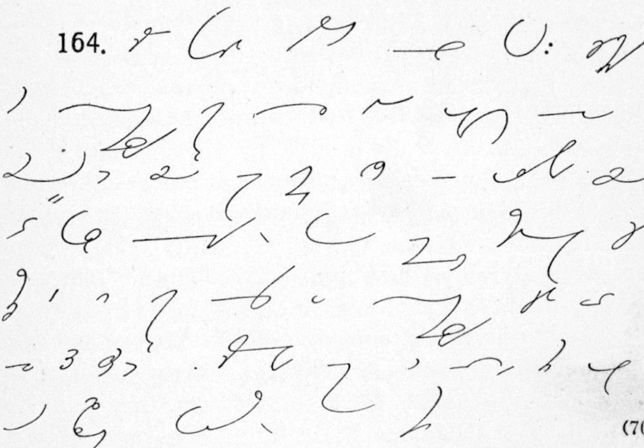

(70)

165.

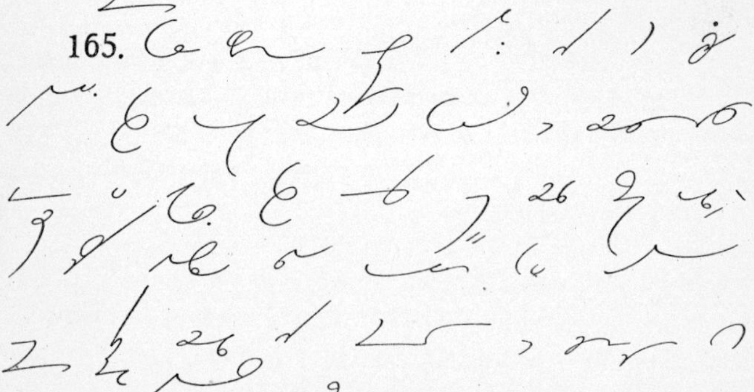

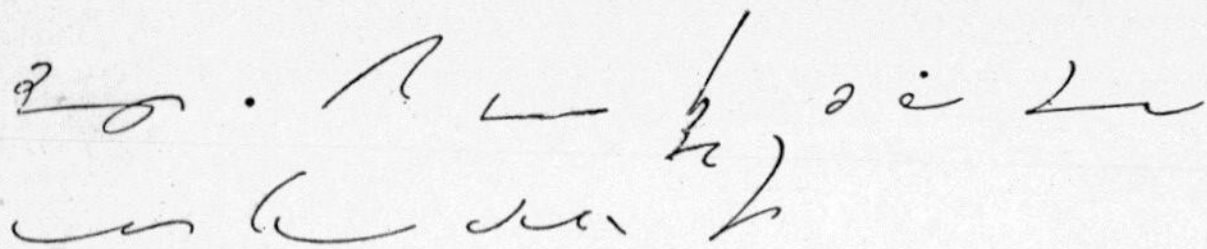

(83)

166.

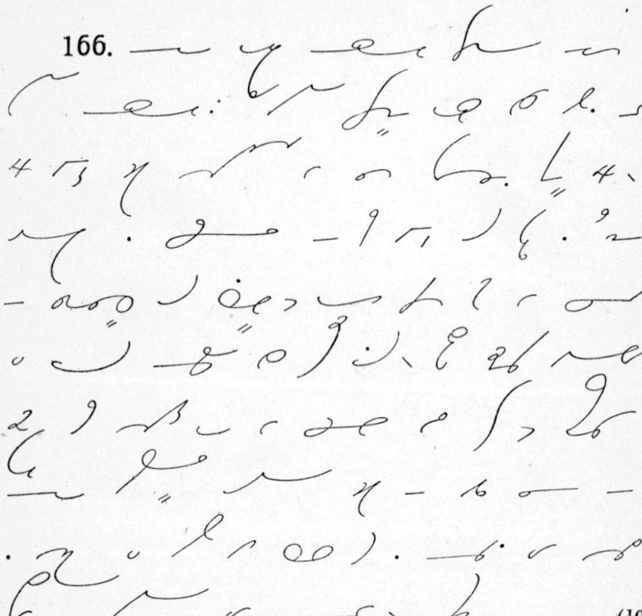

(105)

167.

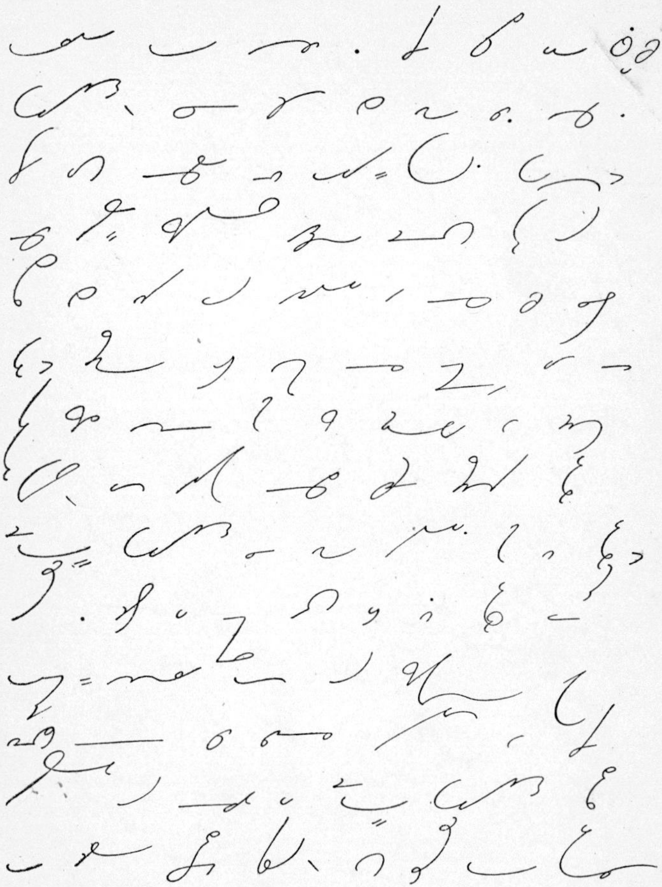

(189)

168.

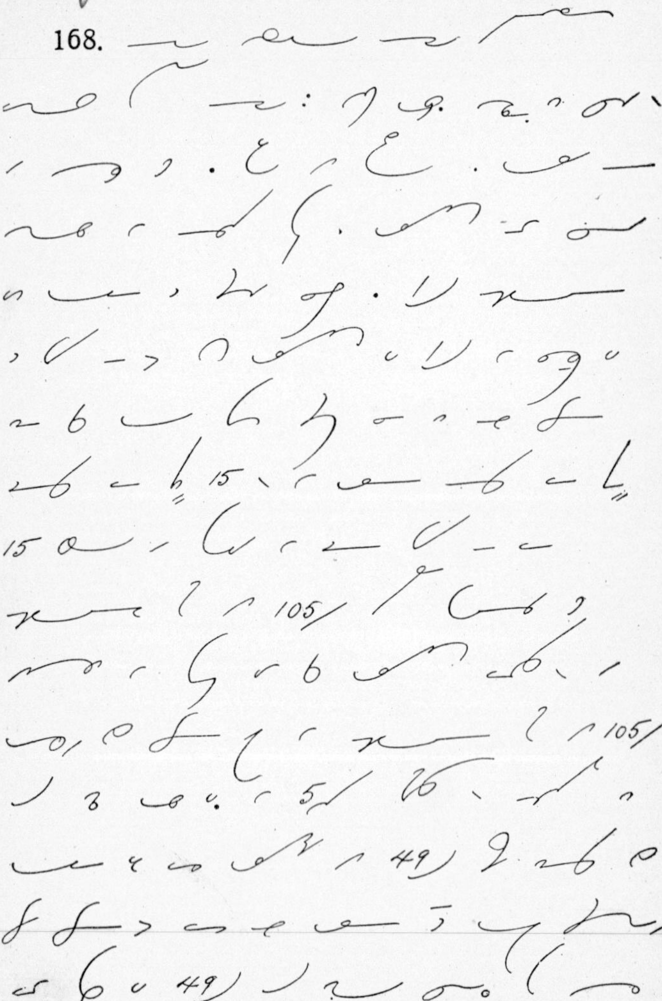

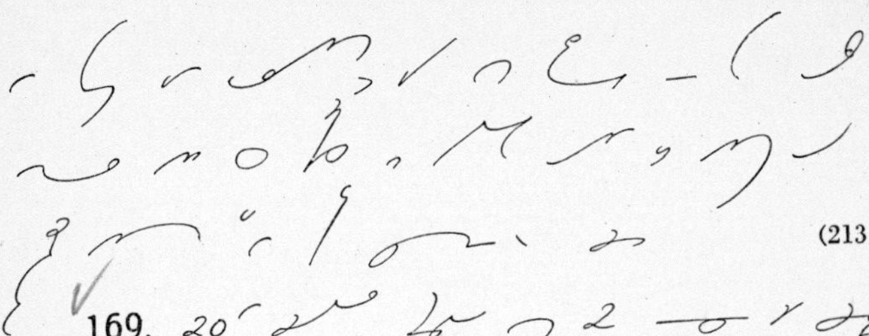

(213)

169.

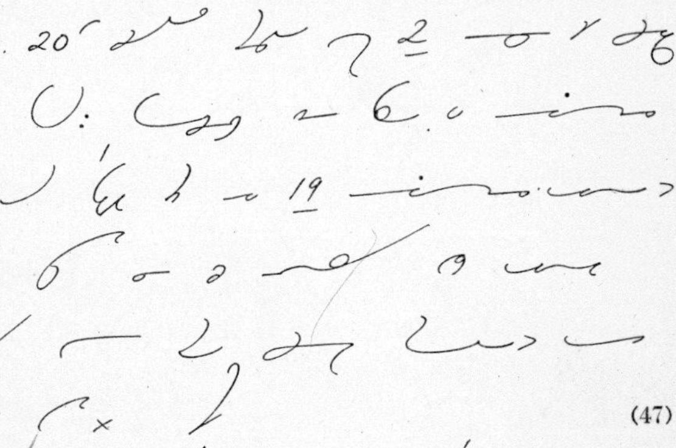

(47)

170.

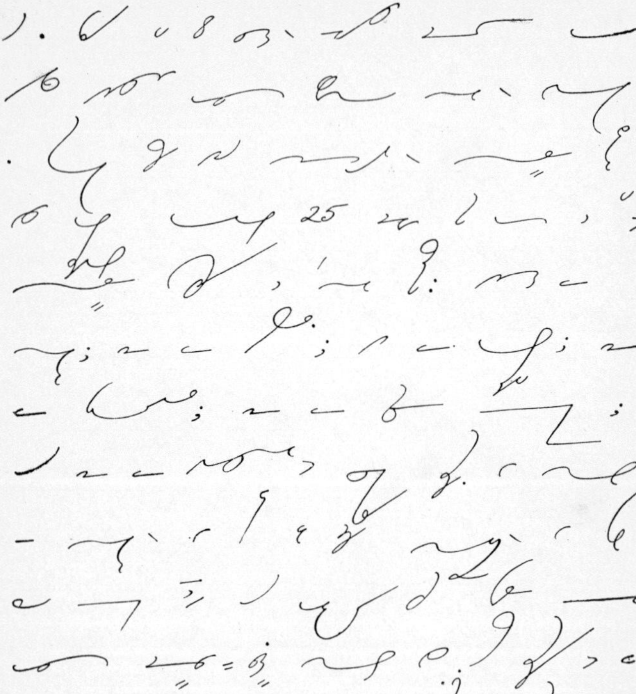

(208)

171.

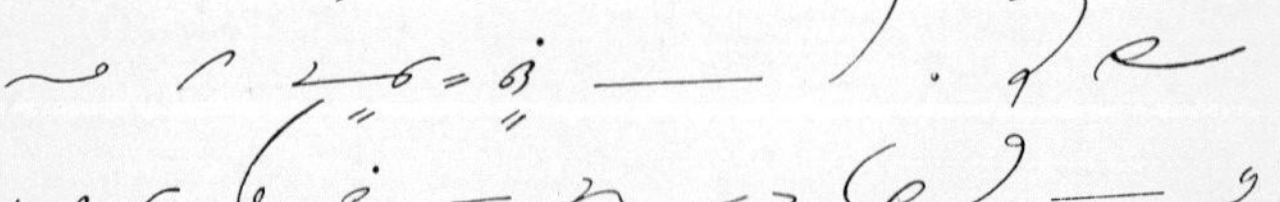

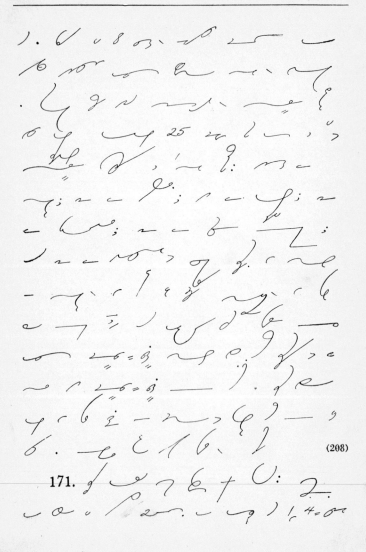

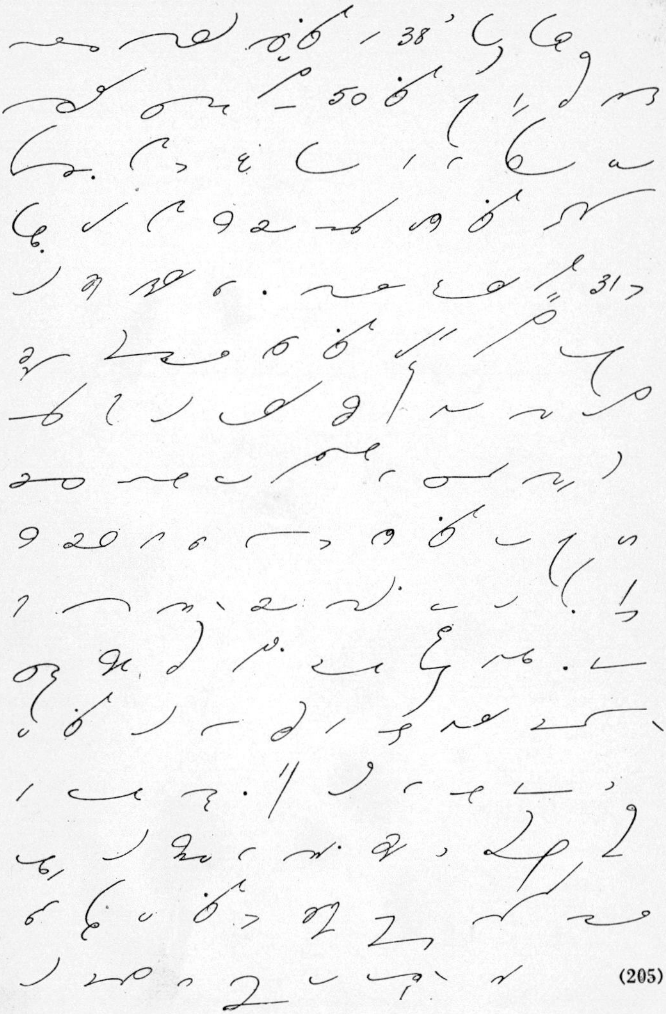

(205)

172. GETTING THE RIGHT START

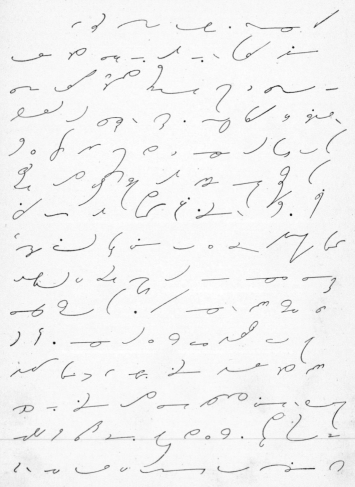

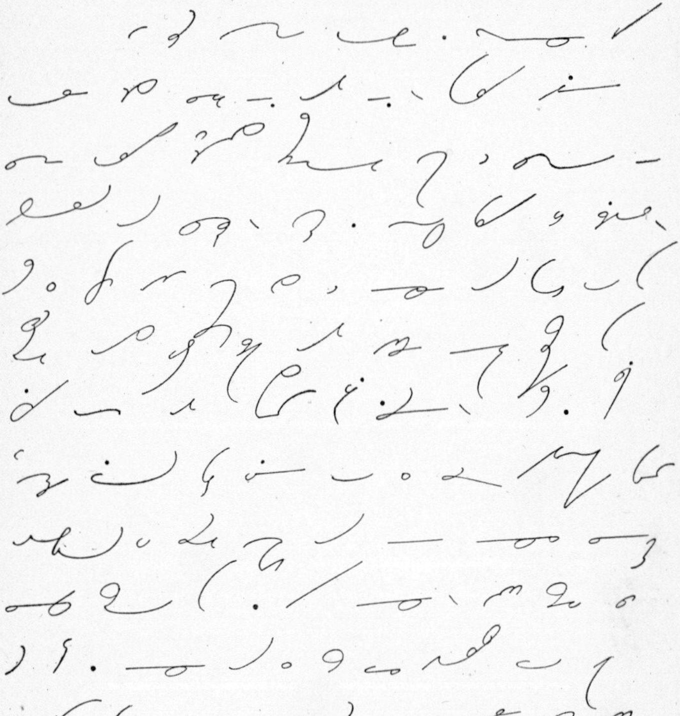

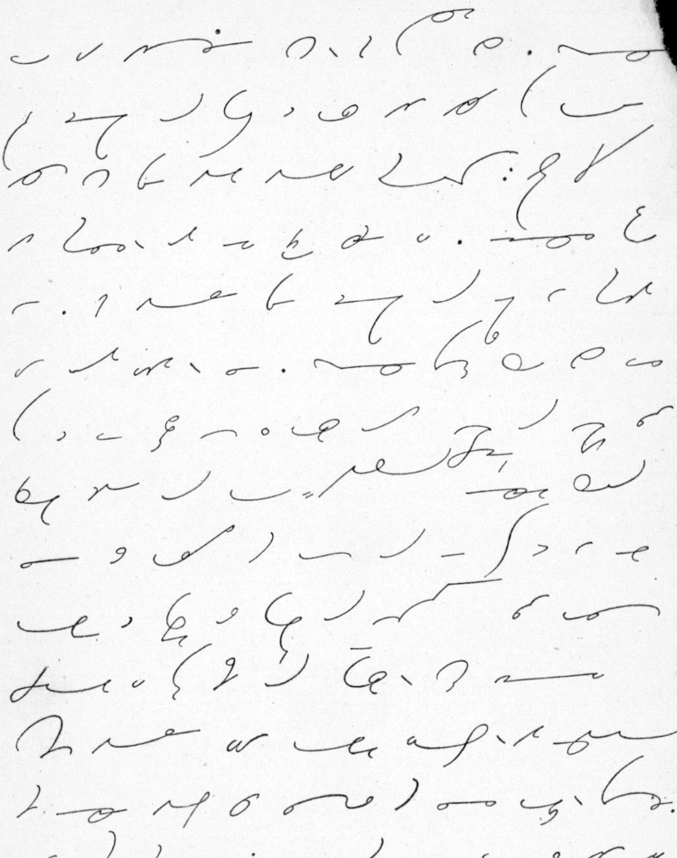

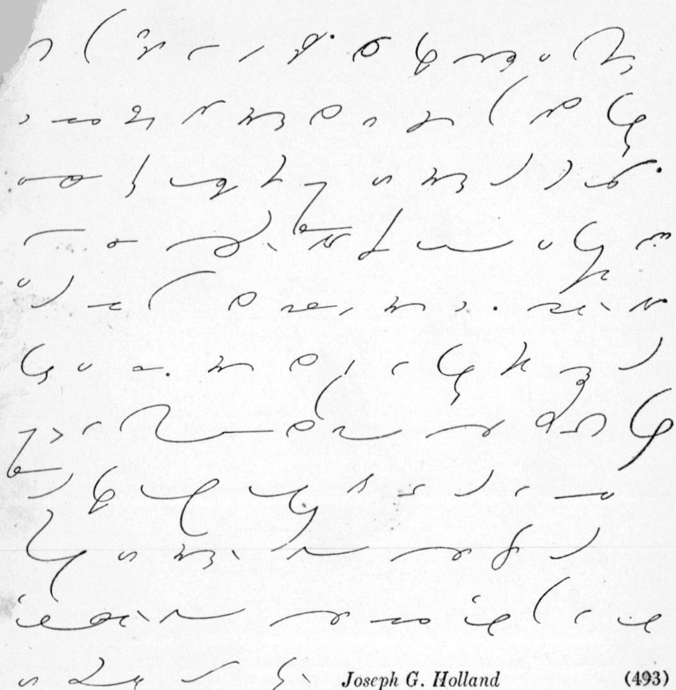

Joseph G. Holland (493)

173. WHITHER THE WIND BLOWETH

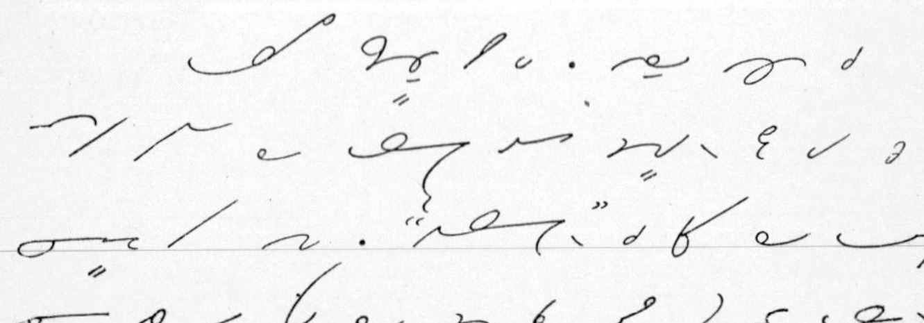

(377)

Dear Sir:

On the editorial page of a recent issue of your magazine I find this statement: "A fair percentage [20] of human beings who read a magazine of this kind do so in the hope of finding in it regularly [40] enough novel and different ideas to pay them for their time and effort."

I believe that statement and I believe[60] that your readers usually get what they are looking for in your magazine. Here is something that is neither novel[80] nor different, but that will fully pay them for the time it takes to read this letter, if they will[100] profit by the suggestions it contains.

Every day in the Chicago post office we receive not less than 75,000[120] pieces of mail without a street address. Letters addressed to large, well-known business houses are not included in[140] this figure. This mail is delayed from ten to twenty-four hours, and some of it cannot be delivered at[160] all.

There are forty-eight carrier stations in Chicago outside of the main post office. Mail coming into Chicago for[180] delivery is separated on the trains according to the postal stations from which the delivery is to be made, and[200] this sorting is possible only if the mail bears a street address. With the same motion that he would dispose[220] of a properly addressed letter, the clerk places a letter without street address in a box labeled, "No street named."[240] Such mail is put together and sent to the main post office unsorted.

There is no use in putting our[260] ordinary clerks to sorting these 75,000 or more pieces of unsorted mail without street addresses. We must use[280] the very best men we have. These men will pick out, as a rule, about 65,000 pieces. The[300] remaining 10,000 pieces must all be looked up in the directory. In this way we are able to find[320] addresses for about 58 per cent of these 10,000 letters, 37 per cent of the letters are[340] returned to the writers, and about 5 per cent are sent to the dead letter office in Washington.

Most of [360] the mail that we receive without street addresses is caused by advertisers not including a complete street address in their[380] advertising matter or on their letterheads. A little thought will show that that is a foolish and shortsighted policy. If[400] we have to return even one letter marked "Not found," it will do the advertiser more harm in the town[420] from which that letter came than he can repair with a thousand dollars' worth of advertising. The person who wrote [440] the letter and to whom it has been returned will give him advertising, but you may be sure that it[460] will all be of the wrong kind, the kind you should avoid.

Yours truly, (474—1.43)

Gentlemen:

Our firm, the largest plant in the world devoted to the exclusive manufacture of thermostatic instruments, has just published[20] a little reference book of 50 pages—with 40 illustrations—covering the many advantages of automatic temperature in textile processes,[40] written by the most experienced technical man in the dye industry.

If you will write on the enclosed postal card[60] the name of your dye foreman, or as he is sometimes called, "The Boss of the Dye House," I will[80] be glad to send him a copy of the book. No charge, of course, and no obligation.

Yours sincerely, (99—1.59)

Dear Sir:

It is, of course, a very simple matter for a man with earning power to accumulate money. But[20] money getting and money saving are widely different; there are so many different opportunities always presenting themselves. To the man[40] who has acquired from $500 upwards, the temptation to increase that sum—whatever it be—is irresistible at[60] times.

In the flood of all sorts of propositions that come to one, how can the "wheat be separated from[80] the chaff"? How can the ordinary business man, without knowledge, experience, or the facilities of handling investments, tell the absolute[100] weak and strong points of each security?

Now our business is the handling of funds—trust funds, bank money, insurance[120] money, and the like. We only invest. We invest the funds of others every day in the year. We know[140] of the varied conditions surrounding each and every one who has money. It is our business to possess that keen,[160] wide, thorough training which causes banks, trust companies, and investors generally to look to us and accept our judgment.

We[180] offer you, therefore, the knowledge, born of wide experience, which we possess. Our judgment very often represents the combined suggestions[200] of the leading investment bankers of the country. Think what an advantage this is to the man with $500,[220] $5,000, or $50,000.

We have made a specialty of high-class bonds. We believe there[240] is nothing better, from the standpoint of security. We can show you why very easily. If funds under your control[260] have been accumulating, or if your personal monies are idle we would appreciate an opportunity to consult with you regarding[280] your investments.

Very truly yours, (285–1.57)

SPEED STUDY XX

174. 

(96)

175. 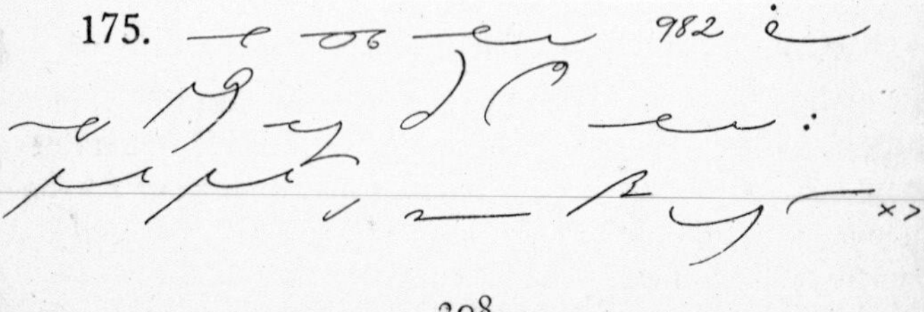

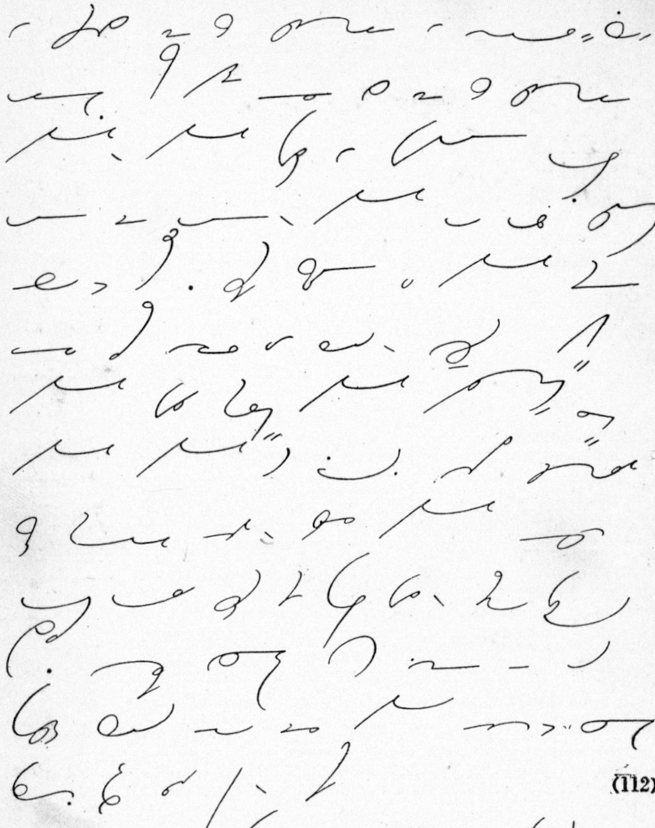

(112)

176.

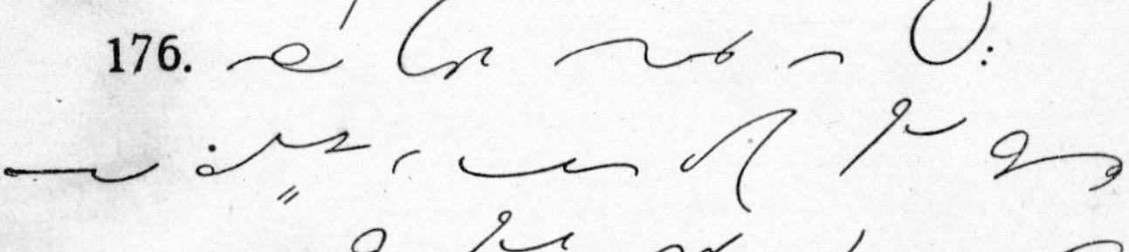

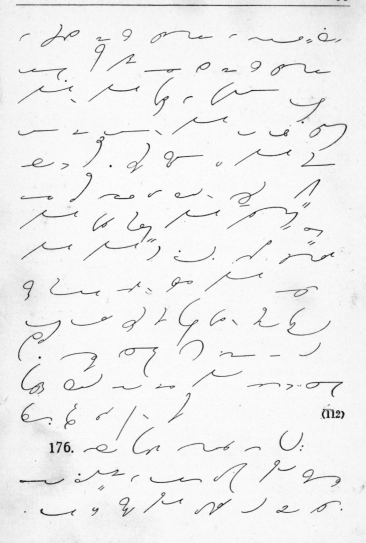

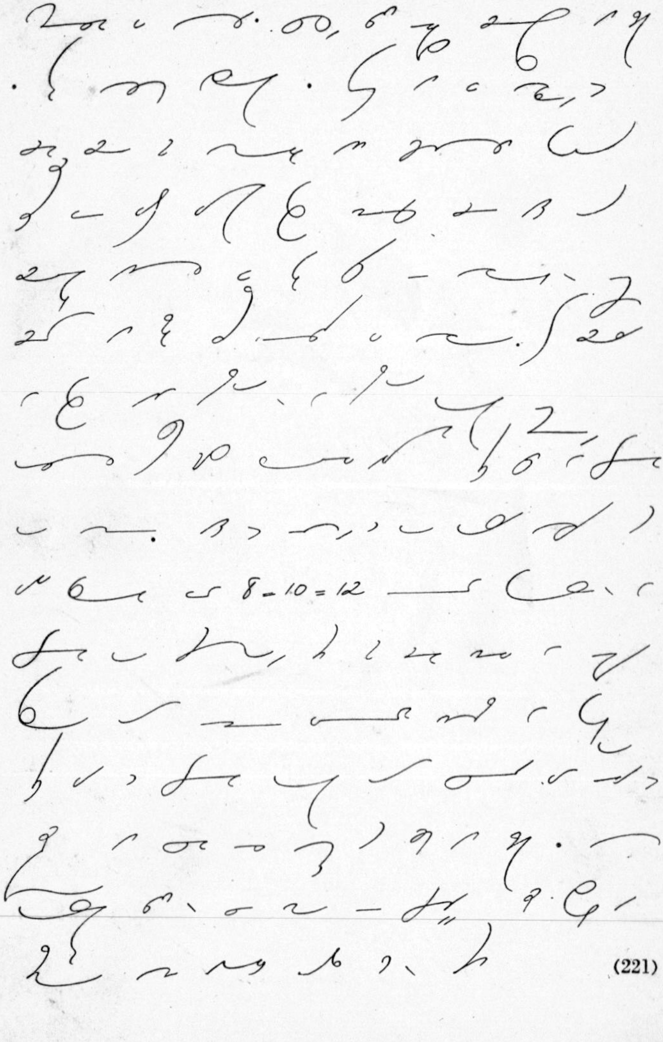

(221)

177.

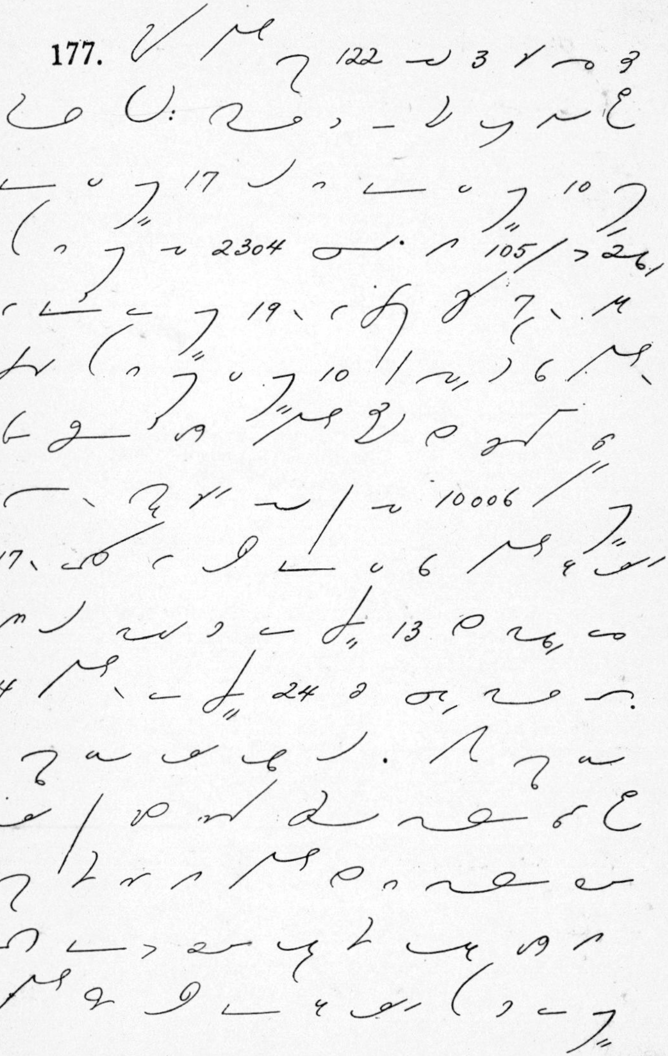

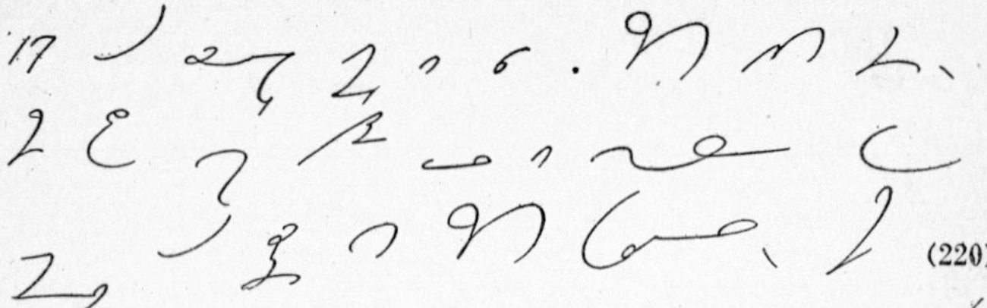

(220)

178.

(40)

179.

(77)

180.

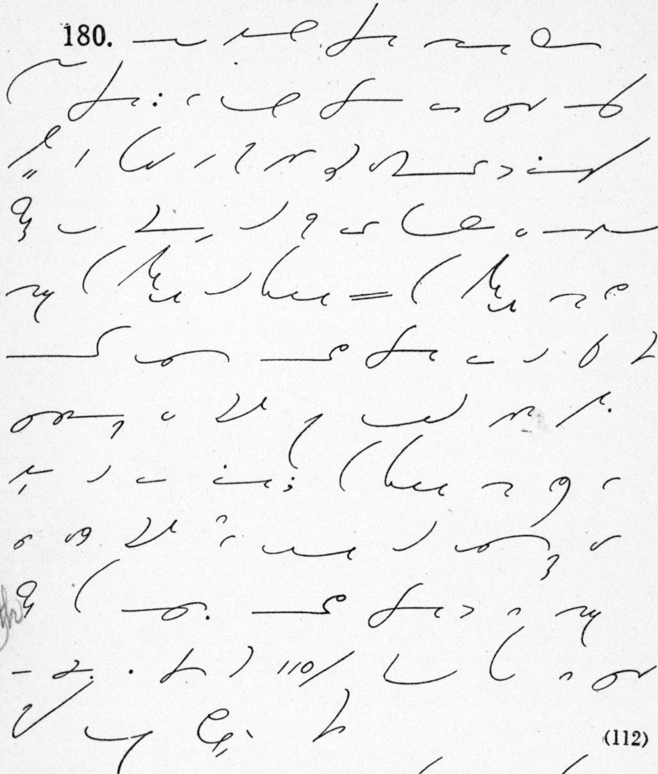

(112)

181.

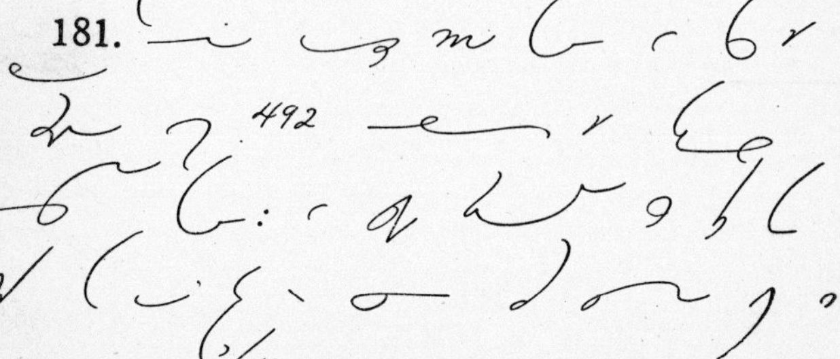

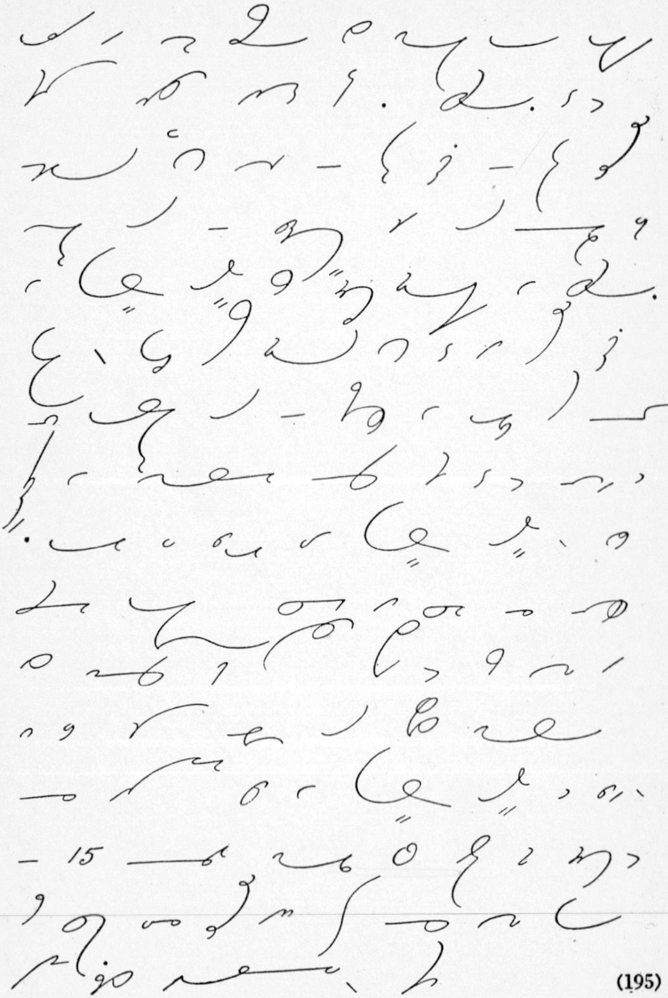

(195)

182. OPPORTUNITY IS PLENTIFUL

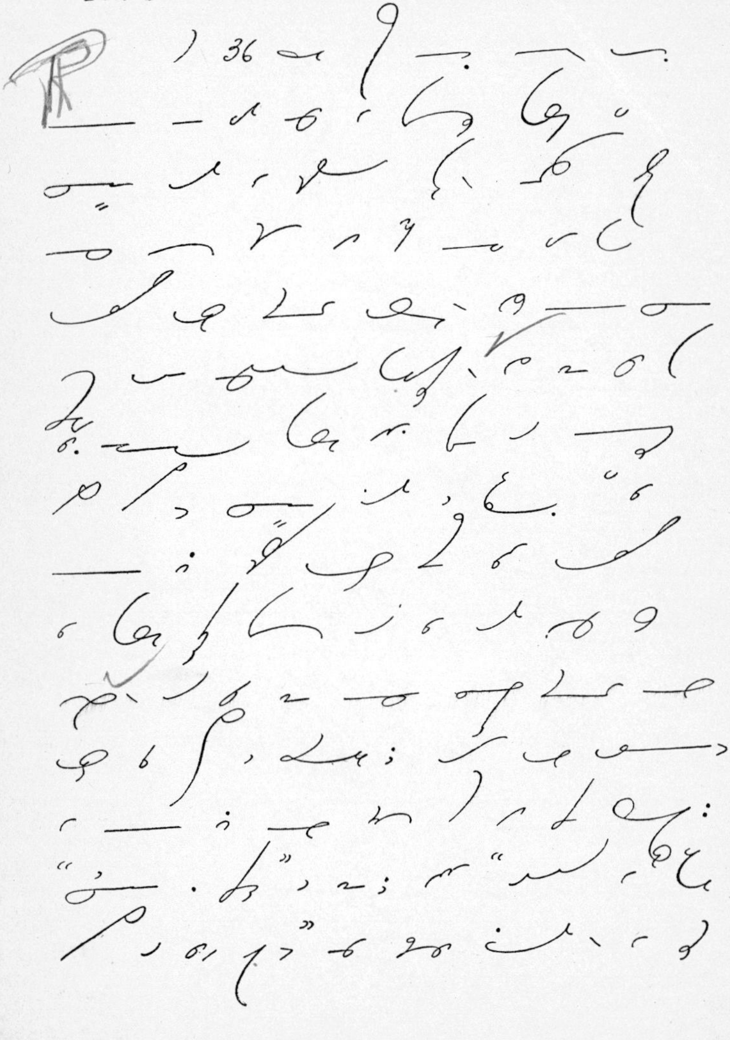

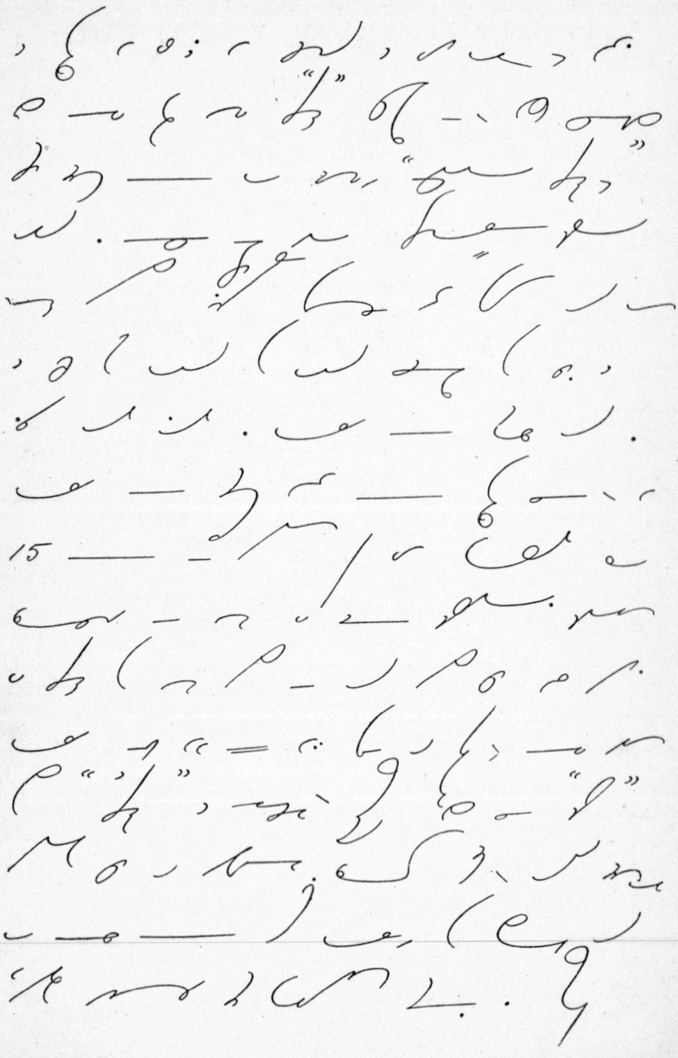
15

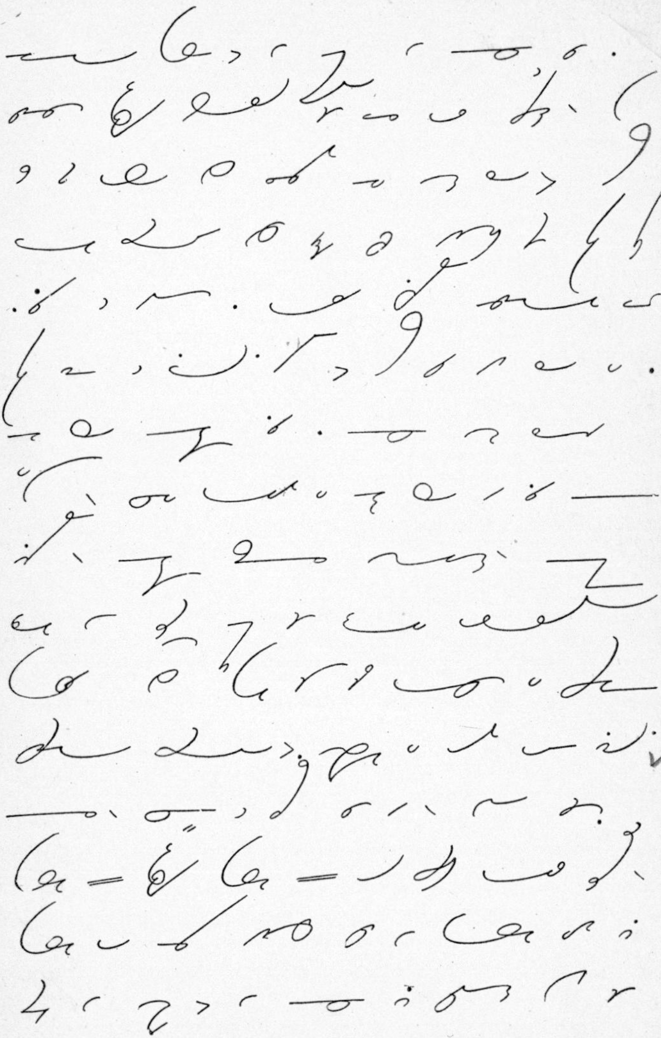

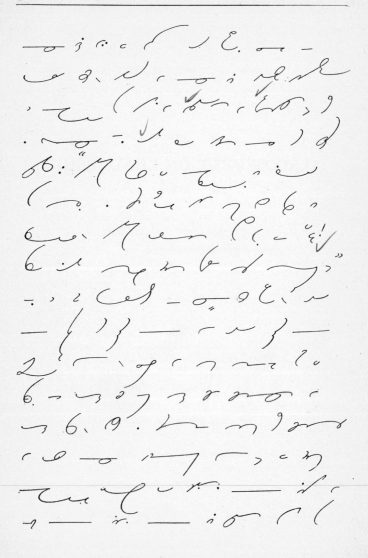

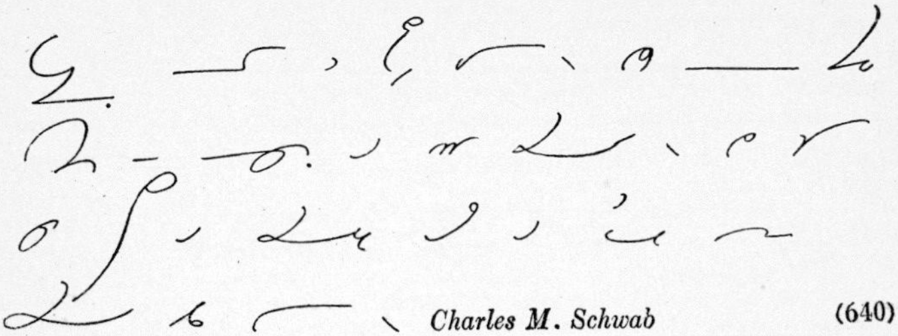

Charles M. Schwab (640)

183. ROOSEVELT ON LEADERSHIP

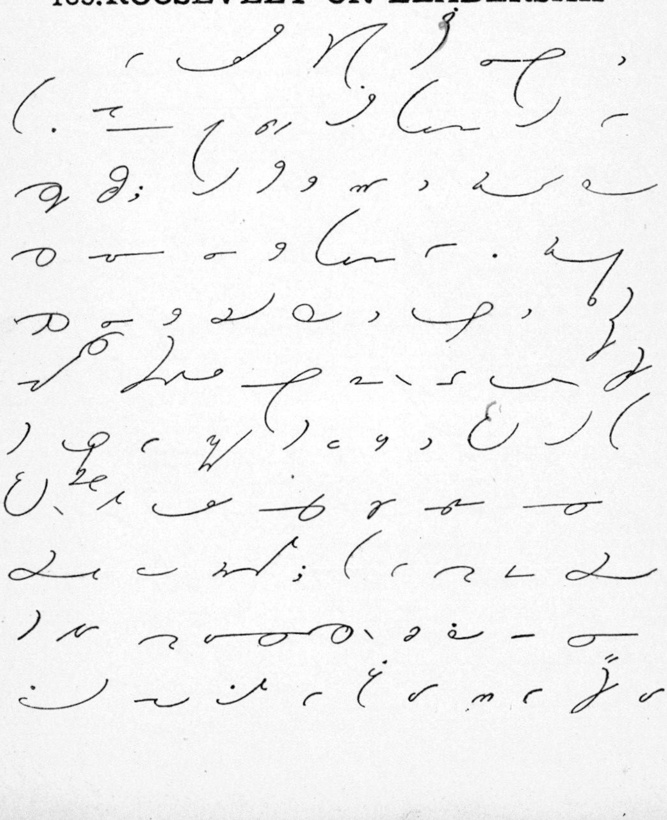

(201)

Dear Mr. Kennedy:

I can't tell you how disturbed I am about the letter I have received this morning from[20] Mr. Jones, telling of the recent conversation he had with you regarding our treatment of the opening order you were[40] good enough to mail us.

Probably there is nothing I can do to correct this unfortunate mistake as, of course,[60] the time to do that was at the moment and not a month later. If you will permit me, however,[80] I should like to say just this:

A big business house like our own is not a machine. It is,[100] rather, an organization of individuals. Of necessity, some of these individuals—and probably most of them—are as nearly 100 per[120] cent in the efficient carrying out of their duties as possible. You will know from your own experience, however, that[140] there are always bound to be errors, because we always have to deal with human nature.

The inexcusable treatment of[160] your order was entirely a mistake. It is not typical of the way we treat all orders, and certainly is[180] not the treatment that our policy, or even our common sense, dictates. It was just one of those things that[200] happen every now and then that are caused by the carelessness of one individual.

I am not trying to get[220] you to reinstate this order. I am simply making an attempt to restore somewhat the good will we are probably[240] losing by this transaction, and hope that some time in the future you may see fit to give us another[260] chance to demonstrate that we can be of service to you.

I am also taking the liberty of asking Mr.[280] Jones to call on you and extend our apologies in person.

Yours very truly, (294—1.47)

My dear Mr. Williams:

We are making a very attractive offer that will interest you. To make your home secure[20] from all financial worries, we are prepared to create an estate for you of as large proportion as you desire,[40] and at once, which will:

1. *Continue your salary for five* years in the event of death, thus tiding your[60] family over the most critical period financially; or provide an income for them as long as they live.

2. Pay[80] final expenses, income and inheritance taxes, any mortgages or loans that you may have, and furnish the funds to give[100] your *children a college education.*

3. Assure you of a monthly *income for life,* with all further deposits waived, in[120] case you become totally and permanently incapacitated by sickness or accident before age sixty.

4. Guarantee the estate to provide[140] an *income for you and your wife* in the "sunset days of life," when you will want to retire from[160] the worries of business or profession.

We are ready to create this estate for you, subject to evidence of present[180] good health, and will gladly furnish further information without obligation, if you will fill in the form below, and return[200] this letter in the enclosed envelope.

Sincerely yours, (208—1.54)

Dear Sir:

Originally developed for wear in India and other tropical climates, Cool Wind worsteds are about as cool as[20] it is possible for clothing to be. That their weave is *extraordinarily cool,* you may test for yourself by holding[40] the attached swatch up to the light and noting the airiness of its structure.

Firm, sturdy-textured, and handsome, Cool[60] Wind worsteds tailor beautifully, keep their shape, wear well, and allow a man to work at highest efficiency on days[80] when the heat would otherwise fatigue and annoy him. Look at the *actual color photographs* tucked beneath this flap—have[100] you ever seen cool summer suits in shades so attractive?

Three-button models—coat, vest, trousers — $45. Found[120] only at The Emporium.

Yours truly, (126—1.52)

Mr. Charles Christy
71 Williams Street
Cranston, Rhode Island

Dear Mr. Christy:

Your comments each month on the direct-mail pieces sent to you by your subscribers are always[20] read with interest by this office. Even more interesting will be your comments on the pieces enclosed.

The broadside was[40] run in early March, followed at short intervals with the envelope enclosures that were sent with the customers' bills. Our[60] gas-meter list, with present users of our heater eliminated, makes a live mailing list. You will note that no[80] provision was made for a coupon or return card.

We felt that ours is a peculiar situation, for most of[100] the towns we serve are of medium size, and a majority of our customers stop in at the office at[120] least once a month to pay their bills and look around. Whether because of this direct-mail series or in[140] spite of it, the fact remains that the sales of our heaters have been steadily increasing. Of course, we used [160] supplementary newspaper advertising also. Your comments on these pieces will be received with interest.

Yours very truly, (177—1.46)

Gentlemen:

Speed. Accuracy. Intelligence. Reliability. Honesty. Ambition. You are looking for a stenographer with these qualities.

Speed. I can write[20] sixty words a minute on the typewriter, and take dictation at the rate of one hundred and twenty-five words[40] a minute. I can transcribe quickly, and you will find that my transcriptions are marked by their

Accuracy. Not only[60] is the mechanical side of my typewriting correct and accurate, but the matter itself is thoughtfully written, with the meaning[80] kept intact. The grammar and punctuation are also correct, as I make use of my

Intelligence. I earned membership in[100] the Minnesota Scholarship Federation while at high school, and had Phi BetaKappa standing during the one year I attended[120] Middle West Teachers' College. I finished the course at Twin Cities Secretarial School in half the time usually required. I am[140] twenty-one years of age—old enough to have

Reliability. I believe in doing every bit of work with the[160] highest possible efficiency. Though loyalty alone would command strict reliability on my part, I realize that it is to my[180] own interest to do your work well; and as to getting it done promptly, I consider that a matter of[200]

Honesty. You will pay me for my time, and none of it will be wasted. If there is any spare[220] time, I can use it to further my

Ambition. I want to learn the business thoroughly, not only because I[240] am deeply interested in it, but because I hope some day to be fitted for a position of responsibility where[260] thoroughness and initiative are required.

May I have a personal interview?

Respectfully yours, (273—1.60)

23-2

46 1